Sport in the Global Society

General Editor: J.A. Mangan

SPORT AND INTERNATIONAL RELATIONS

SPORT IN THE GLOBAL SOCIETY

General Editor: J.A. Mangan

The interest in sports studies around the world is growing and will continue to do so. This unique series combines aspects of the expanding study of *sport in the global society*, providing comprehensiveness and comparison under one editorial umbrella. It is particularly timely, with studies in the political, cultural, anthropological, ethnographic, social, economic, geographical and aesthetic elements of sport proliferating in institutions of higher education.

Eric Hobsbawm once called sport one of the most significant practices of the late nineteenth century. Its significance was even more marked in the late twentieth century and will continue to grow in importance into the new millennium as the world develops into a 'global village' sharing the English language, technology and sport.

Other Titles in the Series

SPORT AND INTERNATIONAL RELATIONS

An Emerging Relationship

ROGER LEVERMORE
University of Liverpool

ADRIAN BUDD
London, South Bank University

Routledge
Taylor & Francis Group

LONDON AND NEW YORK

First published in 2004 by
Routledge
11 New Fetter Lane
London EC4P 4EE

Simultaneously published in the USA and Canada by
Routledge
29 West 35th Street, New York, NY 1009

British Library Cataloguing in Publication Data

A catalogue record of this book is
available from the British Library.

~TOC

ISBN 0-7146-5345-4 (cloth)
ISBN 0-7146-8283-7 (paper)

Library of Congress Cataloging-in-Publication Data

A catalog record of this book is
available from the Library of Congress.

Set in 10.75/12pt Times New Roman by Frank Cass Publishers
Printed in Great Britain by MPG Books Ltd., Bodmin, Cornwall

Contents

Acknowledgements

We would like to thank Frank Cass, Jonathan Manley and J.A. Mangan for their positive response to our initial proposal and for seeing it through to a successful conclusion. Thanks also to the contributors who always responded promptly and with good humour to our petty editors' quibbles, and to our colleagues at the Football Industry Group, University of Liverpool, and in the Division of Social and Policy Studies, London, South Bank University. Particular thanks must go to Mike Pugh, University of Plymouth, who stoically suffered Roger's obsession with the project, especially following the pints consumed at the JSV. Finally, we would both like to thank families, friends and partners for consistent support throughout the project.

Notes on Contributors

Aaron Beacom is a senior lecturer in sports studies at the College of St Mark and St John (Plymouth). He previously lectured in sports management at Exeter Business School and he has worked in the sports industry for a number of years. He graduated with an MA in European Politics at the University of Exeter in 1997 and has recently completed a PhD on British diplomacy and the Olympic movement. He is an active member of the British Society of Sports Historians and has had two recent publications in the *Sports Historian* journal.

Peter J. Beck is Professor of International History at Kingston University, England. He is the author of *Scoring for Britain: International Football and International Politics, 1900–1939* (1999), 'Britain, Image-building and the World Game: Sport's Potential as British Cultural Propaganda' in Alan Chong and Jana Valencic (eds), *The Image, the State and International Relations* (2001) and 'Leisure and Sport in Britain, 1900–1939', in C. Wrigley (ed.), *The Blackwell Companion to Early Twentieth Century Britain, 1900–1939* (2002).

Adrian Budd is a senior lecturer in international politics at London, South Bank University. He has recently written chapters and articles on globalization, the anti-capitalist movement, stakeholding theory and sport under capitalism. He is currently writing a book-length analysis of the critical IR theory of Robert Cox and the neo-Gramscians.

Dr John Harris is a senior lecturer in the School of Sport, PE and Recreation at UWIC. His main research interests focus on gender issues, the sports media and national identity. He has published a number of articles on women's football and is currently undertaking research into rugby union and national identities in Wales.

Christopher Hill is Montague Burton Professor of International Relations at the London School of Economics and Political Science. He was chair of the British International Studies Association in 1999/2000, and is an elected council member at the Royal Institute of International Affairs (Chatham

House). His main scholarly interests are in foreign policy analysis and in the international politics of Europe, including EU external relations and the foreign policies of Britain, France and Italy. He has published widely on these topics, including *Cabinet Decisions in Foreign Policy: the British Experience, 1938–1941* (CUP, 1991), *Two Worlds of International Relations: Academics, Practitioners and the Trade in Ideas* (ed., with Pamela Beshoff, Routledge, 1994), and *The Actors in Europe's Foreign Policy* (ed., Routledge, 1996). His most recent books are a volume jointly edited with Karen Smith entitled *European Foreign Policy: Key Documents* (Routledge, 2000) and *The Changing Politics of Foreign Policy* (Palgrave, October 2002). Having supported Wolverhampton Wanderers for 45 years and Fiorentina for ten he claims some understanding of the sufferings of the ordinary punter.

Barrie Houlihan is Professor of Sport Policy in Loughborough University's Institute of Sport and Leisure Policy. His research interests include the domestic and international policy processes for sport. He has a particular interest in sports development, the diplomatic use of sport and drug abuse by athletes. His most recent books include *Sport, Policy and Politics: A Comparative Analysis* (Routledge, 1997), *Dying to Win: the Development of Anti-doping Policy* (2nd edn, Council of Europe Press, 2002) and *Sports Development* (with Anita White, Routledge, 2002). Recent articles have also been published in *Public Administration, Journal of Sports Management* and *Managing Leisure*.

Barbara Humberstone is currently Professor of Sociology of Leisure (sport and outdoor learning) and director of the OLEE research unit at Buckinghamshire Chilterns University College. Her current research interests include youth transitions through the summer activities initiative; gender, femininities and masculinities in sport and outdoor learning cultures; (eco)-feminist theories; ethnographic research methodologies; leisure education; socio-cultural dimensions of gender; difference and leisure; outdoor education and adventure recreation. She is a member of the editorial board of *Leisure Studies*, the journal of the Leisure Studies Association; a board member of the European Institute for Outdoor Adventure Education and Experiential Learning; and a trustee of the UK Institute for Outdoor Learning.

Simon Lee is a lecturer in politics, Department of Politics and International Studies, Hull University, England. His published work includes articles on the political economy of English football, and the attempted BSkyB takeover of Manchester United. Recent publications include articles on the political economy of the third way, the International Monetary Fund, and English regionalism.

Roger Levermore is both research manager of the Football Industry Group and Director of Studies for International Business BA (Hons) at the University of Liverpool Management School. His background is in international relations, with a PhD (University of Plymouth) completed in 2001 on South Africa in the international political economy.

Rogan Taylor is the director of the Football Industry Group at the University of Liverpool and has been primarily responsible for the development of the first MBA in football industries. He has wide interests in football, including the social and economic history of the game; the relationship between fans and clubs; clubs and the media; post-war football in Hungary; and the modern development of football in Asia. He has published five football books.

Series Editor's Foreword

Sport and International Relations fills a gap. There has been no volume devoted to a specific inquiry into the association between them. It is time there was: 'Sport is now a mirror in which nations, men and women and social classes see themselves. The image is something bright, sometimes dark, sometimes distorted, sometimes magnified. This metaphorical mirror is a source of exhiliration and depression, security and insecurity, pride and humiliation, association and disassociation.'[1] With the result that, 'as sport has grown to a gargantuan size, progressively replacing religion in its power to excite passion, provide emotional escape, offer fraternal (and increasingly sororital) bonding, it has come to loom larger and larger in the lives of Europeans and others. The force of its appeal surprises only the ignorant, yet its appeal is astounding.'[2]

It is beyond any dispute that, athletes of all persuasions now have the capacity to win the attention of not millions but scores of millions within their own nations. Super athletes transcend national boundaries and become International Icons – glamorous, wealthy, 'healthy' and deified. Nations are sustained through economic recessions, political disasters and indentity crises by triumphant athletes who 'symbolize' national virtues. Moreover, men regain some confidence when male athletes win, while women grow in greater confidence when female athletes succeed ...[3]

Consequently, '[sport] encompasses so many dimensions of experience involving politics, gender and class, that this is a "resonant moment", as sport seduces the modern world, for cultural historians [and other academics] as they consider the evolution of one of the most significant human experiences of the late twentieth century.'[4]

One neglected dimension is sport and its import on international relations and vice versa. The global 'brand images' of nations, especially those third world countries with little to boast about to the rest of the world, self-evidently can depend substantially on performances on sports pitches and in sport areas – with the result that across the world 'fair play', over often preached but too often not practised, matters less and less, politicians involve themselves more and more and pressures on athletes grow greater and greater.

To add complication to complication multi-nationals have their marketing strategies and exert their influence and the national and trans-national media have their vested interests and have their impact. And in the middle are the voracious spectators of 'the Global Village' doing their best to enjoy what they are allowed to enjoy.

These elements impinge, to a greater or lesser extent in different places at different times, on international relations between nations, cultures and societies. *Sport and International Relations* gives overdue consideration to these elements. It breaks new analytical ground; constitutes the beginning of a new type of inquiry; and is a welcome first for sport in the global society.

J. A. Mangan
IRCSSS
De Montfort (Bedford)
December 2003

Prologue

CHRISTOPHER HILL

Sport no longer exists in the margins of international relations. A residual intellectual snobbishness still leads some to assume either that sport is a mindless activity or that it poses no interesting questions for the student of society and politics, but this is fast disappearing as the realization dawns of the important part that sport plays in the lives of untold millions across the globe, rich and poor alike. The academic subject of international relations (IR), however, has lagged behind sociologists and historians in giving serious attention to sport, and this book aims to ignite its interest by indicating the many points of interconnection. The neglect may have been initially caused by the subject's obsession with the high politics of inter-state relations, but trans-national relations have been a main focus now for over 30 years, and the assaults on realism have been so common over the same period as to become banal. A more convincing explanation lies in the sheer range of subjects which IR has to cover, from world health to biological weapons, from gender to geopolitics. It is difficult, given the continued minority status of IR specialists in political science departments, to do justice to all the issues generated in world politics. All of us have to be generalists to a greater or lesser degree.

How does sport matter, and where exactly does it connect to the processes of international relations? However much truth there may be in the 'opium of the masses' perspective, it is certainly not a sufficient explanation of sport's importance or impact, any more than it suffices as an approach to the study of television and tabloid newspapers. For one thing it downgrades and patronizes the pleasure, emotion and sense of identity which most people take from some or other aspect of sporting activity. On the other hand it simplifies the processes of economic and social mobilization represented by sport, both amateur and professional. Certainly wherever modernization is under way, large numbers of people participate in organized sport at some level – usually more than attend church or party political meetings – and thereby both consume and generate a significant proportion of their country's wealth. In so doing they form attachments which may well be as important for their identity and sense of community as the conventional factors of state and history. Nor is this always in the direction of reinforcing national sentiments. Support for sporting clubs may privilege club, or

region, over country, while there is an increasing tendency to form attachments to star performers in other countries – as with the global adulation of
Muhammad Ali, or the huge crowds that watch Manchester United during
their Asian tours. As people travel more, or are simply exposed to other cultures through television, they may begin to identify with a second *patria*, as
British golf fans have come to do with the European Ryder Cup team.

Since international relations, by definition, are wider than 'international
politics' they automatically incorporate all cross-border activities, even
those of a purely functional kind. The interesting questions about sport or
other forms of civil association, however, relate to its impact on things outside itself, which in this context means the character and evolution of the
international system. The academic student of IR then has a number of lines
of enquiry to pursue. The most obvious is that of international political
economy (IPE), given the huge growth in professional sport and the money
it generates through the mass media. If farming is best understood nowadays
as agri-business, we ought to coin the term 'ludo-business' for sport, given
that even the Olympic symbol has been put up for sale to multinationals such
as Coca-Cola (we should be shocked if the UN were to seek funds by the
same route) and now that the European Court of Justice has made it clear (in
the Bosman ruling of 1995) that football is a business like any other, with
clubs having no special powers to restrain the movements of their
players/employees.[1] The bigger European clubs have become international
corporations in their own right, farming talent in the Third World and prominent in the media, entertainment and gambling industries of countries worldwide. In this services-dominated phase of international capitalism, sport is a
leading sector of activity.

Nationalism has been one of the subjects that has most creatively linked
together international relations and domestic society in recent decades, but
it has not yet extended its coverage to sport, despite the evident points of
contact. Apart from the clichés about sport either embodying national rival-
ries or providing a safety-valve for them, there are serious issues to research
such as the role of sport in nation-building, whether at the nation-state or the
intra-state levels, and notions of identity and authenticity. Why is a single
British football team still unimaginable when unity works perfectly well in
the context of the Olympic games? Did national teams help Yugoslavia to
survive as a single state for as long as it did? Has the growth in multi-ethnic
club and national teams in football or athletics, and the globalization of race-
horse breeding and ownership weakened mass attachments to the nation-
state and laid the ground for cosmopolitan value systems? Such issues are
important for our understanding of sport, of society and of the international
system.

'The international system' refers holistically to the interplay of states and
non-state actors, which is the only realistic way to conceptualize diverse patterns of action and behaviour in the modern world. In this network, sports
organizations have become steadily more important trans-national actors, in

the sense that they dispose of large resources and are often focal points for political debate. They are both subjects and objects of politics, as in the case of disputes over TV rights for major events on the one hand, and the use of sports teams to promote détente between the two Koreas on the other. In the familiar lists of non-state actors sport can no longer be ignored. Some bodies like the International Olympic Committee or FIFA (Fédération Internationale de Football Association – itself a linguistic hybrid) mirror intergovernmental organizations – but are determinedly independent of them. Some, like Real Madrid or the United States Professional Golfers' Association provide leadership and points of reference in the conduct of their sport internationally.

Even the supposedly traditional area of diplomacy cannot afford to neglect sport – indeed, as Peter Beck shows in this volume and elsewhere, diplomats were quick to see the importance of sport for national prestige from the 1930s if not before.[2] The projection of a country's image or brand, as it would now be termed, is thought to hinge significantly on its ability to stage major competitions and to produce 'world-class' champions. If the exploitation of sport is not always as ruthless as that displayed by East Germany during the cold war, states are still willing to commit large resources, often under the table, to gain a perceived advantage. The political battles and vote-buying scandals associated with decisions on the location of Olympiads and World Cup finals demonstrate that sports are under pressure from states as well as commercial interests as they attempt to conduct their private business. In reality, however, sport no longer is a private matter, concerning only its participants and enthusiasts. Given the central involvement of the biggest political and economic players, it is a wonder that anything at all remains of the Corinthian ideal.

The values of sport find themselves subjected to interference from supposedly higher codes of morality as much as from grubby commercialism. 'Coercive diplomacy', or the attempt to pressure adversaries by all means short of war, has often turned to sport as a relatively cost-free, and dramatic, way of inflicting punishment. Sport was in the front line of the increasing use of sanctions during the last two decades of the twentieth century, as in the attempt to isolate apartheid South Africa or to punish the Soviet invasion of Afghanistan. It has been more successful at maintaining its autonomy since the end of the cold war, but sportsmen and women are still acutely vulnerable to changes in the political climate, as instanced by Australian cricketers' fears over touring Pakistan since 11 September 2001.

Even when direct interference is not evident, it is uncanny how often sport and politics march to the same drum of history. Antonio Missiroli has pointed out the many coincidences between the evolution of Britain's football relationships with Europe and its more general attitudes to European integration, most notably in the failure in 1955 both to allow the English champions (Chelsea) to take part in the inaugural European Cup and to take seriously the Messina Conference that kick-started the EEC.[3] But this is only to say that sport cannot be abstracted from the wider context in which it exists. It does not mean that it is wholly at the beck and call of politicians, any more than it should be seen as a paradise lost to the depradations of big business. There are still battalions of enthusiasts and officials, the majority unpaid, working to preserve the integrity of their sports, just as the millions of spectators and television viewers are perfectly capable of seeing through the hype to the passion, skill and drama that remain. Excessive commercialization and the widespread use of performance-enhancing drugs certainly risk destroying the appeal of high-level professional sport, but there are plenty of other avenues left for enjoyment. Sport is one of the relatively few avenues open for direct mass participation in international relations, not least because sport is a true meritocracy. The best performers always want to test themselves at the highest level, wherever in the world that may be, and spectators always want to see the best, whether that be Maradona, Serena Williams or Michael Schumacher. Accordingly sport is highly internationalized. Even at the humble club level, most participants want to take part in tours abroad and are keen to welcome foreign visitors in their turn. It may be too simple to say, as some idealists do, that sport is therefore inherently a force for good in the world; the exploitation of child labour by sports goods manufacturers is just one of many cases to the contrary. But it does breed 'understanding', in the sense of common interests and enthusiasms (the words 'Bobby Charlton' and 'George Best' have enabled many a linguistically challenged Brit to enjoy hospitality abroad), and it does provide opportunities for the disadvantaged that other walks of life struggle to emulate. Women in many traditional cultures struggle to find sporting opportunities, but they are beginning to do so, escaping from drudgery and oppression through athletic gifts. And it is well-known that basketball and athletics have provided one of the few channels for self-improvement for African-Americans, just as football has for those of Caribbean descent in the UK, and for many young Africans throughout Europe. No one wishes sport to be a mere palliative, an excuse for not engaging in serious reform. But only the deeply cynical do not take pleasure in, for example, hearing working-class British crowds, once capable of throwing bananas at black players, chanting the name of an idol who happens also to be black but whose skin colour has finally become irrelevant.

Sport, community and international relations are deeply entwined precisely because sport combines the importance of vicinity and of the wider world. Sports fans are capable of both deep parochialism, in a wholly understandable devotion to their team as an expression of local community, *and* an intense interest in their sport at the highest, international levels. Television has made the names of stars like Tiger Woods or Zinedine Zidane familiar in back streets anywhere in the world – even if this was also true of Ferenc Puskas and Juan Fangio in the 1950s. To some degree the same applies to politics. Yet sport, like music, engages positive passions, whereas politics is passionate primarily in its antagonisms. It is the ability to cross over between the local, national and international on the one hand, and to connect the mass and the elite on the other, that makes sport such an important phenomenon, in itself and as an object of study. This book starts from such assumptions. It is innovative, wide-ranging and provocative, in challenging mainstream international relations to end its neglect of an activity central to contemporary human experience.

INTRODUCTION

Sport and international relations: Continued neglect?

ROGER LEVERMORE and ADRIAN BUDD

Sport and international relations: A history of neglect

Academic analysis of the mutual impact of sport and society is fairly well established, with literature examining the sociology of sport expanding rapidly, as the titles in this Sport in the Global Society series testify. From this literature it is evident that analysis of sport can tell us a good deal about international relations; from global neo-liberal economics, diplomacy and war to cultural globalization, national identity formation and the media. However, these examples of the relationship between sport and the international environment have been overwhelmingly written by specialists in history, law, sports studies and particularly sociology. Very little text has been devoted to sport from the academic discipline of international relations (IR).[1] This lack of attention has attracted a degree of criticism. In 1986, for instance, Trevor Taylor argued that sport and IR were strangers and that there was a 'mutual neglect'; from an IR position, sport came a very distant second to IR's primary consideration – the 'inter-state struggle for security and power'.[2] More recently, Peter Beck has argued that IR has shown a 'high distaste' for sport, an argument echoed in Christopher Hill's prologue to this volume. Roger Levermore suggests that there are areas in which sport has some, if not a major, role to play where IR is silent; this is particularly the case, he argues, in security studies, conflict resolution, and how competing IR paradigms view the interplay of sport and international relations.[3]

This is not to say that IR has not contributed to analyses of sport in the global society. In the English language,[4] Benjamin Lowe edited a volume on sport and IR in 1978.[5] This vast collection, looking at the use of different cultural philosophies, political ideologies and governmental policies around the world, provides a comprehensive account of the political impact of sport across the globe, primarily from a realist perspective. The publication was, however, limited in the areas of IR it covered, and in the limited audience it reached. Since then, few texts have really attempted a serious analysis of the relationship of sport and international relations. However, those that have have gained more coverage and positive comments than the earlier publications mentioned above. First, Trevor Taylor's chapter ('Sport and International Relations') in Lincoln Allison's edited 1986 collection *The Politics of Sport* details the 'mutual neglect' of sport and IR, while indicating areas where IR scholars could incorporate sport into their analyses. Second, Barrie Houlihan's *Sport and International Politics* (1994) is perhaps the most referred-to academic publication on sport and IR.[6] It had a broader dimension, adding pluralist and globalist (Marxist) angles to realist IR theory. Third, presenting a different theoretical perspective to these mainly traditional realist and pluralist works, is Michael Shapiro's post-structural account of the 'Sport/War Intertext' in world politics, which looks at the sporting metaphors used during war.[7]

More recently, Riordan and Krüger's 1999 publication *The International Politics of Sport in the Twentieth Century* provides an informative and detailed account of the global themes in the politics of sport, without adding greatly to an IR analysis of sport.[8] Aside from these few texts, an increasing number of articles have emanated from IR that have considered sport. One of the first, 'The Role of Sport in International Relations', for the *Indian Journal of Politics*, by Marian Szczepaniak, was difficult to read and also suffered from limited circulation.[9] However, more authoritative articles were written at the same time. In 1981 Kyröläinen and Varis analysed approaches to the study of sport in IR.[10] This was followed in 1982 by Johann Galtung's reading of the Western political and cultural values inherent in global sport.[11] Other, more recent, examples include Christopher R. Hill's 'Keeping Politics in Sport',[12] Pascal Boniface's 'Football as a Factor (and a Reflection) of International Politics',[13] and Allison and Monnington's 'Sport, Prestige and International Relations'.[14]

Some of these texts, particularly before 1982, play down the significance of sport to international relations. Lowe, for example, argues that 'sport is safe because it is peripheral to the international political system'.[15] Furthermore, Szczepaniak notes that 'sports have not been, of course, a decisive factor in international life'.[16] Recent articles, though, have placed a greater stress on the importance of sport to international society. Allison and Monnington, for example, argue that 'modern sport is increasingly and perhaps essentially international and has had an international dimension almost from the outset'.[17] Keys also calls for an analysis of international sports events, such as the Olympics or the football World Cup, which play a significant role in international relations.[18] Most of these articles also note the poverty in IR of a serious analysis of sport. An academic publication examining sport from differing IR perspectives is therefore certainly overdue. This book aims to kick-start a debate on the mutual impacts of sport and international society, from within the IR academic discipline. The majority of theoretical perspectives employed here tend to follow closely the realist, and to a lesser extent pluralist, treatments adopted by most of the above-mentioned publications and journal articles. However, some of the chapters have a more critical theoretical and post-structuralist stance.

The dearth of serious academic literature from the IR discipline was one of the main reasons for Roger Levermore to convene two panels on sport and IR at the British International Studies Association (BISA) conference at the University of Bradford in December 2000. Many contributors to these panels expressed concern over the 'neglect' that IR had paid to serious academic analysis of the international dimensions of sport. Indeed, senior figures within BISA could not recall there ever being a panel at a BISA conference dedicated solely to sport. This book, including some of the papers presented to these panels, therefore represents an attempt to bring the study of sport closer to IR.

The importance of sport to IR

Academic analysis and popular discourse have tended to locate the international sphere somewhere between nation states, as if it hovered in a sort of no man's land. As far as IR is concerned, this is best exemplified in the resistance of realism, IR's dominant perspective, to the opening of the 'black box' of internal social practices and sub-state processes, as if these were of no consequence for the international dimensions of state policy. What is more, for mainstream state-centrism, IR has been chiefly concerned with 'high politics' – issues of security, military power and diplomacy – and, therefore, has tended to exclude analysis of those structural characteristics of the international system that cannot be neatly subsumed under 'politics'. Even where the 'internal/external' has been explored, in James Rosenau's *Linkage Politics* for example, the 'penetrative', 'reactive' and 'emulative' processes he highlighted were seen in largely political terms.[19]

Developments over the last three decades, however, have dealt a serious blow to the notion that societies exist within largely hermetically sealed boundaries and interact with other societies as with external objects – the famous billiard-ball analogy of Hobbesian provenance. Whether through the general and developing impact of what has come to be known as globalization on local economies, environments and so on or, more particularly and dramatically, the forceful eruption of the global within the local on 11 September 2001, the international increasingly impinges upon and constrains our actions. Indeed, IR theory has been grappling with the consequences of what Robert Keohane and Joseph Nye have referred to as realism's difficulties 'accurately to interpret today's multidimensional economic, social, and economic interdependence' since the 1970s.[20] They have suggested that the world has moved into an era of 'complex interdependence', characterized by 'multiple channels' between societies, including both state and non-state channels, such that 'military security does not consistently dominate the agenda'.[21] Other, neo-liberal, IR theorists have expanded the range of what are considered to be significant IR actors (issue groups, trans-national corporations etc.), while regime theory has explored the persistence of international regimes across a range of areas even in the absence of a hegemonic state, albeit that the key actors within regimes remain states. From a more critical perspective, neo-Gramscian theory also 'differs from classical realism in broadening the range of determining factors beyond state power'[22] and conceives the international system as being constructed from the mutual interaction of social forces, states and patterns of world order.[23] These social forces cannot be simply conceived as operating within the bounds of nation states.[24] Notwithstanding the major theoretical differences between these perspectives, all are critical of one-sided state-centrism without arguing that states have been transcended as the major actors in international relations.[25] It is within the context of the growing recognition of the importance of non-state actors that an analysis of sport and IR can be set.

Our intention is not to argue that sport is central to the dynamics and operation of the international system in the same way as economic, political and military processes. There has been no sporting equivalent of 11 September while, even had Argentina won the 2002 World Cup, the impact would have provided only short-term psychological and emotional respite from the economic meltdown afflicting the country. Nor do we argue that the analysis of sport offers an especially privileged access point to the under-standing of the international system. But sport does provide an access point, for it is an important *part of that system*, and, as such, is shaped by it while simultaneously influencing it. Thus, while cricket matches between India and Pakistan are of secondary importance compared with the recent threat of war between the two countries, they are cut from the same cloth of social and international relations and inscribed within the same framework of ideas and social practices. Consequently, we argue that a deeper understanding of the dynamics of global sport may foster greater understanding of the inter-national environment.

The intensification of trans-national and international processes that has impelled IR theory towards innovation in recent decades has been given the label 'globalization'. Anthony Giddens, echoing David Harvey's concept of 'time-space compression', provides a widely used, if rather general, defini-tion of globalization – 'the intensification of worldwide social relations which link distant localities together in such a way that local happenings are shaped by events occurring many miles away and vice versa'.[26] Leslie Sklair has argued for greater precision in defining the key processes of globaliza-tion, arguing that 'the most important global force at the beginning of the twenty-first century is the capitalist global system'.[27] But whether we see globalization as an inevitable product of technological and organizational innovation or as the latest stage of capitalism, it is clear that what Joseph Maguire has called 'global sport' is deeply influenced by, and an exemplar of, the wider globalizing trend.[28]

The 2002 football World Cup in Japan and South Korea provides an example of the way, and reinforces the view, that sport (or certain sports at

certain times) has a significant place in contemporary social life. A range of
trans-national processes, including cultural, political and economic, were
involved. The World Cup was heavily mediatized, providing instant gratification (or disappointment) to distant millions. It was also heavily
commercialized and, like other major world sporting events, was an instrument for the development of the interests of trans-national companies. But
if the World Cup brought millions (virtually) together in a common appreciation of 'the beautiful game' and helped shatter cultural myths about the
'otherness' of Koreans and Japanese (and of hitherto unsung footballing
nations such as Senegal and Turkey), it also reinforced differentiations
between those millions whose point of contact with others was shaped by the
context of national competition at the heart of the tournament. The globalization of sport, then, like its more general set of globalizing practices, is not
a straightforward linear process, but a dialectic of nationalism and internationalism, the distant and the local, the immediate and the mediatized, the
personal and impersonal. Indeed, 2002 was also witness to a revival of the
far right in Europe, and an aggressive turn towards unilateralism in Bush's
America (steel tariffs, National Missile Defence, opposition to the Kyoto
Protocol and the International Criminal Court and so on) whose origins pre-
dated the 11 September attacks. Kenichi Ohmae's claim that we live in a
'borderless world' remains a businessman's chimera.[29]

To repeat, our aim is not to substitute the analysis of sport for IR. Instead,
we argue for the articulation of the two, for an exploration of the international system via analysis of sport, whose specific processes and structures
are related to a wider international social totality. Such an articulation, if it
can be achieved, may help us locate, in global sports processes, developments of wider currency.

Structure and content of the book

In his recent work on IR theory, Heikki Patomäki argued that 'there is no
automatic correspondence between any particular theoretical discourse and
the social worlds they refer to and purport to understand, explain and,
sometimes, change'.[30] Social scientific explanation, then, involves not a
straightforward collection and ordering of the 'facts' of our social existence,
for those 'facts' are presented to us via numerous mediations. Indeed, there
are those social scientists who, prioritizing the ideational dimension of
human existence, question the very existence of an objective reality whether
natural or social, referring instead to plural 'realities'. But, whether 'reality'
is conceived of as a creation of the mind, or as existing independently of it,
all social science is, to an extent, a work of interpretation. Consequently,
ideas, including the frequently unacknowledged ideas of the theorist, are an
important element in social scientific explanation. It is in this sense that
Steve Smith criticized realism's attempts to construct a science of interna-

tional relations based on a positivist methodology, which 'essentially treats order as something "out there", to be observed much in the same way as a natural scientist examines aspects of the natural world'.[31] But this ought not reduce social science to pure relativism, where rival explanations are all equally valid whatever their connection to the 'real world'. Rather, for all that the immediate phenomenal appearance of the social world may, as Marxists have argued, obscure the underlying relations and processes that produce those phenomena, social scientific explanation, to be explanation at all, must offer interpretations that not only take account of the complexity of the social world, without isolating individual phenomena under restrictive *ceteris paribus* assumptions, but also increase the intelligibility of that world.[32]

IR, like the other social sciences, is divided into rival, if sometimes cross-fertilizing, 'epistemic communities' that provide a range of understandings of the structure and dynamics of the international system. All approach that system not with any privileged access to its essence, if such an essence exists, but via the mediated expressions of that essence. One such, increasingly powerful, mediation is to be found in the mass media themselves which provide a rich, or if you prefer, tragically impoverished, diet of images and messages. As far as IR is concerned, these messages tend towards a powerful reinforcement of the dominant perspective, namely state-centric realism. The task of this book, to present a range of understandings in a relatively new area of enquiry, requires a consistent interrogation of realism. Thus, Roger Levermore's opening chapter challenges both traditional IR's reification of states and the ways that the media tend to reinforce it. His central argument is that nation-states (and therefore the inter-state structure), traditionally taken for granted by mainstream IR, are historical social constructs, albeit that they have concrete as well as ideological consequences.

If media images were so powerful as to prevent any deeper understanding of the social world, we would remain trapped within this state-centric discourse. But, as Levermore also argues, in various parts of the world sport has been, intermittently, a vehicle for the expression of oppositional currents that challenge the dominant perspective of a world simply divided into nation-states. Adrian Budd takes Levermore's critical theoretical approach to the inter-state system in a Marxist direction, arguing that while inter-state dynamics are real they are best understood when located within a deeper ontological reality, namely the sets of social practices, relations and structures that are constitutive of the capitalist mode of production. These, he argues, influence the totality of social relations under capitalism, including sporting relations. But if sport under capitalism is commodified and manifests the competitive and exploitative logic of that system, including at the international level, it can also become a vehicle for subaltern resistance such that sport's dominant meanings are never fixed but always an arena of struggle and negotiation.

John Harris's and Barbara Humberstone's chapter on gender relations and sport offers a different critique of hegemonic practices and discourses. They argue that in a patriarchal society hegemonic masculinity underlies social relations, including those of sport, where an idealized masculinity or manliness is presented alongside its corollary – an essentialized femininity. Both are bound within the constraints of a narrow heterosexuality. Harris and Humberstone further argue that this idealized masculinity is globally articulated in conceptions of nationalism. Thus, while not directly connecting gender to international relations, in the way that Cynthia Enloe, for example, does,[33] the linkages that they make between gender, sport and nationalism pose questions of the dynamics of states that IR theory would benefit from exploring.

For all that realism reifies the state system, naturalizes it, gives it a trans-historical timelessness and, for critical theorists, mistakenly disarticulates it from wider social, political and economic processes, Callinicos has argued that it 'seems like a better error into which to fall than the fanciful belief that, thanks to political globalization, inter-state conflict is being transcended'.[34] For state power remains a vital element of the contemporary world order. Indeed, as we write, the world's foremost military power, the United States, has recently launched a strike against Iraq, the power of whose dictatorial leader rested at least as much on his control of a state as it did on economic resources. But states are not the only actors in international relations, and the subsequent four chapters in the book emphasize, to varying degrees, this plurality.

Barrie Houlihan applies regime theory to the issue of doping in sport. Developed when US hegemony, which realism had argued was the cement holding the (Western) world together, faced challenges from the 1960s, regime theory sought to demonstrate how international regimes contributed to the persistence of interdependence. Houlihan illustrates how an anti-doping regime emerged out of cooperation between a variety of national and international governmental institutions and non-governmental sports organizations. He also demonstrates the utility of applying insights from a range of IR perspectives, including neo-liberalism, realism and constructivism, to the development of the emergent anti-doping regime, the benefits of which accrue not only to the dominant sporting powers but also to the less resource-rich 'middle range' sports states which may take advantage of the regime to influence the policies of more powerful states. Here, on the issue of extensive benefits from a discrete regime area, Houlihan touches upon the wider concerns of those IR scholars grouped around the multilateralism and the United Nations system (MUNS) programme sponsored by the United Nations University (UNU) for whom multilateralism represents a possible route to greater balance in the inter-state system at a time when the sole remaining superpower, the US, has reasserted its global hegemony.[35]

The chapters by Peter Beck and Aaron Beacom both explore British Olympic Games policy and diplomacy, but from different angles. Beck's chapter dissects British Olympic Games policy and demonstrates how sport has been used in state diplomacy and as a propaganda vehicle to enhance British prestige, despite governmental claims of a separation between sport and politics. Reacting to, and borrowing from, the Nazi and Soviet models, constructed during the middle third of the twentieth century which was marked by increased state power internationally, the British state politicized sport and established a framework used by all subsequent governments, whether Conservative or Labour. The state's concerns, expressed in nationalist terms, have been replicated at the private level, where sporting organizations have also sought government intervention in sport in order to enhance Britain's international sporting success.

Beck recognizes the importance of non-state actors but his analysis remains largely on traditional realist territory. Aaron Beacom's chapter, on the other hand, highlights the limitations of state-centric realism and its tendency to see sport as a political tool of states. Beacom argues that even in the inter-war heyday of state-centrism, inter-state diplomacy was complemented by the activities of non-state actors. These included commercial interests, regional and municipal government and international sports organizations such as the International Olympic Committee (IOC), which was an important international actor as early as the 1920s. He further demonstrates that, more recently, individual athletes and national sporting associations, such as the International Athletes' Club, have influenced British Olympic policy. Beacom thus challenges realism's attribution of foreign policy coherence to apparently unitary states and highlights their requirement to reconcile contrasting interests within a multi-layered complex of state and non-state diplomatic actors. But if this pluralist perspective gives due weight to the role of national and international sports organizations in sports policy-making, Beacom does not simply dismiss state-primacy arguments. For the British state has continued to bring its influence to bear on, for example, the British Olympic Committee and IOC representatives, whose own influence, he argues, remains marginal beyond a narrow range of issues.

Simon Lee's chapter concentrates on the plurality of non-governmental actors, and their inter-relationships, in the governance and political economy of world football. Indeed, Lee's analysis contrasts sharply with both Beck and Beacom in largely excluding state actors in his review of football's governance. Lee argues that this is indicative of the way national governments or intergovernmental organizations (such as the EU) tend to view sport – as mainly outside the concern of state action. Instead, Lee highlights the tensions that an increasingly prosperous and largely unregulated sporting business, particularly since 1990, has created for the international, national and local (club level) governance of football, those tensions being especially marked between 'significant new private actors' and football's traditional administrators. The lack of suitable levels of ethical corporate governance, the purported increase in bribery and corruption, as well as the

unequal distribution of wealth, indicate that stronger self-governing or external (i.e. government-led) regulation is required to ensure that the unfettered
capitalism in football does not further harm the game. Yet, in addressing
resistance to the dominance of the commercialization and commodification
within English professional league football (with a review of the governance
of Manchester United plc), Lee supports analyses made by Levermore and
Budd that aspects of sport can be used as a vehicle to resist hegemonic
trends within international relations.

Rogan Taylor, a non-IR academic, writing the epilogue from the perspective of a much-travelled sports journalist, reinforces the inherent message of
Lee's chapter, and indeed the book – that the relationship between sport and
international society should be obvious and that serious academic analyses
is required, particularly from IR specialists, if we are to develop a greater
appreciation of that relationship. The content of this book covers a range of
subjects central to IR, such as international political economy, regime
theory, the inter-state structure, gender, diplomacy and state propaganda.
While a number of areas of IR are obviously excluded, the editors and
contributors see the book as an attempt to stimulate debate on sport within
IR. We are conscious of the necessary limitations of such a venture, and of
the suggestions from scholars in other academic disciplines of potential
areas for future research. Blanchard, for instance, suggests that future
research should concentrate on 'the dream of world peace [which] is well
served by efforts to understand sporting diversity, encourage international
and interdisciplinary cooperation, and revisit the original spirit of the
Olympics'.[36] Other, more realistic, directions could include:

- the increasingly important role of sporting federations (such as the IOC)
  as international non-state actors;
- the potential role of sport in international conflict resolution, in diplomacy, and in sanction regimes;
- the construction of global regimes in sport and their role in reinforcing
  interdependence;
- sport as a source of resistance, either by the subaltern to dominant forces
  within Western states, or by those variously 'othered' and subordinated
  by Western states;
- sport and the building of national identity and international projection of
  state interests;
- sport and its relation to social change and to innovation in social theory
  (e.g. sport and capitalism, modernity, progress, inclusion, exclusion,
  discrimination, identity etc.).

To reassert a point made elsewhere in the book, the analysis of sport is not
conceived here as a substitute for engagement with the traditional concerns
of IR. It can, however, be a heuristic device that illuminates practices and
processes of wider significance, thereby contributing to a deeper under-

standing of contemporary international society. Scholars in a range of social science disciplines have already begun this work. Our hope is that within IR, others will welcome our attempt to develop research into what has been a relatively neglected area. While not claiming that we are on the threshold of a revolution in science, or in anything else for that matter, we would, finally, like to point out, paraphrasing Lao-tzu, that even the longest journey must begin with a single step.

1

Sport's role in constructing the 'inter-state' worldview[1]

ROGER LEVERMORE

Defining the 'inter-state' worldview

An increasing body of literature, both academic and 'everyday', argues that sport, and particularly the reporting of sport, plays an important role in 'building' nations, nation-states and national identities. I argue in this chapter that sport, particularly through the narration of international sporting events, shapes concepts (nation, national identity, nation-state and ultimately the inter-state structure) that construct the 'inter-state worldview'[2] – a dominant portrayal of how the political world is cartographically and socially/politically divided into competing states. This worldview is presented as being natural, commonsensical, civilized, modern (yet with historical antecedents) and the only feasible way of ordering political communities, in which the nation-state is often accorded quasi-sacred status. I argue further that such a picture, although questioned occasionally, remains as Cynthia Weber might argue, 'essentially uncontested',[3] thereby excluding the articulation of alternative ideas of how to organize global political life. This is true throughout academia, where the inter-state worldview and its component parts have mainly been portrayed in an unquestioning manner.

Traditional IR theory has keenly articulated this view of international society. The neo-realist Kenneth Waltz, for example, regards states as the primary 'units whose interactions form the structure of international-political systems'.[4] James Mayall, too, asserts that the state system is the 'prevailing conception of international society'. States, he argues, are natural; they 'actually exist; they can be located on a map; they have more or less defined boundaries; they have settled populations and identifiable social and political institutions'. The naming of states helps to 'impose a degree of order on an area of human activity from which there is no escape but which is notoriously anarchic'.[5] In terms of seeking 'justification' for the inter-state worldview, Hinsley and Mayall argue that aspects of the inter-state system can be traced back to ancient Greece, as outlined by Thucydides in his study of the practice of diplomacy.[6]

Mass media ('everyday') reporting is also extremely effective at portraying, in an unquestioning manner, the inter-state worldview as 'real'.

The London *Evening Standard*, for example, argued recently that it would be difficult to 'imagine the world devoid of the tribal, geographical, economic and survivalist forces that herd humans into nation states'.[7] The reporting of sport, particularly inter-state competitive sporting events, is especially persuasive in conveying the message that nations and states are somehow naturally 'apart' and boundaries are 'concrete'. Sports reporting falsely represents a state's population as homogeneous, suggesting that 'we' share a common, yet exclusive way of life, which is more important than other loyalties and identities. At the same time such reporting also contrasts 'us' with other nations, such as through a national team's playing style or the supporters associated with it.

Many writers argue that sport actually eases tensions between contestants and competitors in the international arena, while also unifying often disparate sets of people within a state. Indeed, many world leaders and important figures in the sporting world stress that sport has a harmonizing effect (something that Christopher Hill also mentions in the Prologue to this book). I feel, however, that this dominant reading of global society, particularly through the reporting of sport, is problematic. While recognizing that the inter-state 'world order' does enjoy the benefits listed above (indeed, nation-states and inclusive civic nationalism have provided a degree of unity to areas with very disparate populations), unquestioning allegiance to the dominant worldview has detrimental consequences. The inter-state worldview promotes a form of apartheid that often reduces identity to a single affiliation and encourages populations to be sectarian and intolerant. The xenophobic backlash to certain migrants (such as asylum seekers) throughout much of the world (from Australia to South Africa, and Malaysia to the UK) is one ugly manifestation of such an adherence to nationalism within the inter-state worldview. Many analysts contend that the presentation of the inter-state worldview as natural, commonsensical, civilized and ahistorical is dubious. Hobsbawm, for example, has argued that it has been constructed on selective readings of history, while ignoring alternative representations of the past.[8] In similar vein Llobera notes: 'We are now so infatuated with entities such as France, Spain, Italy, Germany or Great Britain that we tend to believe that they are, if not eternal, at least old enough to be projected into the distant past without committing a dangerous historical fallacy.'[9] Far from promoting international harmony, to which the guardians of the sporting world appear to have a rhetorical commitment, the portrayal of international sport, in practice, often produces opposite effects.

This chapter proceeds by deconstructing the ways in which the reporting of international sporting events, particularly the 1998 and 2002 football World Cups and Euro 2000, the European nations' championship in 2000, has been used to assist the construction of the inter-state worldview and its component parts. This will be the focus of the next section. Illustrating how athletic events contribute to cementing the inter-state worldview provides, however, only a partial understanding of the messages that sports reporting can carry. The subsequent section suggests that sport has been used in far more complex and subtle ways, such as parodying, contesting and resisting those inter-state concepts that it (perhaps inadvertently) assists to create and maintain.

The theoretical perspective that informs this chapter is a mixture of post-structuralism and critical theory. Its post-structuralist origins are based on analyses that have suggested that sport is used by 'the elite' to manipulate the representation of 'reality' to 'national populations'. For example, Baudrillard claims that 'Power is only too happy to make football bear a facile responsibility for stupefying the masses'.[10] The chapter is also influenced by the critical theorist Andrew Linklater. His 'immutability thesis' alludes to the inter-state worldview being presented as a fait accompli, in which alternative versions of political communities cannot credibly replace the inter-state system because of the 'logic of power' inherent in the realist representation of anarchy – only the state can possibly control it. The 'language of immutability' that surrounds this is designed to produce communities that accept the impossibility of changing this worldview.[11] This chapter, while loosely following these perspectives, does not concur whole-heartedly with the rather negative conclusion reached by Baudrillard or Linklater. As argued at the end of the chapter, there is a chance that sport can be used to challenge the apartheid nature of the inter-state worldview.

Sport reporting: maintaining the inter-state worldview

The chapter now proceeds by first describing how sports reporting portrays and maintains the inter-state worldview as if it were commonsensical and natural and, second, by exploring how sports media promote the components of inter-state order as providers of civility, unity and order, while also having quasi-religious and ahistorical attributes.

Inter-state competitive images

By simply highlighting competition between contesting states (or teams that represent states), international sporting events assist in concretizing the impression that the inter-state structure is 'natural'. For instance, Pierre de Coubertin's nineteenth-century essays often portrayed the Olympic Games as 'natural' arenas where competition between 'states-as-nations' took place.[12] Many analysts examining the relationship between sport and global society draw similar conclusions. Johann Galtung, for example, noted that the image of competitive sport perpetuates the inscription of the Westphalian states system. Instead of demonstrating cooperation, sports media tend to concentrate on the competitive element, particularly the simplistic winner/loser binary aspect. This is especially the case in Western culture, Galtung argues, as inter-state sporting contests, as defined above, are the 'clear expression of basic aspects of Western culture', precisely because it sees sport as being 'competitive, in ranking nations, teams and individuals. Western . . . culture is a set of finely entrenched patterns and beliefs, usually unconsciously held and rarely challenged, except from those outside that civilization.'[13]

Contests pitting representative state teams have often carried far more than a simple sporting message – the 'natural' competitive element of the state is frequently highlighted, particularly in the media. Perhaps one of the most notable examples of the political/competitive importance attached to an inter-state sporting contest was during the cold war, when ice hockey matches between the US and Soviet Union were played in a volatile competitive context and where the winning team depicted its political system as the pre-eminent one (described in greater detail in Peter Beck's chapter in this book).[14] The media are often criticized for treating sporting competitions as a 'zero-sum' game. For instance, Phillips-Davison comments that

> A sports event is, in the language of mathematics, a zero-sum game where if one side wins the other side has to lose. In international conflict, both sides may lose, or possibly both may gain something, but there may not be a symmetrical relationship between the gains of one and the losses of another. Sports reporting is unintentionally dishonest in that the focus on the contest obscures the enormous amount of cooperation between the contestants: [for example] the acceptance of the referees' authority and the often-complicated infrastructure of rules, prior arrangements, and sponsorship.[15]

An examination of the British media surrounding the World Cups of 1998 and 2002 and Euro 2000 unsurprisingly reveals that the 'zero-sum game' contest between states is largely reinforced, either in the form of a match between national teams, or occasionally between national supporters. The newspaper headline announcing 'Breathtaking! Argentina and England fought out an epic battle'[16] represented just one of innumerable similar statements made in the media during the three tournaments. Away from traditional media sources, new media forms conveyed a similar message. For example, an official FIFA World Cup '98 computer game was advertised thus: 'Conquer fierce defenders and defeat entire nations on your quest'.[17] Internet websites were also projecting the inter-state world view; one of the more extreme sites declared 'For all the Turks out there, fuck you and Atatürk. Bring those body bags we sent you for the earthquake to Euro 2000, you'll need them!'[18]

The England versus Germany match in Euro 2000 clearly epitomized how the inter-state competitive image was illustrated. A British journalist, Peter Preston, writing in the *Guardian*, noted that beating Germany was seen as a proud national event.[19] The *Sun* (a British tabloid newspaper) pleaded: 'Hammer those Germans tonight because we'd love it ... we'd really love it.'[20] The fervent nationalism that accompanied the match, particularly among English supporters, was noted by many journalists. Oliver Holt, for example, stated that following England then was like 'being on a march with a rampaging army as they lay waste to large tracts of other countries'.[21] This was taken to extremes in England, where, in some areas, those branded as 'German' were attacked.[22]

Reinforcing the impression of inter-state boundaries

In many parts of the world the construction of inter-state boundaries is a relatively recent event, with the majority of borders created and fixed between the late nineteenth and mid-twentieth centuries by political leaders; sport assisted by reinforcing mental images of these boundaries. For instance, throughout the twentieth century, international sporting organizations supported the construction and maintenance of boundaries between states, as if they were real.[23] In 1934, the International Amateur Athletics Federation (IAAF) added a paragraph to its rules confining member associations to the political boundaries of the country they represented, a political statement that effectively denounced those people fighting against established international borders (such as those arguing for a greater Ireland).[24] The statement also had the effect of bolstering the perception that such borders were virtually immutable.

In France, during the 1998 football World Cup, the issue of maintaining national borders was particularly pertinent to domestic politics as the EU's Schengen agreement (allowing free movement across certain EU borders) was suspended. This was because much concern was expressed that the World Cup might generate an 'invasion' of immigrants, Islamic fundamentalists, football 'hooligans' or political extremists. To prevent a 'breach' of these borders, arrests were made in France, Germany, Britain and elsewhere. In these senses, reporting of the World Cup enhanced the reification of inter-state boundaries.

Nationalism, building nation-states and national stereotyping

The perpetuation of nationalism has long been associated with codified sport. International football, for example,

> can act as a surrogate theatre for the working-up of 'passionate nationalism'. An international football match involving 'our' team intrudes into our daily routine, reminding us of with whom we stand with regard to our fellow nationals, and whom we stand against in the international sphere. Sometimes, simply taking part in FIFA competitions can create the conditions for exaggerated displays of nationalism which have a meaning beyond the games themselves.[25]

Furthermore, sport has played a role in constructing 'new' nationalisms and nation-states, especially in efforts to legitimize the creation of a state by being 'recognized'; first, by often diverse populations bracketed within 'their' territorial jurisdiction, and second, by the international community.

Cameroon, with a large number of languages and 'imagined ethnic communities', is representative of much of Africa, in that it is an example of such a state striving to be accepted by its heterogeneous populace. Paul Nkwi and Bea Vidacs contend that football plays a crucial role in creating a sense of 'nationhood': 'the fostering of football is part of a conscious government effort to strengthen national unity. ... [Furthermore], participation in international sport has generated a greater sense of nationhood than any other Cameroonian achievement.'[26]

Sport has often become an important vehicle by which the state is accorded recognition in the international community. Membership of international associations such as FIFA is particularly important, as 'other than being admitted as a member of the United Nations ... it is the clearest signal that a country's status as a nation state has been recognized by the international community'.[27] This is notably the case for many African states, which often only register a 'positive' and successful image in the international community by doing well at international sporting events. Senegal's performance in reaching the quarter-finals of the 2002 World Cup is a particularly apt example of an African state that is often stereotyped as a backward, traditional society; yet its team played intelligent and successful football.

Stereotyping of national populations is also commonplace within the reporting of sport. Examples of such labelling were abundant in the sporting events studied. World Cup 1998 media commentary was peppered with comments about 'Germans' being thorough, efficient, 'cold-hearted' and with 'no sense of humour ... no sense of British fair play'; they are 'mechanical robots with no flair'.[28] Stereotypical references were also made to describe the national characteristics (epitomized by the national football team) of Japan, Iran, South Korea, England, Cameroon and other participants.

Inter-state worldview 'components'

Sports reporting also promotes the components of the inter-state worldview as being able to provide unity, order and civility (in contrast to chaos and anarchy, which is the 'normal' condition of international society). At the same time the sports media tend to present the elements of the inter-state structure as being quasi-religious and ahistorical. The following examples show how the reporting of the 1998 and 2002 World Cups and Euro 2000 assisted such a description of these characteristics.

Unify/civilize

Norbert Elias has argued that the transformation of 'medieval sport', from being anarchic and violent into an event with rules and order, represented a powerful stimulus in the 'civilizing process' that assisted the progression of modern society.[29] Similarly, de Coubertin regarded 'modern' sport (which he modelled on an idealized view of the ancient Olympics) as a vehicle through which society could be 'civilized'. From the 1850s, ancient 'Olympian ideals' were embodied in sport played in British public schools, where the virtues of order, unity and indeed 'civility' were accompanied by a strict adherence to rules. Consequently, in this era, many modern-day sports were codified and transformed from being perceived as anarchic, violent games played by mobs to being ordered and 'civilized'.

Many sports federations such as the IOC, UEFA or FIFA seem to have subscribed to the view that modern sports can promote unity and civility. FIFA, for instance, has as one of its objectives the unification of peoples 'through the expansion of the FIFA family and the promotion of harmony among nations and power blocs'.[30] Notions of unity and progress were endorsed during the 1998 World Cup. At the opening ceremony in Paris four tall inflatable figures, representing the four primary 'colours' of humanity (European, Asian, African and Native American) converged – an act that the organizers intended would symbolize the 'unification of humanity'.

Within this context, the media focused on how France, with its well-known mixture of 'ethnic' groupings, was 'unified' due to the success of its 'multiracial' team, which won the 1998 World Cup. A report in the London *Independent* reflected that the competition represented the remaking of France 'as a football nation, as a confident nation, and most of all, as a multi-racial nation'.[31] This was followed by such headlines as 'French find a new identity'[32] and 'France unites in Football victory'.[33] Writing four years after the 1998 World Cup, such notions of unification appear to have been quietly forgotten in the face of renewed enmity between ethnic groups in France, as the electoral success of the Front National illustrates.

In similar vein, the 2002 World Cup was expected to reduce the political tensions that existed between North and South Korea and South Korea and Japan. Instead, in many ways relations worsened, particularly between Japan and South Korea. Media reports noted that when opposition teams scored against Japan they were celebrated throughout South Korea; Richard Lloyd Parry in the *Independent* argued that 'the two halves of the World Cup have evolved almost as separate tournaments, with very little obvious goodwill'.[34]

However, this is not to say that football has not been used to successfully unify a group of peoples, even if only for a limited period. In Africa, where state failure is a common feature of the continental political fabric, football appears to build bridges between diverse populations. At the 2002 African Nations Cup in Mali, the captain of the Democratic Republic of Congo team, Watunda Iyolo, gravely remarked that 'I am like a soldier, always ready for national duty. My country is ravaged by a brutal war and the economy is a shambles. Football is the only thing that unites the people.'[35] Furthermore, an interesting phenomenon occurred at the 2002 World Cup, in that some of the population in South Korea and Japan 'adopted' national teams to support. Although this may have followed government initiatives in South Korea, the support for other national teams in Japan appears to have been spontaneous and far-reaching. This was remarkably successful in unifying football fans at the World Cup, and it was possibly one of the reasons for the peaceful following of many national teams, particularly England. Whether or not such trends will be replicated during future World Cups and other international sporting events remains to be seen.

Order

Central to a 'civilized world' is the maintenance of a sense of 'order', where people adhere to a set procedure of rules. Within codified football there are two main areas where the notion of 'order' is keenly preserved. The first is on the football field, where the referee is the person who has the authority to impose order. Prior to the 1998 World Cup, the British media in particular focused on the strict rules that referees could impose upon World Cup matches in order to encourage more attacking play, and reduce the risk of 'anarchy' on the pitch. Paul Durkin (an English referee) observed that he would have to stamp his authority on the game he 'controls', in a far stricter manner than he did before the World Cup.[36]

Second, police and stewards have powers to prevent a blurring of the boundaries between sections of the crowd, and also between the crowd and the field of play. The control of spectators reflected a desire for order, not only by security forces but ultimately by national governments and supranational institutions (such as the EU). Discourse surrounding 'hooligans' was filled with references to the lack of order and civility, and to a 'premodern', backward image. Following violence in the Germany versus Yugoslavia 1998 World Cup game (in which a French police officer was left in a coma by German 'supporters'), *The Times* noted that civilized relations between the two countries' (German and French) elites had not filtered down to the lower (*sic*) echelons of society, stating that 'the transformation of [a] historical enemy into the benign axis of an integrated Europe has failed to trickle down into the housing estates and the suburbs'.[37] Consequently, 'German fans organize themselves along tribal lines', and are 'sinister thugs who hate all things French'.[38]

Quasi-religious fervour

Rituals, the worshipping of cult-figures/teams and ceremonies surround many national and international sporting occasions. For instance, de Coubertin claimed that 'the first essential characteristic of ancient and modern Olympism alike is that of being a religion'.[39] The nation (state) and sport are often both characterized by unquestioning fanatical allegiance that frequently embraces religious overtones. Armstrong and Giulianotti draw parallels between religion, national identity and sport, equating football to a secular religion:

> Like the ritualized procedures of a sacred ceremony, footballing events carry similar roles and structuration: a hierarchy of officials; regulating conventions and taboos; a closed space of worship and a pitch that acts as the equivalent of a high altar. An esoteric language is used in this temporal sequence, played to a liturgical calendar in which those seen as the socially powerful are publicly present at important games.[40]

Both the World Cup and European Championships appeared to be events where the 'ultimate' global and European inter-state sporting competitions were 'battled'. Throughout the events, news of the 'national team' was paraded on the front pages of newspapers and in the main television and radio news items. Furthermore, everyday dialogue was peppered with references to how the contest was proceeding. Spectators, either in France or around the world, frequently wore national attire when the national team played. At the 2002 World Cup players, and David Beckham in particular, were worshipped as if they were quasi-religious figures. This led to newspapers in the UK, such as the *Sunday People*, printing David Beckham masks to be worn during England matches. After England defeated Argentina, with a David Beckham penalty, the *Sun* proclaimed that Beckham's goal was struck by the 'Foot of God'.

The use of football in inventing both national and inter-state tradition

There are a number of examples where the 1998 World Cup was used to reinforce the invention of a nation's selective mining of history. First, French celebrations, following the national team's success, involved a huge gathering of people on the Champs-Élysées and around the Arc de Triomphe in Paris. Media reports concerning this gathering compared it to the national liberation of 1944.[41] The Arc, built to celebrate national military victories, was now used to celebrate a modern 'national' sporting victory.

Second, the defeated semi-finalists, Croatia, used their sporting success to highlight the historical existence of the Croatian nation. The national coach noted that 'we are an old nation, but a new country',[42] referring to past international football matches, played between 1918 and 1939, when Croatia was an internationally recognized sovereign state.

Third, media reports surrounding the English team and its followers often referred to past military and sporting 'battles' against previous 'enemies' such as Argentina and Germany. *The Times*, for instance, listed 'the long history of dignity in defeat', from the English (Saxon) military rout by the Normans at the Battle of Hastings (in 1066) to the England football team's loss to their Argentinian counterparts on penalties at St Etienne (in 1998).[43] This rather jocular article contrasted with more serious reporting in the British press prior to England vs. Argentina matches, where some sections of the media tend to equate this footballing contest to the military war, fought between Argentina and Britain, over the Malvinas/Falkland Islands in 1982. For example, before the 1998 match was played many references linked the contest to how the 'war-time leader' Margaret Thatcher 'won' the war, fought 16 years previously. Furthermore, when the Argentinian ship the *Belgrano* was sunk in 1982, the *Sun* emblazoned across its front page the headline 'GOTCHA'. Following England's defeat to Argentina in 1998, the *Daily Star* ran with a front-page headline, 'OUTCHA', and this they followed with 'GOTCHA', when Argentina lost in the following round to the Netherlands.[44] The 'revenge' match in 2002, where England's victory over Argentina in the first round of the World Cup ultimately contributed to Argentina's elimination from the tournament, provoked similar hostile rants in the media.[45]

Overall, this description suggests that sports coverage has assisted in making the components that comprise the inter-state worldview appear immutable, with ahistorical, civilized, ordered, unifying and quasi-religious characteristics. This portrayal appears to lend credence to the argument outlined in the introduction that the reporting of sports events bolsters the hegemony of the inter-state worldview. However, this description of the stereotypical depiction of this worldview has been presented in a rather one-dimensional manner, mirroring perhaps the one-dimensional way in which it usually tends to be illustrated. Parts of this account of the inter-state worldview have of course been queried in the past. For example, de Coubertin's rather romanticized account of the ancient Olympics, and the purported role of sport in Victorian society, have been challenged by Kyröläinen and Varis. They question de Coubertin's depiction of the ancient 'civilized' Olympic games, noting instead that they were abolished in 394 AD because of the 'bickering, conniving and ill-will that the athletic carnival always produced'.[46] Moreover, the modern Olympic era was motivated by more than a desire to introduce 'civility'. De Coubertin, ironically, urged 'Frenchmen' [*sic*] to take part in the Olympics to exact revenge against Germany after defeat in the 1870 war, and therefore 'resurrect French spirit'.[47] Furthermore, alternative definitions to the competitive understanding of sport exist. Jeremy MacClancy notes a number of alternatives to the Western notion of 'zero-sum game' (winner/loser) competition. For instance, when football was first introduced by Western missionaries to Melanesia, it was played for days until both teams had reached a draw.[48]

A number of questions are prompted by the preceding interpretation of the inter-state worldview. For instance, are the 'end users' of the media – the audience – indoctrinated completely by the dominant portrayal? Do all football fans follow the sport religiously, or do they parody to an extent the nationalism that accompanies following a national team? The following section, in touching on these questions, provides a more rounded analysis of the relationship between the sports media and the representation of the inter-state worldview by exploring the ways in which sport can also be used to challenge dominant societal structures.

Sport as a vehicle to contest and resist the inter-state worldview

Without necessarily 'essentially contesting' the immutability of the inter-state worldview, a growing body of literature questions key aspects of it. A well-known example is the work of Benedict Anderson, who notes that a mass belief in the nation (and by extension the global inter-state structure) is far from 'natural' and is instead powered by educational, administrative and mass media (print capitalism) systems.[49] Schools within IR have increasingly attacked the hegemonic position accorded to the inter-state world-view, beginning with functionalism and new world order models,[50] and more recently critical theoretical and 'postmodern' perspectives.[51] Even some realist theorists within IR contest the validity of nation-states as an a-spatial concept (meaning that states are the only proper form of political organization throughout the world), particularly following the 'collapse' of states in Africa. For example, Robert Jackson claims that 'when we speak of the "state" in sub-Saharan Africa, we are creating an illusion'.[52]

Likewise, a re-reading of sport suggests that it has been used to contest, resist and even parody components that comprise the dominant inter-state worldview. Sport, certainly since its mainstream codification in the late nineteenth and twentieth centuries, has represented an area of life that allows for resistance to, and protest against, dominant forms of power in society. This is true, for example, when association football was introduced to colonial Africa; it created space for acts of defiance against the state and the colonial powers.[53] For instance, football was one of the few areas that allowed for the congregation of supporters of the independence movement. It might also be argued that the development of sports distinct to a state, such as Gaelic football in Eire, American football in the US, and Australian Rules football in Australia, while performing a role in constructing the nation-state and national identity, also represented a means of resistance to the dominant spectre of its colonial past. This chapter proceeds by briefly illustrating the limited ways in which sport may be seen to have contested and resisted aspects of the inter-state worldview, particularly in connection with undermining the primacy of the nation-state, and the traditional understanding of nationalism.

Contesting the primacy of the state

Those involved in sport have queried and questioned the primacy of the nation-state in a number of ways. First, the worker sports movement, which was very popular throughout Europe in the inter-war years, focused primarily on non-competition and the virtues of internationalism, which valued cooperation among European workers rather than the primacy of the nation-state.[54]

Second, the growing importance of international sporting organizations (such as FIFA) as global actors challenges the 'primacy of the state' worldview, especially as FIFA and IOC executives receive diplomatic immunity around the world. FIFA's previous president, João Havelange, believed FIFA to be one of the three most influential global actors (the other two being the USA and the IOC).[55]

Third, sport has played a role in disrupting the 'concreteness' of state and national boundaries. Indeed, in Euro 2000 the organizers chose (rather optimistically) as their official motto 'Football without Frontiers', as 'Football crosses frontiers, in sport, culture, politics and economics'.[56] More recently Pope John Paul II called for sports to break down barriers and boundaries (which sporting discourses had assisted in constructing), stating: 'Sport is extremely important because it can help encourage fundamental values among young people. ... So sportsmen [*sic*] have a responsibility: they must make of sport an occasion for meeting and dialogue, beyond any barriers of language, race and culture.'[57]

Contesting dominant understandings of nationalism

In a sense, nationalism has been parodied by national supporters who have toyed with their media representation. Richard Giulianotti, for example, suggests this is frequently the case with followers accompanying the Scottish national football team, as the 'carnivalesque' atmosphere generates a sense of jocularity that erodes the seriousness with which nationalist sentiments of football supporters are associated.[58] Furthermore, the trend for European club football teams to comprise individuals from around the world may actually negate in some ways the demonizing effect that the process of 'othering' by supporters has had in the past. Indeed, on a European level, football has generated such a high level of cooperation between states that some authors argue that parochial nationalism (attached to either a sub-national or national region) is being subsumed by a supra-national European identity.[59]

There are also numerous instances of sport affording opportunities for those wishing to protest against dominant power structures within the inter-state system. For example, those campaigning against apartheid in South Africa, and interested in sport, tended to support opponents of the national side.[60] Simon Kuper also notes that mass non-attendance of the Cameroonian cup final represented a significant show of resistance to the Cameroonian President, Paul Biya.[61] In Afghanistan, under the Taliban regime, football was one of the very few vehicles by which the population could resist the apparently immutable nature of laws laid down by the Afghan government.

A BBC correspondent attending one match noted:

> The crowd was in good spirits. Someone brought me a pot of tea and
> the play began. The football was dreadful – but the match itself was a
> spectacle. Thousands of Afghans having fun is such a rare sight. They
> clapped – an illegal action here. But more daring resistance was to
> come. Half way through the first half, it was time for the late afternoon
> prayers. Pick-ups full of police from Vice and Virtue drove into the
> stadium and circled around. Using loud speakers, they ordered
> everyone to come onto the pitch and pray. A few thousand people strag-
> gled onto the grass, but most remained resolutely standing. Policemen
> leapt into the stands, whips in hand. But the crowd just melted away
> before them, only to reform a little further up the stands. After 20
> minutes, maybe a third of the crowd had been forced onto the pitch …
> and prayers were said. It was a show of resistance. That is unheard of
> in Kabul.[62]

Similar forms of resistance occurred in Iran (particularly in permitting
freedom of expression for Iranian women) following the national team's
qualification for the 1998 World Cup,[63] while opposition to the Iranian
regime occurred during the finals in France but tended to be ignored by
traditional media sources. Harry Pearson commented:

> About 15 minutes before kick-off huge anti-Katami banners and T-
> shirts decorated with pictures of Maryana Rajavi, one of the leaders of
> the Iranian opposition, start to appear around the ground. Three
> minutes before kick-off a large orange balloon with a portrait of
> Maryana Rajavi suspended from it floats across the pitch, bobs over the
> heads of the Iranian players and is eventually captured by the referee
> on the half way line. You look down at the TV monitor on your
> workstation to get a close-up of the image, but the screen is showing
> pictures of some pretty American girls in the crowd. … Later a US
> photo-journalist will paraphrase an old ice-hockey joke, 'tonight I was
> watching a political protest when all of a sudden a soccer game broke
> out', but television viewers around the world will have known nothing
> about it. They will not have seen the dozens of twelve foot by five foot
> banners denouncing the Tehran regime … or the arrival of special
> stewards in black-and-blue uniforms, or the tussles between protesters
> and the CRS that went on continually for two hours. … After the game
> some … journalists are appalled by what the TV has chosen … not to
> show. They cannot believe that such censorship would be exercised in
> a western democracy.[64]

These brief examples illuminate the role of sport as a vehicle that can
assist in providing a platform to contest and resist dominant structures

within the inter-state worldview. In so doing, they illustrate that sport is more than one-dimensional in the messages it carries. This would tend to suggest that people can resist the indoctrination that accompanies dominant power structures, or even play with such structures. It is therefore possible that the 'essentially uncontested' immutability of the inter-state structure could be challenged in the future. Indeed, components that comprise the worldview are being questioned.

That said, the examples provided have illustrated that the level of contestation and resistance is fairly superficial and subordinate to wider issues. The resistance to say the Iranian or Taliban regimes does not necessarily correlate to a fundamental re-thinking of the constructs that comprise the inter-state worldview. It can even be argued that many of the examples presented here, instead of essentially contesting the worldview have actually exacerbated it. Preston, for instance, notes that many supporters applaud 'foreign' players when playing for 'their' local club. Yet, 'put on a national shirt and our everyday heroes are suddenly enemies again'.[65] Indeed, when I was on a recent research trip to France, to observe the policing of Manchester United fans, it was obvious that while the United supporters respected elements of 'France' (such as their three French international players and a previous 'idol', Eric Cantona), this respect was often accompanied by virulent anti-French comments when travelling to and from Britain.

Conclusion

> People keep telling us: 'The idea of nations has been overtaken; it is dangerous, in the past. The future is about the construction of great groupings of people and the withering away of nation states. There is only one goal: a planet without frontiers.' Yet it only needs a national team to go on the pitch, a national anthem sung or a goal scored, for millions of people somewhere in the world to be as one, to unite in joy or disappointment. This is civilized chauvinism.[66]

Although there may be benefits in the inter-state structure, this chapter argues against the sentiments in the above quotation; the maintenance of the inter-state structure is dangerous, it is not a 'thing of the past' – it remains perceived as an immutable feature of the present. As such, it prevents alternatives that could change this current representation from being accorded discursive space. The bulk of this chapter has noted that sport, particularly through its media representation, has helped reproduce this dominant image of the world. Within this context, international sporting events have been viewed as 'civilized' and are an occasion 'for harmless mapping of national characteristics on the activities of those on the field of play ... [where] national teams are the mirror of a territory'.[67]

This raises a number of questions: to what extent do the media exacerbate the competition between states (and the overall inter-state worldview) and simultaneously downplay the level of cooperation that exists in sport? To what extent is there a deliberate attempt to constrain the airing of alternatives to the inter-state worldview? Such questions are difficult to answer, yet, as the section above argues, sport also has the potential to convey a variety of other messages, such as contesting dominant power structures, and thus has the capability to question the inter-state worldview. This suggests that the relationship between sport and the inter-state worldview is multi-dimensional and complex in nature; it not only constructs and bolsters dominant images but can also simultaneously act to contest and resist those very images and their associated practices. Although such acts of resistance at the moment may be derisory and not aimed directly at the inter-state order, the very fact that they are happening, and appear to be increasing in number, may give hope to those looking to use the portrayal of sport to challenge the immutable nature of the inter-state worldview in the future.

2

Sport and capitalism[1]

ADRIAN BUDD

Introduction

In the light of the events of 11 September and their global repercussions, an analysis relating capitalism and international relations to sport may appear perverse. In these circumstances we might be expected to remain on the traditional terrain of IR and studies of world order, which Robert Cox defines as 'the particular configurations of forces which successively define the problematic of war or peace for the ensemble of states', consign sport to the margins of IR and concur with the millions for whom sport is an essentially trivial distraction from more serious matters.[2] Yet sport's importance in contemporary global society suggests that our understanding of that society might benefit from an analysis of the range of social processes that sport entails. This chapter aims to provide a Marxist analysis of the nature of sport under capitalism, conceived as a global social system whose fundamental relations, processes and structures shape more local social practices.

Joseph Maguire has written of global processes of 'sportization', whereby pastimes are transformed into more structured and codified sports, initially in Britain, the birthplace of global capitalism, from where certain sports were exported.[3] Although local sports persist, sport has followed capitalism in becoming global and expresses ever more clearly the competitive, exploitative relations of capitalist society. Sportspeople internationally routinely test positive for performance-enhancing drugs taken to maximize the possibility of victory. Across the world allegations of match-fixing reveal the connections between sport and shady financial interests, including gamblers, while the vast sums offered by media companies for television rights to major sporting events show how more legitimate business interests have increasingly oriented themselves on sport. A major expression of the inter-national dimension of sport, the International Olympic Committee, has also been at the forefront of intensified commercialization in recent decades, awarding global companies such as Coca-Cola and Canon the right to use the Olympic logo in return for huge fees.

These are not accidental phenomena, as if sport were external to capitalist relations but subject to their corrosive influence. Certainly, these excesses may be moderated via regulation, doping regimes, the organization of fans' interests in independent supporters' clubs, boycotts and strikes.[4] But regulation, like trade unionism under capitalism, is like the labour of Sisyphus, compelled by the gods to constantly push a rock to the top of the hill only to see it roll back down. For these phenomena are necessary – not in the sense of inevitability, for conscious human agents may resist particular developments, but as expressions of the inherent potentials of capitalism.[5] Sport under capitalism, as we shall explore more fully below, expresses that system's central features.

For Marxists, the capitalist form of society and the social practices and beliefs that correspond to it are historically specific. Marxists therefore reject the arguments of defenders of capitalism – that people are, for example, naturally competitive and acquisitive, Adam Smith famously arguing that humans have a natural propensity to 'truck, barter and exchange'. Naturalizing and taken-for-granted assumptions also appear in IR, where the dominant realist perspective has attempted to construct a 'timeless science', corroborating its emphasis on states and state-power maximization by a selective mining of history. Justin Rosenberg's critique of realism attempts to '*de*naturalize' social processes and to dissolve reified forms such as states 'back into the historically specific social relations between people which constitute them'.[6] In short, the black box of the state must be opened up and its social contents exposed. Certain theorizations of sport also presuppose an essential and timeless human nature. Ellis Cashmore, for example, argues that our pre-history of hunting-gathering, representing over 99 per cent of human history, has left a genetic imprint which compels us to re-enact the hunt through sport.[7] For John Hoberman 'the competitive impulse is a basic human drive that is more durable than the political regimes that channel and exploit it'.[8] Vanderzwaag argues that school sports 'offer numerous opportunities for competition' as if designed around a natural predisposition.[9] Yet, if Marxists reject the idea of an eternal human nature based on an ahistorical application of contemporary notions, human differentiation from other species is rooted in nature and therefore does have an essential quality, albeit that its forms are shaped by changing historical circumstances. For Marx, labour to appropriate the products of and modify our environment is 'the everlasting Nature-imposed condition of human existence'.[10] So central is labour to human society that as its form changes so, simultaneously, does the totality of human social relationships, including relationships in sport.

The next section will briefly explore the key social relations that constitute capitalist society. This provides a preliminary to the analysis of sport under capitalism, including its international dimension, in the subsequent section. Emphasizing the antagonistic nature of capitalist social relations, the following section explores how sport has sometimes been used as a vehicle for resistance to dominant ideas and structures. Finally, the conclusion will suggest that the rediscovery of play, which stands in a contradictory relation to capitalist sport, should be central to the Marxist project for human emancipation.

Capitalist social relations

Capitalism, like earlier class societies, is based on the exploitation of the direct producers by the owners of the most significant means of production. Compared to earlier modes of production, labour is 'free in a double sense, free from the old relations of clientship, bondage and servitude, and secondly free of all belongings and possessions, and of every objective, material form of being, *free of all property*; dependent on the sale of its labour capacity'.[11] Separated from its own means of production, labour becomes a commodity, labour-power, placed at the service of the buyer in exchange for wages, which represent less value than workers produce – hence exploitation. The product is exchanged on the market and the surplus-value produced by workers is, market conditions permitting, realized as profit. Having lost control over their own labour, workers produce for capital rather than for themselves – Marx referring to this as alienated labour – such that this basic human activity is 'not voluntary but forced, it is *forced labour*'.[12] This is not immediately obvious since when labour contracts are agreed an apparent equivalence prevails. Yet when labour-power is set to work, collectively incorporated via a labour process into the means of production, the labourer becoming, in Marx's famous phrase, 'an appendage to the machine', equivalence disappears and workers face the 'despotism of the workplace'. The buyers of labour-power are now bosses and their prerogatives prevail.

Social relations of class exploitation are reinforced by relations of competition between firms, which force them to maximize exploitation and see workers as merely an element of their capital outlay. Precariousness and insecurity are the normal conditions of existence for workers under capitalism. For capitalists, 'a band of hostile brothers' according to Marx, competition means that they

> cannot exist without constantly revolutionizing the instruments of production, and thereby the relations of production, and with them the whole relations of society. ... All that is solid melts into air, all that is holy is profaned. ... The need of a constantly expanding market for its products chases the bourgeoisie over the whole surface of the globe. It must nestle everywhere, settle everywhere, establish connections everywhere.[13]

Capitalism, then, has an inherent tendency towards a global framework for its operations.[14] But the antagonisms between capital and labour and between competing firms ensure that force, embodied in states with jurisdiction over fixed territories, was not only important in the initial constitution of capitalist social relations but remains central to systemic reproduction. Flux, change and aspatiality thus coexist with elements of fixity and stasis, firms requiring, *inter alia*, stable supplies of raw materials and labour-power with appropriate skills, stable social and political conditions, infrastructure and distribution networks and a rational and stable bureaucratic, legal and administrative system whose outcomes are relatively predictable. States usually meet or guarantee these requirements, funded by part of the surplus value produced at home.[15] Capital may sometimes chafe against the state but, faced with international competition, firms seek guarantees and protection from states, particularly the 'home states' they have become most interdependent with. States then have a dual nature: internally, they attempt to coerce workers, for example, by constituting them as 'free' labourers, and reconcile antagonisms between capitals; externally, they defend and protect the interests of their patch of the global economy and the capitalist interests based there.

Capitalism initially developed in Europe, although the slave trade's importance to British capitalism's early expansion indicated that there was an international dimension to capitalism from the start. But the pressure of competitive accumulation ensured that firms in the advanced states began to extend beyond their national boundaries and confront their rivals internationally. The 'scramble for Africa' in the second half of the nineteenth century exemplified the process whereby capitalism developed into imperialism within a now global system. The impact of international competition posed questions over the boundary between the internal and external, even where, as in the case of island states, geographical boundaries are relatively robust. Boundaries between social practices, however, are more permeable. Thus, in the face of rivals, different national capitals demanded of their states not simply support in distant continents but also modifications of national political economies. Workers' health, education and preparedness to fight for 'their' country became matters of grave concern. These dovetailed with a developing class antagonism across Europe as the newly formed working classes began to feel their industrial and political strength, to resist state coercion, and to demand economic improvements and an extension of democratic and citizenship rights. Although these rights were largely formal, contradicted by labour's subordination to capital, and although the ruling class was careful to evacuate parliament of political power as the franchise was extended, shifting it into state bureaucracies, the granting of citizenship rights did have important consequences.[16] At a practical level, it was hoped that, granted a welfare 'stake', workers would become more efficient, more contented and more deferential to 'their' state. At a more ideological level, states now sought to bind competing class interests together in what Benedict Anderson has called 'imagined communities', and, according to Wallerstein, 'the creation of citizenship rights attempted to shift exclusion from an open class barrier to a national, or hidden class, barrier'.[17] The material and the ideological were as interconnected as the internal and external. While the ruling class engaged in ideological warfare within the working class – 'the *Daily Mail*, founded in 1896, was violently and consistently imperialist. The *Daily Express*, founded in 1900 ... proclaimed in its first leader, "our policy is patriotic: our policy is the British Empire"'[18] – it simultaneously pursued more concrete practices in an attempt to ensure that 'external' or 'alien' ideas and traditions, such as Bolshevism, did not cross national boundaries. For Churchill, the worker's stake was designed to insure against the appeal of revolutionary socialism in Britain; for added insurance he was quick to engage in the international coalition against Bolshevism in 1918, arguing that we must 'strangle the Bolshevik baby in its cradle'.

The social relations of capitalism are not exhausted by the exploitation and competition we have discussed. But, for Marxists these are the central relations and ensure that capitalism necessarily produces both inter- and intra-class conflicts, which, in turn, necessitate state activity. Such activity has always had an international dimension, for states are concentrations of social relations within a global capitalist society. The Russian Marxist Nikolai Bukharin noted at the beginning of the twentieth century that internationalization creates 'a reverse tendency towards the nationalization of capitalist interests'.[19] The balance between the two is not fixed, being shaped, *inter alia*, by the balance of class forces, the interests of dominant powers and the requirements of major firms to maximize or restore profitability. But in the era of 'globalization' the relationship between the contradictory tendencies persists and, although individual firms have become more internationalized, capitalism has not fundamentally thrown off its national moorings.

Capitalist sport

This section, which aims to show how the social relations outlined above are expressed in sport, will not analyse sport in all its variety and complexity. It will, for example, draw largely on professional sport, organized not simply around the drive to victory but also, where clubs are concerned, around profit maximization and capital expansion. In any case, amateur or leisure and professional sport should not be too sharply differentiated, the latter merely expressing the imperatives of capitalism in a more acute form. The analysis will also frequently focus on football and on Europe, especially Britain. Fortunately, developments within football, the world's primary sport, and within Europe, the cradle of both capitalism and modern sport, often exemplify wider tendencies and processes.

Jennifer Hargreaves has written that, for certain Marxist critics, modern sport replicates capitalist industry: it is characterized by 'specialisation and standardisation, bureaucratised and hierarchical administration, long-term planning, increased reliance on science and technology, a drive for maximum productivity, a quantification of performance and, above all, the alienation of both producer and consumer'.[20] The most immediately visible expression of the framing of sport in a capitalist context and its subordination to the economic laws of capitalism concerns its increasing commercialization. Sport is big business, for sports clubs and participants not only compete in the sporting arena but are also connected to wider profit-oriented business interests, including trans-national sportswear companies and media giants who see sport as a form of spectacle that can be broadcast to vast regional or global audiences.[21] As profit maximization, rather than sport itself, is the chief concern, there is a growing unease that the established rules and structures of particular sports will be tampered with to enhance the spectacle and advertising revenue. Over recent years 'reformers' have proposed, *inter alia*, the enlargement of football goals and a review of the offside law to the benefit of attackers, matches of thirds or quarters rather than halves to make way for more advertising and wider use of penalty shoot-outs to provide a winner for each spectacle rather than over a long season.[22] It is feared that these proposals, emanating largely from the United States, will be taken up elsewhere. Technical or organizational innovation, particularly of defences, is of no interest to those who seek to provide instant gratification and a short-term sense of euphoria. The shifting of kick-off times to suit television companies, the scandal of overpriced replica kits produced at a fraction of their retail price by underpaid labour, socially exclusionary pay-per-view games, penalty shoot-outs, end of season play-offs and so on may be only the thin end of the commercialization and mediatization wedge. For sports increasingly compete for global audiences, and failure to accommodate to media company-inspired practices 'would place in question their ability to survive in the global marketplace'.[23]

Intensified commercialization has produced a critical response from marginalized and excluded fans. BSkyB's bid for Manchester United, for example, provoked an anti-Murdoch campaign by the Independent Manchester United Supporters' Association (for further details see Simon Lee's chapter elsewhere in this volume), while, more widely, British football saw a burst of unofficial fanzines in the 1990s as increasingly commercialized clubs became more distant from the surrounding communities in which they developed. But while such campaigns may produce reform and moderate commercial excesses, they nevertheless take capitalist sport largely for granted. The argument of this chapter is that capitalist sport has more fundamental limitations on human freedom: to demonstrate this requires a shift in focus from sports consumption to that of sports production.

To participate in sport means to engage in a labour process which, although technically different from those in other sectors, similarly expresses capitalism's central social relations. For just as other industries combine workers with the means of production in narrowly specialized roles that maximize productivity, thereby removing individual creativity from the labour process and constraining spontaneity and the development of many-sided personalities, so sport, whether individual or in teams, encourages specialization through the rationalization of technique in the pursuit of victory. This may improve performance and thereby the possibility of victory, but where winning is the overriding goal sport ceases to be a pleasurable activity and becomes merely a means to an end. Contrary to the experience of childhood play, which is a means towards personal integration and an expression of all the faculties and abilities of mind and body, for very few adult sportspersons is sport 'only a game'. It is a job and, as with other jobs, specialization has a disfiguring and distorting effect on both the personality and the body. While elite administrators, promoters and club owners may experience the stresses of competitive accumulation, sports-people, drawn disproportionately from ordinary backgrounds, face sport's versions of emphysema, asbestosis and RSI.

Tour de France cyclists suffer intense pain and exhaustion on an almost daily basis. Over the longer term their joints and muscles rebel against the exertions of their short careers. They are, for example, prone to rheumatism, since, having reduced the level of body-fat to between three and six per cent of bodyweight, they are poorly protected against the damp air they encounter, particularly in the mountains. The overwhelming majority of these cyclists will never even experience the momentary compensation of a stage or race victory since their niche function within the team division of labour is to support their leaders. Many footballers, so valuable to their clubs as commodities that their value as humans is neglected, are forced to play, with or without pain-killing injections, through minor injuries, while the pressure to perform on top stars such as Maradona, in the past, and Ronaldo is intense. The latter was forced to 'play' in the 1998 World Cup final just four hours after an epileptic convulsion, allegedly under pressure from Nike, Brazil's multinational sponsor whose $125 million deal allows it to deter-mine who and where Brazil play. Although the evidence now suggests that this conspiratorial version of events is inaccurate, Tostao, one of Brazil's most respected sport columnists and a World Cup winner in 1970, reflected a widespread perception of recent changes when he remarked that: 'in my time it was the army generals running Brazil who tried to pick the team. ... Today it's the sponsors, the businessman, the media moguls.'[24] The physical, and possibly mental and emotional, deterioration of perhaps the two most gifted footballers of the last two decades is a dreadful indictment of the commodification of the human body. Less remarked upon, but if anything more shocking, is the situation that many female gymnasts face. Joan Ryan has shown that young girls, frequently encouraged by state-sponsored coaches, starve themselves to attain an idealized weightlessness, break their tiny necks and backs under the rigours of the training and competition regime; that their mothers hide signs of chicken pox with make-up so that they can retain their team place; and that they sometimes attempt suicide when they fail to make the grade. That most of this goes unreported leads

Ryan to refer to 'legal, even celebrated child abuse'.[25] There is a sporting elite whose rewards are considerable and who therefore escape the routine low-paid drudgery that may otherwise be their lot. This may provide compensation for the alienation that accompanies obsessive repetition and exhaustion, but this elite is a tiny minority of those who set out with aspirations of sporting success.

There are more subtle and acceptable limitations on the human body and personality accompanying sporting specialization than these serious disfigurations and bodily distortions. Harry Braverman famously argued that capitalist industry, in which workers specialize in minute tasks endlessly repeated, and traditional skills are incorporated into ever more complex machinery as workers become appendages to machines, produces a process of 'deskilling'.[26] In one sense this is an over-generalization, for some workers must design the machines, program computers, and perform general services, while complex machines require literacy and other intellectual skills on the part of their attendants. Workers have become better educated and trained as capitalism has aged. But if our yardstick is not the development of technical abilities but the liberation of human potentialities, then the concept of deskilling retains its power as a critique of the capitalist labour process. For competitive accumulation requires that machine designers and computer programmers, for example, only design machines and program computers through most of their working life. Very few engage in a wider range of activities that makes full use of their abilities and creativity.

Sports fans and commentators frequently refer to sportspeople's skill. But this operates within limited domains, and this focus on specific actions obscures the fact that it is only as footballers, for example, that these players are gifted. If skill is conceived of as the full range of human activities then sportspeople may be extremely limited. To reduce sporting ability to its most basic physical aspect, footballers, for example, are groomed from their early teens to become adept at running around, usually in particular parts of the pitch, and momentarily balancing on one leg while the other is swung in such a fashion that it connects with a ball in just the right way to make an accurate cross or shot. Many other sporting skills can be similarly broken down to their basic features. The popularity of football consists, partially at least, in the way that the actions of two teams' players interact in indeterminate ways and in the requirement to adapt bodily movements and team formation to unforeseen circumstances. Rowing and weightlifting, for example, are much more constrained activities. Ability to perform these physical acts and to adapt body movements may serve footballers well during their careers, and the lucky few can become fabulously rich. But these acts and movements are better described as techniques than skills, and are of very little value after a career has finished. Marx and Engels envisaged a society in which all and each would be able to freely develop their interests and aptitudes, where freed from the capitalist division of labour and narrow role specialization, each would spend time in a range of activities.

Sportspeople, constrained by competition, repetition and routinization, have as much reason to look forward to this as others.

The technical division of labour is an aspect of a broader social division of labour which has imprinted its stamp on modern sport since the second half of the nineteenth century. The concentration of workers in factories, mines, docks and so on required the ruling class to exercise despotism in the workplace. The rigid control of routinized labour, later systematized under Taylorism and time and motion studies, meant that 'Sport was a way of filling leisure time with brief, but exhilarating periods of uncertainty. ... The spell of physically competitive activity, far from being broken, was strengthened by the need for momentary release from a colourless world dominated by the monotonous thuds and grinds of machinery.'[27]

This letting off of steam, to use appropriate industrial imagery, is familiar to anybody who has experienced the tedium of routinization and control. Both a reaction to, and relief from, intense time-measured work, it was also, in so far as it soothed accumulated work-related tensions, a preparation for a return to work. Thus, where Braverman argued that when labour-power is a commodity work is 'sharply and antagonistically divided from non-work', it might be more accurate to say that the two are intimately connected.[28] Certainly, the factory origins of many teams, such as Arsenal and West Ham in Britain, indicate such a connection between working-class sport and capitalist industry. The establishment of football among workers in other parts of the world, who emulated their British counterparts working abroad when Britain was the world's leading industrial power, tends to confirm this view.[29] Employers encouraged factory teams as a means to cement workers' company identification, and to instil order and the discipline of teamworking, just as Japanese employers use company songs and meetings today. It may also have helped 'to increase productivity by keeping their workers fit'.[30]

Other developments illustrate the way that working-class sport was shaped by capitalism and the factory system. As industrialization developed efforts were made to regulate workers' free space and leisure time. This was 'not concerned with any simple repression of recognized pleasures, but with defining, regulating and locating them in their appropriate sites. Above all, perhaps, they were concerned to shift pleasures from the site of mass activity (fairs, football matches with unlimited players, carnivals verging on riot) to the site of private and individual activity.'[31]

Working-class sports were also temporally constrained in a way that elite sports were not: golf, cricket, equestrianism and yachting can last many days or weeks. All, of course, require expensive equipment. The regulation and codification of football in the final third of the nineteenth century was overseen by the middle class, apparently fearful of working-class spontaneity and revolution. Yet Adrian Harvey shows that working-class football had operated under sophisticated rules independently of the public schools, while R.W. Lewis argues that distaste for (working-class) sporting professionalism, which posed a potential threat to respect for social hierarchies, was more significant than fear.[32] These arguments suggest that changes in football and in other sports that were codified and bound within tighter structures, rules and spaces, such as pitches and rings, were part of a wider process. Bureaucratization and standardization, and the consequent smoothing-out of administrative and legal irrationalities that Max Weber highlighted,[33] reflected attempts to reconcile contradictions inherent in capitalist competition. Without, to use a sporting analogy, a relatively level playing-field, individual firms faced the prospect of exclusion from markets rigged by personal collusion between their competitors and state officials. For the system as a whole this would entail stagnation and possibly self-destruction. For individual English football clubs, the establishment of a national league under a single set of rules would enable them to promote fixtures likely to draw sizeable attendances of fee-paying customers. Today, with the growing disparity of financial resources between the top football clubs and the rest, there is renewed concern over the absence of a level playing-field.

The potential for class conflict inherent in the exploitative capital-labour relation meant that the element of social control was not absent from the regulation of sport. Indeed, it was assisted by the efforts of the mainly middle-class nonconformist churches which sought to evangelize within the growing urban working class through sport: many of today's professional football teams started life as church social clubs. Codification and social control reinforced the rhythms of factory life: 'The sense of order, discipline, location, and period which sport acquired helped it both complement and support working life. As the form and pace of sport imitated that of industry, so it gained momentum amongst the emergent working class seeking some sporadic diversion from its toil, something more impulsive and daring than the routine labours that dominated industry.'[34]

Participation in sport has been the major emphasis in this chapter so far. But the commodification of sport in the twentieth century is a component of the commodification of virtually all human activities. Sports entrepreneurs therefore seek to maximize markets, even where by aggregating large numbers of working-class people in one place they risk arousing that distaste and fear referred to above. Hence, for large gatherings of wealthy and respectable people, such as at Ascot or Henley, policing is minimal, while similar numbers of ordinary people face surveillance, high-density policing and control of their movements. The Hillsborough tragedy in 1989, and the British Tory government's attempt to introduce football fan identity cards the same year, illustrate abiding disdain for ordinary fans by the police and authorities.

Capital accumulation entails not only local processes of commodification, social control, and bureaucratization discussed above but also efforts by capital to overcome national limitations. Capitalism, as Marx and later Marxists argued, produces a capitalist world system.[35] In the absence of a world state and of the relatively level playing-field provided by national states, firms seek support from states, especially their home states, in breaking open markets and protecting their domestic interests. Hence the inter-imperialist rivalry referred to in the previous section. Under these conditions, sport was quickly seized upon as a vehicle to carry nationalist ideology into the working class and prepare young people for service in the national interest. Lewis argues that the sport encouraged in the English public-school system sought to develop 'qualities of manliness and leadership [which] would help pupils throughout their later lives. This became linked to the other main ideological thread running through the public schools, that of service to the Empire'.[36] More generally, state military interests in a fit and disciplined population encouraged the introduction of drill for British schoolboys (the girls sat quietly doing needlework in preparation for unflappable support for their future husbands). A similar story unfolded elsewhere. In Germany, for example, Friedrich Jahn's gymnastic system, developed in 1811 to prepare youth for patriotic war against Napoleon, became widespread.

According to Eric Hobsbawm, 'the last three decades of the nineteenth century marked a decisive transformation in the spread of old, the invention of new, and the institutionalization of most sports on a national and even international stage'.[37] Thus the modern Olympics were launched in 1896 as the brain-child of Frenchman Pierre de Coubertin. Much of an idealistic nature has been written about the Olympics, both ancient and modern. In ancient Greece they were indeed spectacles of beauty and strength, but they took place against a background of preparation for war, indicating that states' interest in developing their subjects' physical powers is not a recent phenomenon. The modern Olympics, far from expressing the ideal of human integration via peaceful competition, reflected similar concerns. Cashmore, for instance, argued that: 'distressed by France's poor military efforts, especially against Germany, Coubertin felt his country in need of a reminder of the importance of physical endeavour'.[38] By 1912 competitors no longer entered as individuals but as members of national teams. The 1936 Berlin Olympics were a showcase not for the ideal of human unity and solidarity but for Hitler's ideal of racial and national supremacy.[39] Since then national hosts of the Olympics have consistently used them to inflate national pride, as well as to enrich entrepreneurs. Almost as consistently Olympic boycotts have been organized, largely expressing the political interests of national elites. For all the talk of the decline of the nation-state under the pressure of globalization, states and their ideologues continue to use sport for political and economic advantage. Methods include state funding of training and coaching programmes, the promotion of competitive sports in schools, and state grants for research into new sports technologies.

The above observations suggest that sport not only expresses capitalist social relations and practices but also contributes to their reproduction. For critics of capitalism and the inter-capitalist rivalry at the heart of the modern world system, therefore, the conclusion seems clear: sport is part of that constellation of forces barring the path towards greater human freedom, which for Marxists can only be realized under socialism. Yet, such a stark rejection of sport is surely inconsistent with a political project for human emancipation that seeks to mobilize the millions who derive pleasure from sport and engage in sport as something vital and life-affirming. The next section will focus on some of the social antagonisms of sport under capitalism, and in particular analyse how far sport can become a vehicle of popular resistance to oppressive social relations.

Sport and resistance

Sport is structurally determined by capitalism's constitutive social relations which create a sport in their own image, exploitation, routinization, competition, national exclusiveness and all. Yet all relations have two or more sides and workers bring to the capital-labour relation not only some level of consciousness of their antagonistic social interests but also the capacity to act upon them. Thus Henry Ford once asked plaintively, 'how come every time I want a pair of hands I get a human being?'.[40] The commodity labour-power is always connected to sentient, purposeful workers who, however much they depend on the constant sale of their labour-power in order to live, refuse to be reduced to the status of mere commodities. Uniquely among commodities, therefore, 'there enters into the determination of the value of labour-power a historical and moral element', expressed in workers' consistent, if not permanent, resistance to capital's imperatives.[41]

Norman Geras argues that humans' basic needs are not simply physical but include needs 'for love, respect and friendship ... freedom and breadth of intellectual and physical self-expression'.[42] The search for the satisfaction of these needs transcends the boundary between work and non-work, between the workplace and the surrounding community and social relations. Certainly, workers' ideas about their interests cannot be simply read off from class position and experience, for they develop within a powerful set of ruling-class ideas that attempt to naturalize prevailing social relations and are more or less dominant in any period. But although 'one concept of reality is diffused throughout society ... informing with its spirit all taste, morality, customs, religious and political principles, and all social relations, particularly in their intellectual and moral connotation', workers' interests and experiences contradict this concept.[43] Mangan and Hickey are therefore right to reject the arguments that working-class resistance to dominant ideas and the generation of 'independent ideas and actions' are virtually impossible.[44] As Marx argued, humans do not act 'under circumstances chosen by themselves, but under circumstances directly encountered, given and transmitted from the past', but they do, nevertheless, 'make history'.[45]

Sport cannot be separated from wider historical processes, including processes of social resistance. It has thus been argued that for the working class sport is 'part mass therapy, part resistance, part mirror image of the dominant political economy'.[46] In discussing resistance, we should avoid idealizing any activity that does not conform to dominant values, for this can include behaviour that, far from resisting those values, takes competition and individualism to their extremes and offers no possibility of generalization into positive and conscious opposition.[47] Thus, football hooliganism, while an expression of alienation and a reaction to unfulfilled lives, is directed not at the system that produces them but at people experiencing similar conditions. In certain circumstances, however, team identification can entail forms of resistance to dominant social ideas, processes and structures. Under Stalinist state-capitalism in the Soviet Union, supporting Spartak Moscow was sometimes a silent resistance as Spartak was not linked to the state as directly as other Moscow teams – CSKA to the army, Dynamo to the KGB, Torpedo to the Zil car works and Lokomotiv to the railways. More generally, according to Nikolai Starostin, one of Spartak's founders, one-time USSR manager and ten years in Stalin's gulags, 'for most people soccer was the only, and sometimes the last, chance and hope of retaining in their souls a tiny island of sincere feelings and human relations'.[48] Additionally, the crowd provided a camaraderie that contrasted sharply with the atomized suspicion under the dictatorship. At a more conscious level, under Franco's dictatorship Barcelona fans, fearful of abusing Franco openly, abused instead his favourite team, Real Madrid. In East Germany, the Stasi team Dynamo Berlin was hated – despite, or perhaps because of, winning the championship every year between 1979 and 1988 – while when Western, especially West German, teams visited party members filled the ground for fear that the majority of the crowd would cheer the opposition.

These actions combine private opposition and displaced resistance to the core social and political relations of given societies at specific times. In other circumstances resistance through sport can become a moment within a wider movement with the potential to reshape social structures. A popular alternative to Hitler's 1936 Berlin Olympics was organized to take place in Barcelona in 1936. That it reflected working-class opposition to fascism was clear, but it was also clear that resistance through sport was seen as secondary to less symbolic and more direct forms of resistance. For the games were called off on their eve when Franco's military rising began, many contestants staying in Spain to join the International Brigades. At the 1968 Mexico Olympics two black American athletes, Tommie Smith and John Carlos, turned their backs on the US flag and raised their gloved fists in the black power salute at their medal ceremony. Smith explained: 'When we're winning, we're Americans. Otherwise, we're just negroes'.[49] Muhammad Ali's refusal to fight in Vietnam, since 'no Vietnamese ever called me "nigger"', expressed similar concerns. But if Ali, Smith and Carlos gave expression to a rising tide of resistance, the ebb of that tide also impacted on sportspeople. Thus as black power subsided, when Wayne

Collett and Vince Matthews received Olympic medals in 1972 they merely 'stood casually, chatted, joked and turned away from the American flag during the victory ceremony'.[50] Beneath this ebb and flow, the antagonisms at the heart of capitalism ensure that, whether conscious or unconscious, resistance to the dominant practices of the political-economy of sport and contestation of the dominant meanings attributed to sport constantly lurk beneath the surface of working-class attitudes to sport. The establishment of the Football Supporters' Association and the growth of the unofficial fanzine movement, both seeking to amplify the voice of ordinary fans within British football, provide illustrations of this resistance and contestation, albeit of a relatively moderate kind. Latin American football offers further illustrations.

At the time of the 1970 World Cup Brazil had a military government. Seeing footballing success as an opportunity to deflect opposition and a distraction from social grievances, the government identified with the team by adopting its song *Pra Frente, Brasil* ('Forward, Brazil') as its own. This ideological construction of an 'imagined community', under military leadership, appeared successful as millions celebrated thrilling performances and ultimate victory. The reality behind this appearance was, however, more complex. During the 1970s military men began to dominate Brazilian football, and sport more generally. Admiral Heleno Nunes became sports minister, and Claudio Coutinho, team manager in 1978, used physical education methods developed for the armed forces on the national squad. His ambition was to 'modernize' Brazilian football along European lines, producing physically stronger players and a less expressive style of football. Popular criticism of this style at the 1974 and 1978 tournaments, although not signifying a diminishing desire for national success, indicated that nationalist sentiment coexisted with alternative reasons for popular identification with the national team, a view reinforced when the 1982 team simultaneously recaptured some of the expressiveness of 1970 and a wide measure of popularity.

The architect of the 1970 victory had been Joao Saldanha, although he had been sacked as team manager shortly before the finals, apparently for refusing to pick President Medici's favourite player.[51] Saldanha argued that 'Brazilian football is a thing played to music', to a samba rhythm. The reason for this, and the resultant form of expressive football, lies not in any essentialized athleticism among Brazilian players but in the particular pattern of Brazilian capitalism's historical development. Brazil's cities are surrounded by sprawling shanty towns, *favelas*, where black Brazilians are concentrated and where *capoeira*, a sort of dance-cum-martial art, is practised. *Capoeira* was traditionally danced by slaves, upon whose exploitation Brazilian capitalism initially depended; for them, *capoeira* provided a space for momentary exhilaration and free bodily movement denied them elsewhere. Professor Muniz Sodre of the Federal University of Rio de Janeiro argues that 'to understand our football you have to understand the *capoeira* ... a way of tricking your opponent'.[52] After the 1930s, when the ban on black players was lifted and 'mulattos' could participate without powdering their faces, Brazilian football began to assume its expressive character and to become a temporary relief from mundane problems. It offers no insurance against poverty, insecurity or marginalization, but thrilling players such as Pele, Garrincha, Jairzinho, Didi and, today, Ronaldo do provide a glimpse of a less alienated and constrained future.[53] Resistance to Brazilian capitalist development produced, by a circuitous route, an invented footballing tradition which, although still inscribed within capitalist social relations, presents a microcosm of a future festival of the oppressed. Its international popularity, even among those with no other knowledge or interest in Brazil, indicates the shared aspirations of subaltern social strata internationally.

Social antagonisms in Argentina have also found expression in football. Assuming power in 1976, after FIFA had named Argentina as the hosts of the 1978 World Cup, the military junta attempted to use the event to legitimize its rule, building modern stadia and introducing colour television. Meanwhile political prisoners were murdered to prevent their discovery by foreign journalists. To ensure Argentina's passage into the semi-finals an inter-state bargain, awarding Peru *inter alia* 35,000 tons of free grain and $50 million of financial credits, was apparently used to guarantee victory over the Peruvian team in the second group stage.[54] There is a suspicion that performance-enhancing drugs were used as added insurance, detection being avoided by the fact that the team's water-boy provided the bulk of the post-match urine samples, one of which showing its provider to be pregnant! Argentina's victory in the final, amid scenes of national jubilation, suggested that the junta's plan had succeeded. Yet, as in Brazil in 1970, nationalist outpouring masked a more complex reality: 'The joy is not joy. It is a kind of explosion of a society which has been obliged to keep silent.'[55] Inscribed within a nationalist framework that posed no challenge to the junta, the intensity of the explosion can nevertheless be seen as a displaced expression of latent social and political tensions. The persistence of such tensions ensured that military rule was never fully secured and legitimized, and the erosion of social toleration of the junta was one factor behind its decision to invade the Falklands/Malvinas in 1982, when it recycled the 1978 World Cup song *Vamos Argentina, Vamos a Ganar* ('Go On Argentina, Go and Win'), in an attempt to reinforce legitimacy. This has parallels with Brazil in 1970, a further similarity being the relationship between footballing style and social oppression. The 1978 team manager Cesar Luis Menotti came, like Saldanha, from the political left and equated creative football with pre-junta freedom, regarding defensive football as an imprisonment of ordinary Argentinians' authentic spirit. Although Menotti's worldview did not transcend capitalist social relations – involving, for example, nationalism and competition – and although he may well have been complicit in the bribery of Peru and drug-taking, it seems reasonable to suggest that Menotti saw his team's performance as an indirect form of resistance to military rule.

Conclusion

Sport under capitalism is competitive, nationalistic and elitist, and imposes a rigid regimentation and division of labour on participants. Ideological attempts to naturalize these characteristics conceal the real nature of the productive and social relations involved, and reduce those relations to the actions and capabilities of isolated actors. Some of these actors, whether participants, sports entrepreneurs and promoters or corporations, derive considerable rewards from sport. The majority of people, however, experience sport as a theatre of dreams, a spectacular distraction from social grievances, an arena for the safe expression of accumulated frustrations, and, as far as mass spectator sport is concerned, a means to make social connections and identifications and, therefore, briefly put the isolation, alienation and mundane troubles of their lives to one side.

Locating the mass attraction of sport in this context enables us to qualify the apparently uncontroversial argument of Elias and Dunning that sport entails the 'arousal of pleasurable forms of excitement'.[56] For even the more spontaneous sports such as football are constrained by routine and a team division of labour that sees most players largely limited to patrolling discrete parts of the pitch. Meanwhile, they constantly risk the ending of their careers by industrial injury, finish their weekly labours exhausted and may only enjoy a few seconds of their work, when their team scores and they can make contact with their fellow humans without risking injury. Only a tiny proportion of players genuinely excite supporters, and this not because their talent is alien but because anyone who has been coached and ordered to 'stop dribbling' and 'play properly' (i.e. subordinate spontaneity to a regimented team pattern) recognizes in players such as Maradona or Ryan Giggs that part of him/herself that once thought life could be free.

Despite all the limitations imposed by capitalism, sport can be a positive element in people's lives, and reforms to increase the voice of ordinary people in sport and widen access are worthwhile. But free, spontaneous human activity is to be found in play rather than sport. In his discussion of human nature, Norman Geras argues that play is common to infancy in all societies and that 'the need for and enjoyment of play itself is just a feature of humanity as such, rooted in its biological nature'.[57] Play allows humans to connect with, and integrate, their selves without fear of social disapproval, rediscover childhood intoxication with the joys of contact with the elements and the body, improvising its shape, running till they drop, jumping for joy. Alienation, time constraints and the division of labour ensure that adults only approximate to this when on holiday, swimming in the sea, playing in the sand, running on the beach or, perhaps, lazily touring France on bicycles. Here there is no notion of specialization, hierarchically organized business interests, team rules, record breaking, driving ourselves to our limits for victory – no winners or losers. And here the sense of belonging to social groups, which can be so emotionally powerful as a counterpoint to atomization, isolation and individual powerlessness, is not limited by the competitive identification with one group against all others.

If the resistance that sport can sometimes become a vehicle for is to really transform social relations, it must articulate with wider social forces. According to John Wilson, the French events of 1968, when student protests rapidly developed into mass society-wide protests, including a general strike, 'contained elements of the festival; spontaneity, gaiety, a reverence for the past and a playful irreverence for the future prevailed'.[58] They were a harbinger of a day when, told that people once paid to watch others 'play', tried to go faster, jump higher and further, throw further, or knock others unconscious, people will simply ask 'why?'.

3

Sport, gender and international relations

JOHN HARRIS and BARBARA HUMBERSTONE

Introduction

While the discipline of international relations has rather neglected the study of sport, the internationalization and globalization of sport have received much attention from other scholars, particularly during the 1990s, and continue to be popular and extensively researched subjects in the new millennium. All the leading sports journals have devoted extensive coverage to the area and numerous academics have produced texts looking at the subject.[1] Works on global football also continue to appear frequently.[2] Nevertheless, there is little articulation of the three areas of gender, sport and international relations, and little recognition of the implications of gender and gender relations in the representation of nationalism. This is a significant gap in the IR literature, in which nation-states remain important, if not the central, actors. IR theory has, consequently, largely ignored the implications of the ways in which hegemonic masculinity, embroiled in sport, reinforces nationalistic ideology and concomitantly 'normalizes' discourses around the position and practices of women in sport and society. Sporting images, packaged for the consumption of worldwide audiences, are heavily gendered; yet academic literature on sport and globalization, particularly within IR, has largely ignored the role of women as participants and consumers.[3] For adherents of the realist perspective on IR's traditional problematic, namely inter-state relations and the issues of war, peace and security, this is not seen as a problem; but for those chiefly using critical theoretical perspectives who seek to explore the power structures underlying states, gender imbalances may provide important explanatory mechanisms for state behaviour. This chapter, while it will, for the large part, not focus directly on the consequences for IR of gender divisions in sport, will nevertheless demonstrate the importance of gender stereotypes in sport to conceptions of 'the nation' and thereby raise a number of issues which have an important bearing on our understanding of state power and therefore the inter-state system.

'Hegemonic masculinity' and 'emphasized femininity'

Why is it that women are largely ignored, or, if made visible, represented in less celebratory ways than men? Arguably this has much to do with the ideologies surrounding sport as a male preserve and the 'othering' of those who do not meet the idealized form of 'masculine' perfection. To understand the role of female athletes within the global sports arena it is necessary to first explore notions of manliness/masculinity in sport, since it is upon these that notions of femaleness/femininity are differentiated or 'othered'. Femininity is created against masculinity and one cannot exist without the other.[4] Moreover, societies and nations throughout the world are character-ized by structures whose continuity may largely depend upon the maintenance of 'hegemonic masculinity' and 'emphasized femininity'. Connell argues that these gender forms are stereotypical and idealized and that 'their interrelation is centred on a single structural fact, the global dominance of men over women'.[5] Furthermore, Mac an Ghail maintains that 'manliness … is a contested territory; it is an ideological battleground'.[6]

Within this context, sport provides a visible ideological national and international arena in which forms of masculinity are played out. Arguably, sport is in the frontline of this struggle for hegemonic masculinity, provid-ing particular social contexts where discourses and practices normalize traditional forms of masculinity, while excluding other forms of masculinity and femininity.[7] It is through the media coverage of sport that 'otherness' is continually being created, challenged and changed. Connell's definition of 'hegemonic masculinity' addresses this struggle: 'At any given time, one form of masculinity rather than others is exalted. Hegemonic masculinity can be defined as the configuration of gender practice which embodies the currently accepted answer to the problem of the legitimacy of patriarchy, which guarantees (or is taken to guarantee) the dominant position of men and the subordination of women.'[8] This analysis of masculinities is based around life-history interviews with diverse groups of men, including sports-men. The rigid boundaries of what it means to be a 'real' man are delineated. His work is crucial to an understanding of the ways in which hegemonic masculinity shapes men's actions and emotions and, simultaneously, the ways in which women are perceived, understood and represented.

Analysis of the life story of the Australian champion 'iron-man' (who competed in endurance events including swimming, running, and surf-riding) demonstrated the paradoxes and contradictions associated with the everyday experience of a male athlete who for Connell 'lives an exemplary version of hegemonic masculinity' which is still highly relevant today. For the 'iron-man', being male is about 'not be[ing] gay' and 'be[ing] strong' and it is also about keeping his sport exclusively male. As Connell notes:

> [for] a particular form of masculinity [to be] hegemonic means that it is culturally exalted and that its exultation stabilizes a structure of

dominance and oppression in the gender order as a whole. To be culturally exalted, the pattern of masculinity must have exemplars who are
celebrated as heroes. Steve [the iron-man] certainly enacts in his own
life some of the main patterns of contemporary hegemonic masculinity: the subordination of women, the marginalisation of gay men, and
the connecting of masculinity to toughness and competitiveness. He
has also been celebrated as a hero for much of his life, in school and in
adult sport. He is being deliberately constructed now as a media
exemplar of masculinity by the advertisers who are sponsoring him.[9]

Considerable pressure is placed on individual men to conform to heterosexual hegemonic masculinity. Sport in particular is embedded within informal
codes and powerful sanctioning mechanisms, which spell out the boundaries
of what real man are and should be. Although there are exceptions (David
Beckham, for instance, reaches out to diverse gendered and sexualized
audiences), this is largely a global phenomenon. Hegemonic masculinity is
socially and culturally constructed, reinforced by media portrayal, and is
arguably not the 'natural' condition for men. It varies over time but it contin-
uously embodies toughness, physical and sexual prowess, aggressiveness
and the distancing of femininity.[10] The considerable challenge by women at
all levels of society makes the maintenance of hegemonic masculinity
imperative if men are to retain their power in societies, and thereby over the
international relations agenda.
    As all the chapters in this book illustrate, messages conveyed through
sport impinge upon all aspects of society, both nationally and globally. Sport
is therefore a significant and powerful arena through which various
processes construct and legitimate dominant forms of masculinity and where
what is to be excluded is also defined. The consequence is the construction
of 'emphasized femininity'; for women are largely rendered invisible in
sport or portrayed as overly 'feminine', heterosexual and meeting the needs
of men. Rarely are their sporting skills and expertise celebrated or are they
upheld as sporting icons or hero(in)es. The prevailing cultural messages
through sport celebrate the idealized form of masculinity at the same time as
inferiorizing the 'other' – women and forms of masculinity that do not
conform. Arguably, 'sport's very physical nature gives it special significance
because of the fundamental link between social power and physical force.
Sport is a major arena in which physical force and toughness are woven into
hegemonic masculinity and the resultant ideologies transmitted.'[11] With this
in mind, we would dispute recent writings that suggest that sport in some
way equalizes the relations between male and female sportspeople. For
Mangan, 'sport makes modern men and women . . . in the same image. The
global espousal of modern competitive sport puts a premium on aggression,
assertion, strength and self-discipline – for *both* men and women.'[12] We
argue that sportsmen and sportswomen are not seen or represented in the
same way or with the same level of 'respect' in the media, either nationally

or internationally. We will show that women in sport continue to be 'othered' as different to, and less worthy than, men.

We have briefly touched upon the significance of gender in making sense of nationalism and global sport. The importance of hegemonic masculinity in defining sport and the identification of forms of masculinity espoused through national sport in perpetuating extreme nationalism and violence have been discussed in some detail elsewhere.[13] Since hegemonic masculinity is maintained through sport by the exclusion and denigration of sportswomen, our intention here is to draw attention to the position of women throughout the world in sport and to show the ways in which women are 'othered' through prevailing discourses. We will also illustrate how discourses around sportswomen are differently constructed in different countries and within various sports. Football is a particular focus for this analysis.

Women and football

Association football is, without doubt, the most popular sport in the world. For many countries it forms an integral part of their constructed/imagined national identity and their standing in the world order (for more detail on these issues see Roger Levermore's chapter earlier in this book). It is also linked, in many cases, to notions of manliness and hegemonic forms of masculinity within cultures the world over. Because of this there has historically been a strong resistance to women playing the sport in many parts of the world.[14]

Since the mid-1970s women's football has developed rapidly, due in part to the Sport for All movement in Europe and North America and parts of Asia. In this part of the chapter we aim to offer an insight into the wider world of women's football. Our aim is not to 'stop at every port' around the world, and simply list all we can about the world game, but to provide a thumbnail sketch of the global picture, highlighting the divergent nature of women's football around the world. We do this to identify the cultural 'locatedness' of a particular sport in an attempt to examine and explore the gendering of a global commodity. Association football differs markedly from country to country not only in terms of its perceived 'value' within a particular culture but also in terms of its gendered 'positionality'. To truly understand femininity/masculinity within any given sport it is important to be aware of the international picture also.

In most parts of Britain, football for men forms an important part of the masculine identity. Its locatedness, though, is not the same the world over and some other nations have their own form of 'football' as integral parts of the masculine ideal. In the US, the word 'football' refers to a totally different game, known as American football, or 'gridiron' in Britain, where it was for many years a relatively alien concept. However, since UK terrestrial television started screening the sport in the mid-1980s it has assumed a strong fan base in Britain,[15] and a number of American football teams have emerged across the country and in other parts of western Europe. For Americans, association football is known as soccer. Here the sport is not part of the male psyche, as 'real men play football', a sport whose masculinity-validating dimensions have always been one of its prominent cultural features.[16] Soccer, meanwhile, is presented as a junior co-educational activity; as a game for immigrants and their children, from countries where the association game is an integral part of the culture (e.g. Italy and Mexico); and for women.

The USA is a leading force in women's football. It was not until the 1980s that the first national championship took place. In recent years, US success on the field has been phenomenal. In 1991 the US were the inaugural world champions, beating Norway 2–1 in the final in China. Five years later, in front of their own spectators in Atlanta, they became the first Olympic champions, beating China in front of a then world record crowd of 76,489 people. The victory of the home team in the 1999 Women's World Cup finals, proclaimed as the 'largest women's sporting event in history', saw soccer assume a prominent position within American culture.[17] Every game was broadcast live on television in the US, attracting an estimated 40 million viewers. Following the home nation's victory in the tournament, the team found itself elevated to iconic status, with its leading players appearing on the David Letterman show, the covers of numerous magazines and even at the White House at the request of the then President Bill Clinton.

Some similarities to the USA are to be found when we examine the place of association football in Australia. Here they also have another sport called 'football' which serves as an integral part of the male identity, providing an arena where notions of manliness, masculinity and muscularity are promoted and celebrated both on the field of play and in the stands. This game is known in many other countries as 'Aussie Rules', which is also characterized by high-impact tackles. Women's soccer is growing at a considerable rate, and has risen markedly in recent times.[18] However, in terms of women entering a male preserve, it is probably more pertinent to look at the females who play Aussie Rules.[19] Aussie Rules occupies the same exalted status as soccer in most parts of Britain and gridiron in the US. It is a sport that embodies dominant notions of hegemonic masculinity.

Within both of these countries then, other forms of football are more significant in forming an integral part of the male identity. An analysis of newspaper coverage of these sports would highlight pronounced notions of manliness, utilizing militaristic terminology and emphasizing physicality. It may be that many nations cling to a particular form of football as a kind of male preserve as it becomes more and more important to a faltering ideology of male supremacy. It is important, though, to further contextualize this aspect. It would be wrong, as can be seen from the locatedness of football in some of the other countries we will focus upon, to group association football in England, American football, and Aussie Rules as one. Although they may be very similar in terms of their social construction in relation to spectatorship and social class, football in England is arguably closer to another American sport, namely baseball. However, the two other codes of football both rely on fierce physical contact. In this respect, the games are more similar to the rugby codes than association football. This is further evidenced by the fact that both also use an oval shaped ball.

Football has a universal appeal. The following section looks at a selection of countries to achieve a broader understanding of how sport can be 'located' in and between nations. In 1997 we attended the International Sociology of Sport Association's congress in Norway. During our visit the national female team was playing an important football match and many of the bars and restaurants showed the game live on their screens. This enthusiasm and support had certainly never been seen in England, where the culture of most public houses would have seen this event ridiculed. On the day after their victory, much space was afforded to the match in the newspapers, and most publications on the newsstands led with the sports story. This may be a reflection of Norway's relation to football being similar to that of the USA, where football is seen as a sport more suitable for 'women', since it is largely through the Norwegian 'outdoor life', or *friluftsliv*, that hegemonic masculinity may be more readily identified.[20]

Of all the countries where women athletes have been at the forefront of raising the sporting profile of a nation, China is perhaps the most significant.[21] During the early part of the 1990s Chinese women made rapid progress in a number of events and set new world records in, for example, athletics, in times that obliterated previous records. Much negative publicity has also followed, particularly through the subsequent positive drug tests of a number of these athletes (see Barrie Houlihan's chapter later in this book for more detail). To the best of our knowledge, their female football players have been untouched by this controversy. Their performance in reaching the 1996 Olympic final was all the more remarkable given that such a small number of females actually play the sport there. There is a major difference in the way the sport is conceptualized within Chinese culture. Brownwell notes how a woman who plays soccer might be considered 'vulgar', but she is never considered 'butch'.[22] This highlights a very different framing of sport, where 'maleness' and the sport are not necessarily always seen as one and the same. A similar situation is found in Japan, where women's soccer does not have to differentiate itself from a sexual stereotype.[23]

In Brazil, spiritual home of 'the beautiful game', on the other hand, there is a strong resistance to the idea of women playing football.[24] As other authors have shown, the same has been true of Germany.[25] Even in Sweden, one of the leading powers in the women's game, the players are often viewed with suspicion and contempt.[26] However, the differences between gender relations in football there and in England were most vividly highlighted by the relative media interest in the 1984 encounters between the two countries.

The first leg was shown live on Swedish television, and for the second leg 36 Swedish journalists travelled to England, while the games barely received a mention in the English press.[27] Whereas the recent (male) World Cup finals in Korea and Japan received unprecedented media attention across the globe, the women's premier tournament, in countries other than the US, often passes by relatively unnoticed. The level of sponsorship afforded to the respective World Cups further highlights the discrepancy between the male and female game. The 1998 male World Cup in France, brought in $360 million from its 12 official sponsors, while the following year's women's World Cup raised a total of $6 million in sponsorship.[28]

The examples included above clearly highlight the differential cultural locatedness of a sport within the global arena. USA star player Mia Hamm is reputed to earn more than $1 million a year, while many top players in other parts of the world work full-time and receive no payment for their football. This further highlights the 'value' afforded to the game in different cultures. The reality for many women football players, unlike their highly paid male counterparts, is that their game does not have such an exalted status within their home nations. Studies in England,[29] New Zealand[30] and a comparative study across four European countries[31] have all highlighted the opposition and oppression encountered by female football players at a variety of levels. Issues centring around sexuality and the 'image' of the game are of particular concern to many of the athletes.

The lesbian athlete and compulsory heterosexuality

Cox and Thompson point to the way in which a 'mythical construction of the lesbian athlete is still embedded in women's soccer', strongly affecting both lesbian and straight players.[32] There is, they argue, a homophobic climate in sport perpetuated by the normalizing heterosexual discourses that compel female athletes to adopt emphasized feminine appearances and exaggerated heterosexual behaviours. Women's entry into traditionally and predominantly male sporting spaces, although suggesting possibilities for women to resist and contest male definitions, values and control in sport, has been met by material barriers and resentment. Women transgressing such barriers are frequently depicted as not quite female and, when not adopting emphasized femininity, as 'butch'.

Rugby union, a form of football that Nauright and Chandler claim epitomizes hegemonic masculine characteristics 'such as toughness, loyalty to team and country and aggressive competitiveness',[33] is a particular case in point. Wright and Clarke's research into the media representation of women rugby union players in the UK, Australia and New Zealand, reveals the ways in which women players' (hetero)sexuality is policed and heterosexism is 'normalized' for the players.[34] Wright and Clarke show the ways in which players in the then women's English rugby team were described in terms of their looks, 'feminine' attributes and their particular relations with men. Where heterosexual credentials were not established, women were talked about in terms of their 'motherly' actions, self-sacrifice or given little attention. In such a climate, it would clearly be difficult for a woman to talk about or be associated with a female partner or relations with other women. Consequently, lesbian athletes are largely rendered invisible and afraid of being stigmatized should they publicly reject these powerful scripts of heterosexuality. Sport is one of the most powerful social arenas in which heterosexual ideology is perpetuated and even demanded for both men and women.

Despite the obvious ambiguities and problems for women who attempt to play male-defined sports, it is estimated that 30 million females world-wide now play the game of football.[35] Seven years ago football's world governing body (FIFA) proclaimed that 'the future is feminine' and the events of USA 1999 did much to promote the female game. Kimmel notes how the 1999 world champions provided a revealing insight into the way that sport has become one of the primary sites for the reproduction of gender relations. He refers to the 'persistent (and insistent) references' to the heterosexuality of the championship winning team.[36] The image of Brandi Chastain taking off her shirt (and revealing Nike's latest sports bra) in celebration after her winning penalty kick attracted global attention. Brookes refers to the image as being a 'paradigmatic example of how post-feminism and commodification are interrelated'.[37] In many ways this may be read as an expression of 'girl power' whereby women show that they can be athletic, fit, and successful in sport, without compromising their (perceived) femininity. Arguably, these images collude with the hegemony of heterosexual, emphasized femininity which is embedded in the commodification of women's bodies.

As highlighted previously, the success of the US women's soccer team and the resultant coverage of its achievements promoted female team sport in a way that has seldom been witnessed before. Players like Chastain and Mia Hamm represent 'accepted' images of commodified sports idols (something that rarely occurs with female team sport athletes). The 'visibility' of female athletes within the media is often linked to heterosexist images that involve some degree of undress and it is to this issue that we now turn.

The (in)visibility of female athletes

The role of the mass media in shaping opinion and framing attitudes has long been recognized. Research has pointed to the under-(re)presentation of women in the media, and the fact that when females are (re)presented, existing societal norms are highlighted through stereotypical portrayals.[38] Many authors have suggested that female athletes are underrepresented in the sports media, as a mechanism to preserve sport as a male domain.[39] It is also evident that female athletes are subjected to 'non-task' relevant commentary, or portrayed in a non-active role, in order to construct and/or reinforce hegemonic masculinity.[40]

Within the global sports arena there are many differences between the (re)presentation of male and female athletes. It is evident that in a number of cases female athletes are judged primarily in terms of looks rather than sporting ability. No female football player enjoys the global profile of, say, a David Beckham, Zinedine Zidane or Ronaldo. The Russian tennis player Anna Kournikova is probably the most highly visible female athlete in modern sport. She has major sponsorship deals with companies such as the sportswear manufacturer Adidas and Berlei bras (under the slogan 'only the ball should bounce') and is reputed to be one of the world's highest paid tennis players. Yet the media attention and her exalted visibility are not matched by her performance as a tennis player. To date, Kournikova has yet to win a major singles tennis tournament and since sustaining a foot injury in 2001 has plummeted down the world rankings.

Over the past few decades the number of sports open to women has expanded considerably, and they now compete at the same level as males in a number of sports.[41] Yet the absence of women athletes from the public eye, in a variety of countries, is an explicit reminder that sport is a male domain in many newspapers the world over. This male dominance is evidenced by the noticeable absence of females in a recent American survey listing the one hundred greatest athletes of the twentieth century – only eight women were deemed worthy of inclusion on a list that included three horses![42] It is suggested that the media constructs and maintains masculine ideals in sport by highlighting those characteristics which are associated with hegemonic masculinity outlined earlier, while either rendering sportswomen displaying similar sporting attributes invisible, or acceptable if they pass the test of heterosexuality. To suggest that women can demonstrate sporting excellence independently of a man would threaten the gender regime.

This can be exemplified in the world of mountaineering, which although not generally perceived as a sport, clearly exhibits many of its characteristics. In particular, men who engage in risky mountain expeditions can be portrayed as heroes, while women are seen as out of place.[43] The reporting of the death of Alison Hargreaves while she descended the difficult K2 mountain in 1995 is illustrative. Hargreaves was considered as one of the UK's most experienced and competent women mountaineers, and had successfully climbed a number of Himalayan peaks that year. In the same month as her death two men were also killed descending a Himalayan mountain. These men were reported as mountaineers, 'of great integrity and huge stature', while Hargreaves was proclaimed as an unfit mother and 'obsessed' by her desire to reach the summit. No mention was made of the fact that one of the men who died was also a parent. Such phenomena of hero creation are highly evident in sport and frequently implicated in the creation of national identification.

Creating hero(in)es and national identities

Rowe, McKay and Miller have described sportsmen as the representatives of national character.[44] Boyle and Haynes support this view and highlight how few other cultural forms lend themselves as easily as sport to being used as an indicator of national identity.[45] In England, for example, national identity is established predominantly through the achievements of male sports teams and individual male athletes. This has become increasingly apparent in recent times as sport has been utilized by the newspapers as a replacement for warfare. Militaristic terminology and emphasized masculinity is evident within the sports reporting of both the tabloid and the broadsheet press. Stevenson posits that the majority of a nation's heroes today are sports stars and the ideal of the fit and athletic male is central to discourses of national image and identity.[46] As such, male sports stars embody the masculine status of the nation's men, and the media construct a masculine ideal through the elaboration of the country's achievements and the promotion of male athletes and teams. In doing this, the media construct a masculine status in sport by glorifying male efforts in defeating foreign opposition, and encouraging male support and patriotism among newspaper readers.[47]

In many countries this mediated (re)presentation of masculinity and manliness is most visibly presented through football stories. An example of this is highlighted by the feature on England defender Tony Adams, draped in the flag of St George, before his team's opening Euro 2000 match (*Sun*, 12 June 2000). The back-page article is headlined 'Adams in Euro opener war cry', implying the commencement of battle and conflict, and demonstrating the national importance of the team's success. Jansen and Sabo suggest that the war metaphor idealizes masculinity, celebrating confrontational differences between men and women.[48] Later in the tournament the phraseology of the newspaper's back-page appeal to 'Hammer those Germans' (17 June 2000) establishes unified, patriotic collectivity, centred around the national team's sporting prowess.

Mass-circulation tabloid newspapers such as the *Sun* and *Daily Mirror* utilize their expansive national influence to direct the country's men towards an aggregated unified force, protecting all that is masculine in the sport. It is not our intention to suggest that football is the only sport where national identity is established by the media. However, as the national sport of many nations, it is the perfect example to demonstrate the print media's application of this as a mechanism to construct masculinity and, simultaneously, nation-states, nationalism and national identity. The tabloid press places a high level of expectancy upon the back of the nation's sports teams, radiating a patriotic, masculine vibe. In order to protect this masculine status of a country many newspapers modify their portrayal of athletes and teams, dependent upon their adherence to expectations.[49] After losing to Portugal in the Euro 2000 championships, descriptions of the England football team took a sudden change in direction, from 'determined', 'assets' and 'heroes' to terms such as 'sorry England' and 'blundering'. While the word 'heroes' is demonstrative of the male dominance in sports coverage, and of the psychological and physical ordeals faced by male athletes, succumbing to these ordeals and failing to meet the expectations placed upon them damages the ideology of male dominance. As such, if a male athlete or team lose unexpectedly, the print media attack their masculinity, in order to preserve the greater masculine status of the country. Following a lacklustre display against Switzerland in the opening game of Euro '96, the England team were labelled 'plonkers' (*Sun*, 10 June 1996) and fans wrote in to protest about the national team. The England football team have been a regular target for the tabloid newspapers over the years as their performances have often been read, and measured, alongside a suggested 'crisis in masculinity' and major changes to the gender order. This differs markedly from coverage of the England women's team, whose international matches are often played without being mentioned at all in the media.

Newspapers sometimes utilize the same technique to establish sport as a masculine domain, when focusing upon individual male athletes. The *Daily Mirror* (28 June 2000) focuses its back-page coverage on British tennis no.1 Tim Henman after his first-round victory at Wimbledon. 'Henman lifts British Spirits' and 'Henman restored some British pride' are prominently printed to communicate his heroic status and simultaneously assert his importance in British sport. The words 'British sport has finally found a winner' (*Sun*, 30 June 2000) imply that Henman is the only Briton worthy of acclaim and is the sole hope for British sport. Such insinuations fail to recognize other athletes' efforts and achievements (including female British tennis player Lucie Ahl, who had also won her match) thus handing Henman 'hero' status.

The focus on Anna Kournikova in a variety of newspapers across the globe is clearly demonstrative of how physical appearance is often deemed more important than nationality within women's sport. While strong nationalistic discourse is prevalent in articles on a whole host of male sporting activities, the focus within women's sport remains on the 'look' and perceived attractiveness of athletes. The *Sun*'s 'countdown to Wimbledon' (17 June 2001) provides an example. The nationalistic discourse in the men's game is evident in an article on Tim Henman and his new, improved bid for the title. Just over the page, however, the 'countdown to (women's) Wimbledon' begins with a reader's vote to find the 'sexiest woman in tennis'. Harris and Clayton suggest that this introduction to the 2001 championships is concerned with 'seeking out' a suitably feminine replacement for the absent Anna Kournikova.[50] As the *Sun* states, 'Anna Kournikova has left her army of adoring male fans frustrated by pulling out of Wimbledon' (20 June 2001). More importantly, perhaps, the sport is left without a carrier for the emphasized femininity standard. That the tabloid newspapers were so keen to initiate a new 'face of femininity' in tennis suggests that Kournikova's role was viewed as being one of only glamour and sensuality. Additionally, that none of the 'candidates' for the new 'sexiest woman in tennis' were British, strengthens the argument that nationality is perceived to be less important than physical appearance in women's sport.

This example highlights the conflict between some of the fundamental themes within the gendered sports world. Tennis is deemed as a female-appropriate sport, particularly when practised by athletes such as Kournikova, yet nationalistic discourse and masculinity are inserted within the British/English press when cheering on Tim Henman or Greg Rusedski. The irony of this seems lost on many of the newspapers, particularly when such nationalistic discourse is focused on Rusedski, a Canadian. Similarly, tabloid newspapers have regularly utilized English football to apply mechanisms for the construction of masculinity and national identity.[51] A host of sub-standard performances by the national team, particularly during the latter part of Kevin Keegan's reign as manager, resulted in some of the most damning media scrutiny since the team's failure to qualify for the 1994 World Cup. Only recently have the tabloids re-employed the nationalistic narrative, with the appointment of a Swedish manager. Conflict and confusion were prevalent within the press coverage following Sven-Göran Eriksson's appointment, but much of this was soon forgotten as he oversaw England's qualification for the 2002 World Cup finals. As the examples above have highlighted, in terms of media coverage, and even 'status', male sport is ranked and perceived as being much more important than female sport.

Conclusion

This chapter has highlighted the ways in which organized sport is used to bolster a fragile ideology of male supremacy, celebrated through hegemonic masculinity embedded, albeit in different ways, in sport throughout the world. Manliness and masculinity are often linked to national identity and concepts of nationhood. Women are largely neglected within theorizations of the nation and international relations, and sport provides a microcosmic representation of international society 'reflecting contradictory and paradoxical messages about the roles of women that are transmitted into other societal institutions'.[52] Consequently gender relations and representations of women and men in sport have clear implications for the ways in which international relations in sport are explored and understood. In recent years female scholars have identified the role played by women athletes in the global sports arena. Football, as a team sport, carries with it a clearly identifiable national image when countries meet in the international arena. Benedict Anderson's locution of an 'imagined community' is, in many cases, created and understood through sport, and particularly football.[53] As Eric

Hobsbawm has stated, the imagined community of millions seems more real as a team of 11 named people.[54] It is evident that coverage of female sports stars, meanwhile, is more often linked to 'looks' and perceived heterosexual attractiveness rather than to sporting performance and national pride. As we have shown, women athletes are still rarely reported for their athletic prowess but rather for the way in which they live up to an idealized hetero-sexualized femininity that reinforces the hegemony of the 'Adonis' male sport icon, its connections to nationalistic ideologies and its implications for international relations and sport.

It is important to recognize that much of our discussion has focused upon dominant and exalted (re)presentations within the media. Football, as the world's most popular sport, provides an interesting site for examining the (re)production of gender relations within the global sports media. Our analy-sis emphasizes the cultural locatedness of media (re)presentations whereby there is a 'societal value' attached to various sports forms. The examples of the 1999 World Cup-winning soccer team and tennis star Anna Kournikova have further exemplified the currency attached to heterosexual femininity within the sports media.

Stevenson's Australian study highlights many similarities to those issues identified and discussed here.[55] Such (re)presentations work towards promoting an emphasized femininity which is denied a lesbian script and which is itself implicated within the (re)presentation of a particular hegemonic masculine sporting ideal. Hargreaves is one of the few researchers to have explored issues of 'otherness' in the global media portrayal of female athletes.[56] There is a definite need for further research exploring the multidimensionality of identities within the global sports media. (Re)presentations of elite female athletes are subject to many complex and contradictory frames of analysis. We have already highlighted the currency attached to a particular white, heterosexual femininity through our description of the press coverage surrounding Anna Kournikova and compulsory heterosexuality of other sportswomen. Future research needs to focus also upon the (re)presentation of black female athletes and the invisi-bility of Muslim athletes within the sports pages.[57] The current dominance of women's tennis by the Williams sisters (Venus and Serena) provides a particularly pertinent opportunity for scholars to further explore the inter-sections of race and gender in media sport. Hargreaves offers an interesting analysis of the (re)presentation of Australian (aboriginal) athlete Cathy Freeman. Freeman was chosen as the face of the Sydney 2000 Olympics and was featured in news stories across the globe (particularly after winning the gold medal for the 400 metres, when she celebrated by parading both the Australian and Aboriginal flags). Such an event adds another dimension to analyses of sport and nation. Freeman was viewed by some to be a signifier of a new 'constructive nationalism', while others viewed her act as a sign of tokenism and assimilation into the white world.[58]

Despite limitations of space it is important to at least mention different identity (re)presentations and, in recognizing and signalling issues relating to the multidimensionality of identity, to draw attention to disabled athletes of both sexes who are marginalized and inferiorized in sports media coverage. Arguably Britain's most 'visible' disabled athlete of recent times is Tanni Grey-Thompson. Yet even an athlete of this standing is largely overlooked by the media and only receives (limited) coverage at the time of the Paralympics. Furthermore, she was unable to receive her 'BBC Sports Personality of the Year' award following her successes at the Sydney Paralympics as the organizers had assumed she would not win and neglected to provide wheelchair access to the stage. Grey-Thompson's case highlights practices and discourses in need of further exploration. Despite being largely ignored by the British press, as a Welsh woman her achievements are promoted and celebrated more extensively within the Welsh media. The *Western Mail*, self-styled *papur cenedlaethol Cymru* (national newspaper of Wales), presents the achievements of a variety of Welsh athletes. Although rugby union remains Wales's national sport and the focus of much of the newspaper's coverage, articles relating to nationhood and national identity feature prominently in its sports reporting. It could be that female and disabled athletes receive greater coverage in nations such as Wales than that identified in previous studies, which have focused on larger nations.

For traditional IR, and even many of the innovatory perspectives in the discipline, nation-states remain key actors and their interactions within the inter-state system are of abiding interest. We hope that this exploration of the gendered and sexualized content of contemporary nationalism will not only provoke a questioning of any taken-for-granted assumptions about nation-states and the inter-state system but also contribute to the elaboration of future research agendas.

4

Building an international regime to combat doping in sport

BARRIE HOULIHAN

Introduction

The Sydney Olympic Games were a great success not just because of the efficient organization, quality of competition and high standard of the facilities but also because no world records were broken in track and field events – something that had not happened at any Olympics since 1948. The absence of world records, together with the large number of athletes who withdrew before the Games – 27 from the People's Republic of China team alone – and the near record number of positive drug tests recorded, provide some of the most telling evidence that doping at the Olympic Games is getting more difficult. Many would place the credit for the apparently more effective anti-doping policy jointly at the door of the Australian government's domestic anti-doping body, the Australian Sport Drug Agency (ASDA) and the newly formed World Anti-Doping Agency (WADA). While ASDA was established in 1990, WADA is much more recent, having been established only in November 1999. Yet it was the establishment of WADA that offered the prospect of, at last, securing the formation of an effective international anti-doping regime. In discussing international regimes, this chapter follows Krasner's definition of regimes as 'sets of explicit principles, norms, rules and decision-making procedures around which actor expectations converge in a given area of international relations'.[1] As such, regimes are seen as a sub-set of international (often inter-state) institutions. WADA is an unusual, and possibly unique, international organization in so far as it brings together states and non-governmental sports organizations and is jointly funded and jointly managed by a board that has equal representation from states and sports bodies. The agency is located at the heart of a complex pattern of agreements, written conventions, norms, values and domestic legislation that constitutes the putative regime.

This chapter starts by tracing the gradual emergence of the issue of doping and its transition from a private matter to a public policy issue. Attention is paid to the evolution in the nature of the problem and particularly to the movement of doping in sport beyond the capacity of national governments and national sports organizations to a problem that required cooperation between a range of national and international governmental and private sports organizations. The values and interests of key policy actors are explored within the context of international regime building. The chapter then examines the current structure and pattern of international efforts to combat doping in sport, especially the role of WADA, and assesses whether they constitute an effective policy regime. The chapter concludes with a discussion of the problems that face WADA in contributing to regime effectiveness and an evaluation of the prospects for success. The chapter's contribution to our understanding of policy regimes is in its analysis of regime formation in relation to a policy issue that exhibits a number of distinctive characteristics: first, that it falls between the public and private spheres; second, that both public authorities and private organizations, such as the IOC and the major international sports federations, have been reluctant to claim ownership of the issue; third, that policy leadership is assumed reluctantly and often as a defensive measure; and fourth, that the establishment of an effective regime requires the close and continuing cooperation between public and private bodies.

From Mont Ventoux to Lille: The slow process of regime formation

The modern history of doping in sport is intimately linked with the history of the world's most prestigious cycling race, the Tour de France. It was the death of the British cyclist Tom Simpson, during his climb of Mont Ventoux in the 1967 tour, that raised awareness of the issue of doping within international sports federations and a small number of governments. Simpson was the first in a succession of international sports stars who became enmeshed in doping scandals – which came full circle with the near collapse of the 1998 tour when Willy Voet, the Festina team *soigneur* (masseur), was stopped while trying to bring erythropoietin (EPO) across the border between France and Belgium. The subsequent investigation by the French police uncovered extensive doping and led to parallel investigations across much of Europe and a major trial in Lille involving Voet and eight others, including the leading French cyclist, Richard Virenque.

The 1998 'tour trial' could be seen as simply one more scandal involving drugs to join the long list that included: the exodus of US athletes from the 1983 Pan-American Games, allegedly because the drug-testing regime was more sophisticated than they had expected; the positive results that mysteriously disappeared from the IOC Medical Commission chair's hotel safe during the 1984 Los Angeles Olympic Games; the steroid-assisted 100m world record for Ben Johnson at the Seoul Olympics; and the recent spate of positive test results for nandrolone that included Linford Christie. What made the 1998 scandal different was that it led directly to the IOC proposing the establishment of a new international anti-doping agency, thus initiating the process that was to lead to the formation of WADA.

The establishment of WADA undoubtedly marked a watershed in the evolution of anti-doping policy. However, the level of cooperation that it reflected, and promises, has been a long time in the making. Barely 15 years earlier the policy infrastructure was radically different, with policy-making, such as it was, taking place within a series of relatively discrete arenas largely divided between governmental and non-governmental actors but also with significant divisions within these two primary clusters.[2] Actors on the governmental side in the 1980s could be divided into four groups: the 'activists', the apathetic, the poor and the subversive. The small number of 'activist' governments, most notably Sweden, Norway, the UK and France, had begun to address the issue of doping around the early 1970s, and while their actions were important they were relatively modest, often limited to expressions of disapproval, funding of limited programmes of 'public interest' tests, occasional legislative action and cajoling their domestic governing bodies to take action. The assumption underpinning the policy of activist governments was that the problem of doping could be tackled effectively at the domestic level, a position that was reinforced by the implicit priority given to establishing their own ethical credentials over a concern to reduce doping in international sport more generally. Apathetic governments included those of such major Olympic 'powers' as Canada, Australia and the United States. Within this group the problem was recognized but the policy response rarely exceeded ritual condemnation. The relatively marginal involvement of poorer countries in international sport, especially the Olympic Games, in the 1960s and late 1970s provided little incentive for them to recognize the issue of doping in sport even if they were able to find the resources necessary to be participants in the emerging policy discussions. By far the most significant group was the subversives, such as the Soviet Union and the GDR, where state-organized doping was firmly established behind a public front of pompous condemnation of drug use as contrary to the spirit of Olympism and a problem confined to the commercialized West.[3]

Among international sports organizations there was slow and fitful action towards doping. The IOC began discussing doping in the early 1960s and initiated limited testing in the early 1970s. At about the same time some of the major international federations, most notably the International Amateur Athletic Federation (IAAF), were moving through a parallel, and equally modest, process of policy development. For both the federations and the IOC, measures to control doping were tentative for a series of inter-related reasons: first, at a time when the amount of international sport, and associated broadcasting income, was increasing rapidly, doping was perceived by some policy actors as an aspect of commercially successful sport that was best quietly ignored; second, knowledge of the nature, extent and likely development of the problem was scant and few organizations were willing to invest in research; third, the dominant, and highly convenient, perception of the problem was that it involved a few 'rogue' athletes and that it could be contained, if not eliminated by, in-competition testing; and finally, because both the IOC and the major federations were, at best, simply concerned to ensure the probity of their particular events or sports.

Contact between these disparate policy actors was limited. Indeed, only the Council of Europe displayed a sustained concern with the issue and provided a regular international forum for its discussion. The council began considering the issue in the early 1960s and by the late 1970s published a 'Recommendation on Doping', enhanced to charter status in 1984, designed to give a lead to member states with regard to their domestic policy. The council provided a forum for member governments to exchange information and examples of 'good practice' in doping control and, as such, helped to lay the foundation for the international anti-doping regime. However, while the significance of the role of the council should not be undervalued, the limited resources at its disposal, the lack of involvement of sports NGOs and the infrequency of its meetings meant that it should be seen as a secondary, rather than primary, source of regime formation.

The position in the mid- to late 1980s was of a series of fragmented and mutually suspicious organizations only gradually, and often unwillingly, accumulating evidence that doping was extensive rather than isolated, at the heart of modern sport rather than peripheral and systematic rather than opportunistic.[4] The shift in problem perception was the outcome of a number of diverse factors which emerged in the late 1980s, some endogenous to the loose 'issue network' of interested policy actors and others of an exogenous nature. Among the endogenous factors was the slow acknowledgement that the growing geographical mobility of athletes meant that many spent more time beyond the jurisdiction of their domestic anti-doping authority and governing body due to the pattern of international competition, warm weather training and scholarships. For example, American and Australian road cyclists rarely needed to return to their home country, given that the primary grand prix circuit was based in Europe. A second factor was the increasing acceptance that in-competition testing was of declining effectiveness due to the shift away from the use of amphetamines at the time of competition to the use of anabolic steroids during training. Out-of-competition testing was not only more expensive, but also often meant that the anti-doping authority in the athlete's home country had to arrange for testing to be completed by the equivalent body in the country where the athlete was training. Such international arrangements required a degree of complementarity of regulations, if not harmonization, that was frequently beyond the capacity of the national bodies and international federations to deliver, thereby enabling a number of successful appeals against a penalty for doping on the grounds of flawed or incompatible regulations. The third factor was the growing willingness of wealthy athletes to use the courts to challenge the findings and decisions of their governing bodies. Even a successful defence could be financially crippling for a domestic governing body.

Exogenous factors included a series of scandals that radically altered the attitude towards doping held by the Australian and Canadian governments. The uncovering of extensive doping at the prestigious Australian Institute of Sport led to a Senate inquiry[5] and the subsequent establishment of ASDA with strong support from the government. In Canada, the Dubin Inquiry,[6] established in the wake of the. Ben Johnson scandal, led to a similar shift from apathy to activism on the part of the government, reflected in the establishment of the Canadian Centre for Drug Free Sport. A further exogenous factor, which had a less direct, but still substantial, impact on the nascent anti-doping regime, was the ending of the cold war. The collapse of the Communist system throughout central and eastern Europe, but especially in the Soviet Union and the GDR, undermined the highly effective government-financed and (it was widely argued) drug-dependent sports system. The end of the cold war also diminished the value of international sport as a surrogate for super-power rivalry and the implicit rationale for the ambivalence towards intervention on doping in the United States.

The position in the late 1980s was that there was an increasing recognition of the need for action at the international level and a marked weakening of the factors inhibiting regime development. However, substantial barriers to policy development still remained, the most important being the level of mutual suspicion that persisted between the main policy actors. Among sports organizations there was a deeply rooted tension between the IOC on the one hand and the major international sports federations, especially the IAAF and swimming's Federation Internationale de Natation, on the other. The federations valued the income and publicity that the Olympic Games generated but also saw the games as a threat to their own world championships. In addition, the federations wanted a greater share of the rapidly rising wealth of the IOC and were generally concerned that an event-organizing body was having such an effect on their development plans. Among states, the long-held suspicion among western European and north American governments that Communist states were systematically doping their athletes made cooperation unlikely. More importantly, activist states on the issue of doping distrusted both the federations and the Olympic movement, arguing that they had a vested interest in ignoring the issue or in only taking such action as would maintain a facade of concern.[7] However, the federations and the Olympic movement were equally suspicious of the motives of governments, arguing that they were largely responsible for encouraging drug use in sport.

Regime formation

Perspectives in international relations, whether neo-liberal, realist or constructivist, for example, offer different lenses through which to examine the movement of anti-doping policy, from consideration within a series of largely self-contained policy arenas to the status of an emergent international regime. Each also offers only a partial insight into the process of regime formation in relation to doping.

Neo-liberalism focuses on the interests of states and non-state institutional actors, such as the IOC and international sports federations, and suggests that 'self-interested parties [endeavour] to coordinate their behaviour to reap joint gains'[8] and that actors are 'strategically rational but otherwise mutually indifferent'.[9] This produces cooperation in the formation of regimes on a strictly limited basis, usually as a means for overcoming market failure and where the anticipated outcome is a *positive sum position* for all actors involved.[10] The perspective is well summarized by Krasner who argues, in relation to state interests, that 'success or failure of regime-building can be explained by the extent to which regimes provide information, monitoring capabilities, or focal points that allow states to move towards the Pareto frontier; everyone better off at the same time; absolute rather than relative gains matter'.[11] States benefit from participation in regimes in a number of ways, including: the reduction of uncertainty through the pooling of information about rival states, in areas of trade, defence and sport for example, and a reduction in the cost of gathering that information; the provision of a greater degree of continuity, stability and predictability about other actors' behaviour; and an increase in the cost of non-compliance due to the damage to reputation and thus the risk of 'forfeit[ing] potential future gains from cooperation'.[12] In relation to doping, state anti-doping agencies benefit not only from pooling information on testing procedures for new drugs and sharing the costs of testing their globally mobile athletes through multilateral testing agreements, but also from the pooling of information about the emergence of new drugs and the rigour of anti-doping efforts in rival countries.

The neo-liberal emphasis on interests and the desire to reduce uncertainty is often coupled with a recognition that resource constraints are an important prompt for states to seek solutions through cooperation. The regime is consequently seen as a network or arena for issue discussion and definition, and also often for policy implementation by providing incentives for compliance. In relation to anti-doping initiatives, the regime therefore provides an opportunity to overcome limitations on resources, such as money for testing, limited scientific expertise for research or urine analysis and authority to conduct tests outside the home country.

Conversely, the more intensive sharing of resources provides an important factor in explaining the formation and persistence of regimes.[13] Neo-liberalism provides a useful explanatory framework in this regard as it directs attention to the gradual development and strengthening of international agreements and links, especially between states but also, during the 1990s (when considering the sporting sphere), between states and international sports organizations. Furthermore, neo-liberalism also emphasizes the growing awareness of the resource costs of an effective policy response. The value of the neo-liberal perspective may be demonstrated in an examination of the actions of a number of governments and intergovernmental organizations, such as the Council of Europe, particularly from the mid-1980s.

The quiet endeavours of the Council of Europe during the 1980s began to pay dividends in the 1990s. In the mid- to late 1980s acknowledgement of the standing of the Council's anti-doping charter came from UNESCO, the European Community, the World Health Organization and the IOC, and encouraged the Council to redesignate the charter as a convention available for signature from 1989. By the late 1990s there were 38 signatories from among members plus three from non-members, including Australia and Canada.

The growing interest among intergovernmental organizations was complemented by the growth in networking between governments. In 1987 a group of northern European countries formed the Nordic Anti-Doping Convention which provided for harmonization of procedures and penalties as well as the mutual testing of athletes. 1990 saw the development of a similar agreement, initially between the UK, Australia and Canada and later joined by New Zealand, Sweden, Norway and the Netherlands, which adopted the additional objective of lobbying within sports forums for greater commitment to drug-free sport. There was also a series of bi-lateral agreements involving, among others, China, Australia, Ireland and Canada.

Paralleling the growth in density of contacts between governments, international sports organizations, which are more readily acknowledged as significant policy actors within the neo-liberal perspective, were also establishing an infrastructure of inter-organizational relations, which extended the role of the IOC's Medical Commission and the work of the medical committees of the major federations. In 1988 the IOC co-hosted with Canada the first 'Permanent World Conference on Anti-Doping' at which the Olympic Anti-Doping Charter was endorsed and adopted. Six years later, in 1994, the IOC brokered an agreement, among all the members of the 'Olympic family' of organizations, aimed at closer harmonization of procedures and penalties. However, it was the lack of progress following the 1994 agreement that both enabled and prompted the more proactive states to continue with their own international efforts at policy development.

Underpinning the increasingly elaborated network of international relationships was the stark recognition on the part of sports NGOs that while the initial phase of policy-making required resources that they possessed, such as authority, organizational capacity and rule-making legitimacy, the current phase required resources that states either possessed in greater quantities, such as money and access to scientific expertise, or else monopolized, such as legislative power. In addition, deepening dependency relationships were also emerging between states. As more countries established state-funded anti-doping agencies and began to finance 'public interest' testing there was a greater need for international cooperation regarding the exchange of information, mutual testing of athletes and a more closely coordinated approach to negotiations with the IOC and the international federations.

To the important caveat that the assumption of rationality on the part of policy actors is frequently hard to sustain should be added the further caution that interests are often inferred and often ascribed a degree of coherence and intention that they do not deserve. With these qualifications in mind, it is possible to build an explanation of regime formation around an analysis of the interests of the various central policy actors. Starting with the more powerful states, it is suggested that they were seeking to ensure the continuing utility of international sport as a framework for diplomacy. Over the years a number of studies have confirmed the attractiveness of international sport as a low-cost, low-risk and high-visibility opportunity for diplomacy.[14] In addition, it is generally the case that if international sport is to be used for diplomacy, then countries need to have the necessary elite sporting resources, preferably a successful national team/squad of athletes or a range of world-class facilities. Furthermore, the 1990s marked the period during which states that had most successfully exploited sports diplomacy, especially as a surrogate for cold war rivalry in the boycotts of the 1980 and 1984 Olympic Games, realized that the strengthening association between elite sport and drugs was undermining the utility of sport at a time when it was offering a broader range of benefits, particularly to the economy through tourism and urban regeneration.[15] While success in competition remains important, it is hosting the event itself that is increasingly significant and valuable, with the consequence that the former is seen as a means of achieving the latter. For example, the close association between doping and the recent success of elite Chinese female swimmers and runners damaged China's bid to host the 2000 Olympic Games and might explain the decision by Chinese sports authorities to drop 27 athletes from its Sydney Olympic squad as an attempt to avoid the potential embarrassment of positive drug test results and thus undermine its (ultimately successful) bid to host the 2008 games.

Benefits from the development of a regime also accrue to 'middle range' sports states, such as Portugal, Ireland, India and many countries in South America. Lacking the resources to either compete effectively with athletes from states that supported or ignored drug abuse or control the behaviour of those states, this middle range group may hope to use the collective influence of the regime to impose anti-doping behaviour and lock it in to the domestic policies of the more powerful states.[16] Where it is difficult to see benefits of regime formation is in relation to weak/poor sports states. Even assuming the formation of an effective anti-doping regime, drug use is only one source of resource inequality that puts them at a disadvantage: inequalities in general sports science, training facilities, coaching and sports medicine still remain.

The absence of general benefits for all regime members suggests that the realist perspective, and its concern with the use of state resources in the pursuit of what Hughes refers to as the core interest 'to preserve its essence: territorial boundaries, population, government and sovereignty'[17] will provide additional insights into the process of anti-doping regime formation. Specifically, it may be argued that international sporting success provides a state with a useful diplomatic resource which, though not of the same significance as economic or military resources, nonetheless enriches the diplomatic repertoire. Consequently, a benefit of regime formation to the more powerful states is that a strong regime would, at the very least, generate a degree of stability in terms of the relative status of participants in international sport by making shifts in the hierarchy of sporting success more difficult, thus preserving the relative diplomatic utility of sport. On the one hand tighter control over doping strengthens the scientific advantage of the current 'international sports powers'. Many factors contribute to a country's overall scientific advantage: doping is one such factor, but others include support from dieticians, nutritionists, equipment technologists, biomechanicians and psychologists. In comparison to the cost of investing in equipment technology, biomechanics, physiology and so on, the science of doping is simple and relatively cheap. On the other hand, an effective anti-doping regime will have most impact on those poorer countries that only have access to cheaper and usually more easily detected drugs. Those athletes using human growth hormone and Hemopure, a substitute for the now detectable EPO, or awaiting the arrival of gene therapy, are much more likely to come from the richer and established sports powers. At best, an effective anti-doping regime will freeze the existing inequality between states and at worst will enable the richer states, or at least the athletes within them, to widen the gap between the European/Oceanic/north American elite and the rest.

The realist perspective, which suggests that regime creation is the result of the distribution of power and the calculation of self-interest by states, offers a forceful explanation for regime formation.[18] For the more powerful states the motive is to establish, extend and reinforce competitive advantage, while for weaker states the acceptance of international obligations is the result of compulsion. Recent trends in swimming provide some supporting evidence for this view. Although strongly challenged by the East Germans in particular, both the United States and Australia saw themselves as major swimming powers. When, in the mid-1990s, Chinese female swimmers began to move rapidly up the world rankings, win medals and break world records, the swimming federations in both the USA and Australia first expressed scepticism at this dramatic improvement and then voiced open allegations of doping. The motivation was not just outrage at cheating or at the loss of status, although both were important, but also financial, as the funding for both federations by their respective national Olympic committees was derived from a formula based on their level of international success. An effective anti-doping regime was attractive as a means of controlling the diminishing but still significant number of subversive states.

Constructivism offers a third perspective on regimes. In part a critique of realism and neo-liberal perspectives, constructivism covers an extremely

broad and eclectic range of positions and draws on an equally broad range
of sources in the social sciences, including Weberian interpretive sociology
and symbolic interactionism. To greater or lesser extents constructivists
emphasize the significance of ideas in shaping the behaviour of actors in
international relations. For Wendt, ideational explanations imply that structures of human association are determined significantly by shared ideas and
that the identity and interests of policy actors are socially constructed
through ideas.[19] Nadelmann, in his study of global prohibition regimes,
argues persuasively that 'moral and emotional factors related neither to
political nor economic advantage but instead involving religious beliefs,
humanitarian sentiments . . . conscience, paternalism, fear, prejudice and the
compulsion to proselytize can and do play important roles in the creation
and the evolution of international regimes'.[20]

Ideational explanations of regime formation tend to take one of two
forms: the first emphasizes the role of epistemic communities and the
second the significance of 'transnational moral entrepreneurs'.[21] Haas
defines an epistemic community as 'a network of professionals with recognized expertise and competence in a particular ... issue area'.[22] Due to their
control over the important resource of knowledge and the dependence of
other policy actors on knowledge to reduce uncertainty, epistemic communities have the potential to influence the way issues are framed and solutions
selected. Doping is an international issue about which there is substantial
uncertainty, where individual states are weak and where there is considerable technical complexity – in short, an issue where there is substantial
scope for the formation of an epistemic community around the growing
cadre of scientists, sports medicine specialists and doping control administrators. However, as I have argued elsewhere, the potential members of the
epistemic community are, currently at least, too closely tied to the interests
of their employers, government anti-doping agencies or international federation doping control units, to constitute an effective independent voice.[23]

It is difficult to identify clear equivalents to Nadelmann's 'transnational
moral entrepreneurs' in the area of doping. There are no organizations that
carry the moral authority of Amnesty International, Greenpeace or Oxfam
and have had a similar impact in mobilizing popular opinion and political
support. The Council of Europe might perhaps lay claim to the role, as its
opposition to doping is complemented by its ethical stand on racism and
intolerance in sport, but its international profile is low even within Europe.
OATH (Olympic Advocates Together Honorably), an international organization campaigning under the slogan 'integrity in and through sport', grew out
of the 1998 corruption scandal surrounding the IOC and took a clear anti-
doping position. However, it was poorly resourced and struggled, ultimately
unsuccessfully, to sustain an international profile.

The emergence of the international anti-doping regime cannot easily be
explained with reference to interests alone or to power or ideas in isolation.
It is clear that a reassessment of interests by key policy actors was

significant following events that either affected them in particular or affected the much broader pattern of international relations. Examples of the former include the doping scandals that affected particular countries, especially Canada (Ben Johnson), Australia (Australian Institute of Sport) and more recently France (1998 Tour de France) and international sports bodies such as the IOC (Salt Lake City bidding corruption). The recalculation of interests that these scandals prompted not only led to a reform of domestic policy in Canada and Australia, but also made both countries more concerned to establish an effective international regime so as to avoid a situation where their more rigorous approach to the use of drugs in sport was exploited by athletes from other states which, for whatever reason, gave doping a lower domestic priority.

Perhaps the most perplexing recalculation of interests was within the United States government, which had for many years studiously avoided acknowledging the issue of doping in sport only to emerge at the end of the 1990s as a leading supporter of WADA and a more rigorous anti-doping regime. In part the change of attitude has been attributed to the post-cold war climate and in part to the continuing association between drug use and professional sports in the USA. However, neither of these explanations is sufficient. A more likely combination of causes was the appointment of Barry McCaffrey as the White House 'drug czar' and the identification of 'drugs in sport' as an aspect of the general drugs problem where publicly discernible progress could be made; and a recognition that recreational and sport-related drug use were no longer discrete problems, as steroid use was becoming increasingly prevalent among young people outside a sports context. McCaffrey's powerful intervention in the debate concerning the formation of WADA was important not just because of the sporting and financial status of the US in the Olympic movement (US corporations provide 60 per cent of IOC income), but also because of the offer of $1m 'start-up' funding for the new agency. However, McCaffrey's intervention highlighted the weakness of the USA's domestic anti-doping policy and prompted him to put pressure on the government and the United States Olympic Committee to emulate Canada and establish an independent anti-doping body.

The primary example of broader changes in international relations having an impact on the calculation of interest by actors relates to the end of the cold war and the collapse of the Communist sports infrastructure throughout much of central and eastern Europe. Not only did the end of the cold war remove an important rationalization for doping, but it also provided an opportunity for organizations such as the Council of Europe to offer support to potential new members to help establish an infrastructure of civil society within which sports organizations could play an important part. A second example concerns the gradual embrace of sport by the European Union following the publication of the Adonnino Report in 1985 as an element in its strategy for developing a stronger sense of European identity.

By the mid-1990s, the European Union had significantly broadened its interest in international sport and by the late 1990s was emerging as a central actor in international anti-doping policy, not least because of the extensive resources that it had available.

Yet while the recalculation of interests was important, of at least equal significance was the capacity to act on perceptions of interest. As mentioned above, what made the emerging participation of the EU in anti-doping policy discussions important was not simply the acknowledgement of its interest in international sport but its power to commit resources and influence other actors. Equally important was the transition of the United States from a marginal to a central actor in debates on doping in sport. Also as noted above, the United States brought with it substantial financial, legal and organizational resources. While the US government, so far at least, is an enthusiastic supporter of WADA and the anti-doping regime, its motives are mixed. Its forceful intervention in the discussions about WADA, which helped to ensure that the body would be independent of the IOC, was prompted, in part at least, by a desire to 'put the IOC in its place' and deflate the collective ego of the committee following the series of bribery scandals surrounding the host city bidding process.

The status of the current anti-doping regime

The evolution of the current anti-doping regime is far from linear; rather it reflects shifts in the nature of the problem of doping and key actors' changing perceptions of the significance of doping and international sport. Moreover, there are many actors whose attitude towards doping is shaped by non-sports policy objectives, including maintenance of the brand image of the Olympics and other international sports events, the identification of sport as a means of economic development and as an opportunity for city or country marketing.

These caveats notwithstanding, the anti-doping efforts have been substantially strengthened by the establishment of WADA. It has been suggested that the more stable and successful regimes exhibit a series of common features. First, a degree of stability and hierarchy (though possibly implicit) among key actors. While there might not be an explicit distinction between 'insiders' and 'outsiders' or between central/senior and peripheral/junior members, most regimes will exhibit signs of the development of a set of tacit understandings that help it operate. Second, functions associated with regime maintenance are fulfilled: these include agenda setting, forecasting of problem development and the monitoring, and in some regimes enforcement, of compliance. In other words, effective regimes tend to have a clear organizational capacity which is most often provided by states. As Keohane, Haas and Levy observe, regimes, as a sub-type of international institutions, 'do not supersede or overshadow states. ... To be effective they must create networks over, around, and within states.'[24]

Third, within effective regimes there is often an arena, whether actual or virtual, which facilitates regime interaction, maintenance and development. For some regimes the arena might be a permanent secretariat with regular meetings, conferences or working groups of policy actors, but for others the arena may exist as newsletters, journals and websites. Within the doping policy area the core set of policy actors has become more clearly defined, with activist governments, major international federations and the Olympic movement comprising the key members. Over the last 20 years the policy distance between these sets of actors has remained, though modified by the increasing pattern of mutual resource dependencies that has developed. In addition, policy leadership has moved steadily out of the hands of the two sports clusters and towards those of activist governments. This latter development is, in part, a reflection of the regime requirement for resources which are most easily available to governments and, in part, a consequence of the lack of leadership provided by the IOC and federations at a time when their income was growing exponentially. Increasingly, regime persistence and development is secured through the elaborate and expanding network of intergovernmental agreements and the steady rise in government-controlled and -funded domestic anti-doping agencies.

The fourth and final characteristic of successful regimes is the existence of an arena for the exchange of information and policy-making. While there has been a growing number of international conferences and multilateral meetings, it was the establishment of the World Anti-Doping Agency that gave the anti-doping regime an organizational core.

Conclusion: the future of the anti-doping regime

While the establishment of the anti-doping regime has been rapid and in many ways reflects an impressive degree of cooperation between previously antagonistic organizations, considerable caution needs to be exercised in reaching an assessment of the regime's chances of medium- to long-term persistence and effectiveness. There are three overlapping sets of concerns that need to be taken into account, some of which are primarily associated with the characteristics of the regime, some more closely associated with WADA and others associated with the nature of the problem.

Foremost among those concerns associated with the regime is its high dependence on state resources and continuing support. Over the last 40 years many, indeed most, of the major sporting states have, at worst, ruthlessly exploited international sport in general and the Olympic Games in particular for a variety of ideological and nationalistic purposes: at best, states have treated international sport as a potential partial solution to a variety of economic, diplomatic and social problems. Instrumentalist perceptions of sport dominate and few states have been prepared to value sport for its intrinsic qualities, such as excitement, personal satisfaction and sense of well-being. The clear danger inherent in an instrumental perception of international sport is that enthusiasm can wane when it proves less effective than hoped or when alternative policy tools, such as trade, the arts and education, catch the imagination of policy-makers. Commitment to anti-doping policy might lessen if the perceived utility of international sport diminishes or if the opportunity cost is seen as too great. There are already one or two countries where the amount of public money being spent on doping control is being challenged on the grounds that it exceeds the sum devoted to encouraging mass participation. Alternatively, commitment to drug-free sport might be reduced because of a desire to maintain the existing levels of success.

The operation of WADA is itself also a source of concern. First, its initial chair is IOC vice-president Richard Pound and the agency is currently located in Lausanne, along with the IOC headquarters. Moreover, some of the members of the WADA board are from federations that have been notably unsuccessful in limiting the growth of doping in their sports. Taken together, these factors make it more difficult for the agency to establish an organizational culture that is not simply derived from that which prevailed for so long within elite sports organizations and did so little to stimulate a proactive stance towards doping. Second, the agreement on the formula to determine the contribution of individual governments to the financing of WADA took a long time to be reached. Formulae derived from OECD practice, or constructed around numbers of athletes that a country sends to the Olympic Games or the number of medallists, were all considered before a compromise was negotiated. The failure of bodies such as UNESCO to ensure that agreements on financial contributions are fulfilled is a source of concern regarding WADA. Third, governmental representation has yet to be settled. Some regions have bodies that provide the basis for representation: for example, Europe is represented through the EU and the Council of Europe and Africa through the Supreme Council for Sport in Africa. However, no similar bodies exist in the other continents.

The final set of concerns relates to issues that are internal to the operation of WADA and constitute the most potent threats to its future. First, WADA has yet to agree a definition of doping. In the past federations have relied on definitions that referred to 'intent', 'harm to health' and 'performance enhancement', but none of these has proved to be watertight when challenged in court. More recently, some federations, most notably the IAAF, have adopted a 'strict liability' definition according to which an athlete is absolutely liable for the presence of any banned substance in his/her blood or tissue. However, the strict liability definition itself has been successfully challenged in courts or tribunals in the United States and Germany. A second problem facing WADA is the basis on which it should seek to achieve harmonization of penalties for doping infractions. Most federations and most states favour a tariff range which sets, for example, a minimum ban of two years for a first offence of doping with steroids.

However, a small number of federations, notably soccer and cycling, refused to accept the two-year minimum; consequently, the regulation allows variation of the minimum penalty at the discretion of the federation. The federations that have resisted the regulation are, not surprisingly, those which are faced with rich and powerful commercial teams, leagues or individual athletes and therefore may feel that they would be unable to enforce a two-year penalty. Apart from the reluctance of these federations to support the two-year ban for a first offence involving steroids, there is the more significant debate that has, so far, received very little attention and concerns the issue of equity in making all sports and all athletes, whatever the stage of their career, subject to the same penalty. For example, it is open to question whether it is equitable to impose the same two-year ban on a middle-distance runner, whose international career might last for over ten years and who has a series of high-profile events in which to compete, as on a rhythmic gymnast, whose career is usually much shorter and whose one chance of high-profile success comes every four years at the Olympic Games. A third problem is the escalating cost of defending doping decisions. An increasing number of domestic governing bodies are proving reluctant to penalize an athlete, even when the evidence is strong, for fear of litigation. As a result international federations are imposing penalties, but doing so from the relative security of Switzerland and Monaco where challenge to corporate decision-making is difficult and the protection of individual interests noticeably weak.

When the anti-doping regime is compared with those dealing with environmental issues or human rights, its achievements to date are by no means insignificant. However, it is difficult to avoid the conclusion that, WADA notwithstanding, the regime is standing on less secure foundations than its nearest comparators. Probably of greatest significance to the future success of the anti-doping regime is its ability to retain a high level of popular commitment to drug-free sport. But not only is almost nothing known about public attitudes towards doping in sport, there is also no sign that policy-makers perceive public support as an important factor in ensuring continued government commitment and ultimately regime persistence.

5

'The most effective means of communication in the modern world'?: British sport and national prestige

PETER J. BECK

Introduction: Sport as propaganda

Despite frequent claims that politics and sport do not mix, it has proved difficult to prevent sport from acquiring an extra-sporting dimension in the eyes of governments, the media and public opinion in today's globalized society. Speaking as South African President in July 1996 and undoubtedly influenced in part by sport's high profile in the anti-apartheid campaign, Nelson Mandela observed that 'sport is probably the most effective means of communication in the modern world, bypassing both verbal and written communication and reaching directly out to billions of people worldwide'.[1] Mandela was speaking in Britain, where throughout much of the twentieth century governments and the media professed to uphold, at least on paper, the autonomy of sport. Even during the 1980s British ministers for sport, glossing over the Thatcher government's proposed boycott of the 1980 Moscow Olympics, proved regular exponents of this line.[2] By contrast, the 1990s witnessed a change of course. Successive Conservative and Labour governments, motivated in part by prestige considerations, adopted a more overt and systematic approach towards sport in order to improve the international performance of national sports teams as well as to win the right to host major events, most notably the Olympic Games and football World Cup finals. Inevitably, in 2000 the Blair government, like the footballing authorities, was disappointed by the abortive British bid for the 2006 World Cup finals, but the personal role played by both John Major (Prime Minister, 1990–97) and Tony Blair (Prime Minister, 1997 onwards) in support of the bid established the political significance attached to staging such high-profile events. Unsurprisingly, in April 2000 the government's sports strategy document, entitled *A Sporting Future For All*, recorded that 'we will continue to work with national and international bodies to try to attract more events to the UK. We remain committed to supporting a viable bid for the Olympic Games'.[3] Such sentiments were reiterated more recently in the Labour Party's 2001 general election manifesto.[4]

These *political developments* reflect the high visibility of sport in contemporary Britain. Despite traditionally suffering from high-minded distaste, and glossed over by most historians and international relations specialists, 'sport matters' – to quote Blair – to politicians, the media and large numbers of Britons.[5] Apart from accounting for a growing proportion of their space, sport has moved increasingly from the back to the front pages of newspapers. Indeed, Peter Clarke's *Hope and Glory: Britain 1900–1990*, the final volume in the Penguin 'History of Britain', even depicted sport as a secular religion:

> For some people, the joke goes, sport is not a matter of life and death: it is more serious than that. When it is referred to as a religion, the comment may be suggestive as well as ironic. The ability of sport to capture the popular imagination, to infuse a sense of common commitment in the outcome of an epic contest, to provide a strong narrative line – this is not just a trivial matter.[6]

Moreover, *A Sporting Future For All* represented sport as 'a booming industry, worth £12 billion of consumer spending every year and employing around 420,000 people'.[7] Nor can the past be forgotten in a country whose sporting heritage draws heavily upon Britain's role in inventing and developing many modern sports. In this vein, John Major, whose government assigned responsibility for sport to the new Department of National Heritage, identified the centrality of sport in Britain's past and present: 'Some people say that sport is a peripheral and minor concern. I profoundly disagree. It enriches the lives of the thousands of millions of people around the world who know and enjoy it. Sport is a central part of Britain's National Heritage. We invented the majority of the world's great sports.'[8] Hitherto, British governments were guilty, in Major's view, of 'undervaluing a national asset and missing a political opportunity'.[9] As mentioned in the previous paragraph, the Blair government readily reiterated such supportive rhetoric.

The political implications of sport have been explored in depth by Barrie Houlihan and James Riordan, who have suggested a range of criteria – which includes the promotion of health, defence, labour productivity, nation-building, international recognition and prestige – for conceptualizing government policy towards sport.[10] However, this case study of Britain focuses on only one policy element: that is, sport's propaganda potential in terms of reflecting and enhancing, as well as diminishing, British prestige at home and abroad. Historically, what might be defined as the Nazi and Soviet models exemplified the propagandist exploitation of sport. British governments, though publicly espousing a distinctive alternative apolitical approach, were not unaffected by these models; indeed, they were pressurized to emulate the sporting success of Nazi Germany and Soviet bloc countries, so that even before the 1990s, British sport was more politicized than governments liked to admit in public. In turn, during the past decade British developments were still encouraged and inspired by foreign countries, most notably by the example of Australia; indeed, the growing emulation and use of Australian models and expertise has fostered press references to British sport's 'fixation' with Australia.[11]

Britain and the Nazi model

Hitler's 1936 'Olympic *blitzkrieg*', as depicted vividly in Leni Riefenstahl's 1938 film *Olympia*, means that Nazi Germany is regarded still as providing the stereotypical model for the instrumental use of sport.[12] Already, in 1935, Sir Eric Phipps, the British ambassador in Berlin, had described how German sport, headed by Captain Hans von Tschammer und Osten, the *Reichssports Führer*, was being forced into the National Socialist mould in pursuit of state glorification and Hitler's totalitarian aspirations: 'the National Socialist Party are slowly but surely tightening their hold on German sport'.[13]

Working alongside political education, sport was employed to inspire the German people, especially the youth, to believe in both their often-proclaimed racial superiority and place in the construction of a dynamic new Nazi order. Indeed, for one critic, the German people were 'indoctrinated with grotesque conceptions of national prestige' through sport.[14] Soon after Hitler's advent to the chancellorship, Bruno Malitz's *Die Leibesübungen in der Nationalsozialistischen Idee* (1933) articulated the key message:

> There is one sentence in German sports which we, who are National Socialists, ... negate. The sentence is 'Politics do not belong in Sport'. For the Nazi, 'Politics belong in sports'... Sport must be recaptured ... and used as a weapon for the genuine building of a nation ... We Nazis want to educate the people through sport.[15]

Subsequently, Kurt Münch's *Deutschkunde über Volk, Staat, Leibesübungen* (1935) became the political bible for German sport. Readers were left in no doubt about the regime's distinctive vision of sport, including its use 'as the outward expression of a strong German Reich'.[16] As Phipps observed, 'the political importance of sport is insisted upon throughout the book', most notably in a section which he drew to the British government's attention: 'Gymnastics and sport are thus an institution for the education of the body and a school of the political will in the service of the State. Unpolitical, so-called neutral gymnasts and sportsmen, are unthinkable in Hitler's state'.[17]

In November 1935 Phipps informed London that 'the German Government attach enormous importance to the Olympic Games from the point of view of propaganda, and hope to be able to take the opportunity of impressing foreign countries with the capacity and solidity of the Nazi regime'.[18] Inevitably, any kudos resulting from hosting the 1936 Olympics, which were awarded to Germany before Hitler's accession, or from winning Olympic medals was presented to domestic and external audiences as the product of Hitler's leadership. Henry Channon, a British MP, was one of numerous foreign visitors to the Berlin Olympics, where 'German wins were frequent' and duly celebrated: 'One was conscious of the effort the Germans were making to show the world the grandeur, the permanence and the respectability of the new regime'.[19] Notwithstanding Hitler's irritation that Jessie Owens, an 'inferior' black athlete, won the high profile sprint races, an impressive medals tally (33 gold, 26 silver, 30 bronze) gave Germany top place in the unofficial points table and facilitated attempts to emphasize the much vaunted, albeit difficult-to-prove, link between national power and sporting prowess. Looking back on the event, the British embassy in Berlin recorded the reaction of Goebbels, Hitler's Minister for Public Enlightenment:

> It is difficult for anyone in England to understand the importance attached to these games in Germany. No trouble or expense was spared to make them an advertisement of the National Socialist regime, both as regards the organisation of the games themselves, and the performance of the German athletes. ... Taken all in all, however, the games were an extraordinary success for Germany and for national socialism. Dr Goebbels, with shining eyes, told a member of my staff that the national spirit created by this regime was responsible for the German victories and this view is widely held.[20]

During the 1930s the overt intervention characteristic of the Nazi model helped British government efforts to present the distinctive separation of politics and sport in Britain as a key liberal value in what Lord Lloyd (chairman of the British Council, 1937–41) described as the 'fierce war of ideas' between democracies and dictatorships.[21] However, in practice, attempts to steer clear of sport were hampered by the fact that any official move, even inaction, was bound to be interpreted at home and abroad in political terms, especially as the labour movement and Jewish groups in Britain saw sport as an instrument through which to propagate an anti-Nazi message, as illustrated by their abortive campaign for a British boycott of the 1936 Olympics. As a result, British governments, though attempting to conceal any moves, were forced to be more interventionist towards sport than they would have liked. For example, in 1938 the Football Association (FA) was reminded *privately* of the need to select a strong England team in order to ensure a good performance against Germany.[22] Subsequently the Foreign Office, impressed by reports of the positive impact of England's 6–3 win in Berlin on British prestige in the wider world, informed the FA of the government's pleasure at the result. Meanwhile, the British Council, created during 1934–35 to 'make known the achievements' of Britain on the world stage, assigned sport only a supportive role, although its overseas representatives reminded the British authorities that sport was equally capable of exerting negative impacts. For example, Chelsea's rough and unsporting behaviour on the club's 1936 Polish tour was reported as providing 'admirable examples of British propaganda as it should not be'.[23]

One enduring British consequence of the Nazi model was the 1937 Physical Training and Recreation Act, since what were perceived as German norms impacted upon the ongoing British debate about low national standards of health and physical fitness. Neville Chamberlain (Chancellor of the Exchequer, 1931–37; Prime Minister, 1937–40), imbued with a long-standing concern for social reform and impressed by reports of German practice, pushed for action, most notably in a speech delivered at the 1936 Conservative Party Conference: 'Nothing made a stronger impression upon visitors to the Olympic Games in Germany this year than the splendid condition of the German youth, and though our methods are different from theirs in accordance with our national characters and traditions I see no reason why we should not be equally successful in our results.'[24] Soon afterwards (in 1937), a Board of Education pamphlet that drew heavily on the findings of a delegation's visit to Germany provided a further stimulus for legislation, recognizing that 'bodily fitness makes for national efficiency and personal happiness'.[25] Before the outbreak of the Second World War, the National Fitness Council (NFC), established by the 1937 Act to fund improved sports facilities (e.g. swimming baths), undertook a domestic propaganda campaign extolling to what was viewed as an uninformed public the benefits of physical training and sport.

More importantly, the 1936 Berlin Olympics impacted on the mindset of most Britons. Feelings of disquiet, particularly on the part of those involved in the abortive boycott campaign, were complemented by a general appreciation of the manner in which the event projected positive images of both the host and participants on the world stage. This legacy explains in part the willingness of the British government to support the British Olympic Association (BOA)'s bid to host the 1948 Games, the first Olympiad to be held since the 1936 Berlin Olympics because of the wartime cancellation of the 1940 and 1944 Games. Significantly, in January 1946 the Labour government responded both immediately and positively to the BOA's initial soundings. No Olympics could be held in any country in the face of government disinterest or opposition, if only on account of the need for competitors' entry visas, but post-war disruption accentuated the usual need for official support. In the event, an extremely positive response, given personally by Ernest Bevin, the Foreign Secretary, prepared the way for a successful British bid to host the Games.[26]

The Labour government, which anticipated that any post-war accommodation, food supply and other logistical problems would have eased by 1948, perceived a range of substantial political, economic and other non-sporting benefits from hosting the Olympics. From an early stage, the case was argued primarily in terms of using the Olympics as a 'shop window' for developing tourism, earning much-needed dollars through ticket and programme sales and gaining national prestige through a job well done for an event attracting global visibility.[27] Nor should the personal enthusiasm of ministers such as Philip Noel-Baker (Secretary of State for Air, 1946–47, and for Commonwealth Relations, 1947–50) be overlooked; indeed, Clement Attlee, the Prime Minister (1945–51), gave Noel-Baker, a former Olympic competitor, special ministerial responsibility for the games, since 'the Government is anxious to maintain our national prestige in sport'.[28]

Notwithstanding widespread British disapproval of its more blatant manifestations, the 1936 Berlin Olympics highlighted the national projection benefits accruing to the host country; indeed, in January 1948 Noel Curtis Bennet, the BOA's vice-chairman, reminded Attlee of the way in which 'the Germans used them [the Games] to prove what a wonderful system National Socialism was'.[29] For many Britons, any prestige arising from a leadership role in sport acquired added value at a time when serious questions were being raised about Britain's role in the post-war world. Despite emerging as a victor in the Second World War, British governments were preoccupied with status at a time of post-war austerity, the strains of reconstruction and the difficulty of keeping up with the USA and Soviet Union. According to Hector McNeil, Noel-Baker's successor as minister of state at the Foreign Office, the key priority was 'to combat the impression that Britain is in decline', most notably by arguing that post-war difficulties were merely temporary checks to British power across a broad range of activities, not excluding sport.[30] Likewise, Noel-Baker saw 'an important Foreign Office interest in the Olympic Games':

> My own view is clearly that it is now in the national interest that they should [go ahead]: if we can organise well, as I hope we can, I think we shall gain both in prestige and in foreign exchange. If, on the other hand, we were to cancel them, I feel sure that there might be a considerable blow to general confidence in our recovery.[31]

Thus the games were seen as offering Britain a major public relations opportunity – a *Manchester Guardian* editorial presented the Olympiad as 'a test of British organisation' – but as Noel-Baker warned in a minute agreed by Attlee, the event, if badly managed, was capable of harming the 'national reputation'.[32]

Government support was reaffirmed repeatedly during the next year or so in the face of both deteriorating economic conditions and sustained press criticism about holding the games in 'crisis-crushed' Britain; in fact, in September 1947 an *Evening Standard* editorial demanded 'Call off the Games'.[33] Noel-Baker advised the government to stand firm against such 'foolish' criticism, for cancellation would be interpreted as 'a great blow to British prestige. It would greatly encourage those people abroad who desire to think that we are down and out.'[34] This argument, given added force by the need to support Britain's status in a cold-war world dominated increasingly by the two superpowers, was backed up by official pressure, such as was exerted on the Beaverbrook press, which promised no more 'call off the games' articles.[35]

There was also considerable speculation that the 1948 games would mark the entry of the Soviet Union to the Olympic movement for the first time since 1917. In the event, these hopes proved abortive. Nor were the ex-enemy countries, Germany and Japan, allowed entry. Nevertheless, the 1948 London Olympics attracted more competitors and countries than its Berlin predecessor. Generally speaking, the British government and media regarded the event as a major success.[36] At an early stage, the government took a close interest in feedback from the opening ceremony, which was adjudged to have worked well in terms of impressing foreign diplomats and media; thus, according to one official 'It constituted the best possible "propaganda"' in terms of typifying the 'dignity', and 'faultless organisation' expected of official occasions in Britain.[37] For the *Sunday Times*, the ceremonial splendour offered a 'lesson to the world about Britain's capacity and will for great achievements'.[38] Film rights were awarded to the Rank Organisation, whose 'XIVth Olympiad: the Glory of Sport' (1948) film, together with newsreel coverage, provided a supportive visual record enhancing the public relations aspect. However, the propaganda benefits gained from hosting the event were qualified to some extent by what was interpreted as a relatively modest British performance (23 medals, including three gold), which warranted no more than sixth place in the unofficial medals table. The USA headed the medals table by a long way, even if Soviet entry to the Olympic movement during the early 1950s meant that this proved the last Olympiad at which the USA was so predominant.

Hosting a major sporting event forced the British government to qualify its non-interventionist stance and to treat international sport more seriously. Even so, the Attlee government, opting for an arm's-length approach, left organizational details to the BOA-based organizing committee and confined its role to support activities such as providing and improving accommodation at Richmond Park and RAF Uxbridge, issuing visas for competitors, dealing with transport arrangements and providing official hospitality. Nevertheless, Attlee, using a text originally drafted by Noel-Baker, introduced an extra-sporting element into his radio broadcast welcoming competitors to the first Olympiad held in London since 1908:[39]

> It is indeed astonishing how in these years since the Games were held last in London, sports and games known only in a few countries have been taken up with enthusiasm by so many nations. Sport today is truly international and a common love of sport creates a bond of friendship between men and women separated by distance and by the lack of a common language. It over-steps all frontiers.[40]

But his message was already being undermined by events; the escalating Berlin crisis reflected the deteriorating state of East-West relations. On 30 July 1948, the *New York Times*'s front-page report, 'King George Opens Olympics for 6,000 from 59 Nations', illustrated by a photograph of a British athlete carrying the Olympic torch in front of a board quoting de Coubertin's famous message about taking part, not winning, was printed alongside another article headlined 'Britain Considers Halt in Army Cuts in Berlin Impasse'. Soon afterwards, the two superpowers began interpreting sport as merely another front in the cold war. Indeed, during and after the 1950s the Olympics became a major East-West battleground in a divided world, and victories were interpreted and presented as evidence of far more than mere sporting prowess – as recognized in an UNESCO report: 'athletic or games supremacy has become the *sine qua non* of general national superiority. For example, the Olympic Games are now regarded by many as merely a testing-ground for two great political units'.[41] Sportsmen and women might have seen themselves as engaged in purely sporting activities, but they were frequently viewed by governments, the media and public opinion as playing, scoring, running, jumping or throwing for their respective countries or cold war bloc in terms of projecting national values and strengths as well as weaknesses.

The Soviet model

In 1980 the Foreign and Commonwealth Office (FCO), prompted by the Thatcher government's advocacy of a British boycott of the Moscow Olympics in protest against the Soviet invasion of Afghanistan, displayed the continuity of British official thinking about Soviet sport: 'Since it began participating in international sporting events after the Second World War, the Soviet Union has always attempted to link the victories of its athletes with the claimed superiority of the Soviet social and political system'.[42] The Soviet Union, having performed a virtual non-role in international sport since 1917, emerged suddenly after the 1948 Olympiad as a 'new and formidable challenger', playing an increasingly significant and successful part in international sport.[43] A series of impressive performances – the Soviet Union tied with the USA at the head of the 1952 Helsinki Olympics points table – ensured that the Soviet model now became the object of widespread study, admiration and emulation elsewhere.

Subsequently, the German Democratic Republic (GDR) vividly displayed the international recognition and prestige accruing from the Olympic success of a relatively small state following the Soviet lead; indeed, the Soviet Union and the GDR relegated the USA to third place in the medals table at the 1988 Seoul Olympics.[44] However, following the 1989–91 revolutions, the Soviet model, though surviving in China, Cuba and North Korea, was discredited in the wake of a series of revelations and court cases disclosing the unsporting nature and human costs of politicizing sport.[45] Looking back from 2000, it became clear that the GDR's formerly much-admired sports machine, whose one-time head (Ewald) had links to the Nazi youth movement, created for political purposes the 'best athletes that chemistry could buy' in Entine's words; thus, Carola Beraktschjan, a former swimming world-record holder, complained that 'we were vehicles chosen to prove that socialism was better than capitalism. What happened to our bodies was entirely secondary to that political mission.'[46]

However, these problems were not apparent in December 1948 when the Communist Party Central Committee redefined policy goals to ensure that 'Soviet sportsmen win world supremacy in the major sports in the immediate future'.[47] The 'world supremacy target', acquiring added meaning from its promulgation at a tense stage in the cold war, placed a premium on sporting success to establish that – to quote a 1949 Soviet resolution – 'the increasing number of successes achieved by Soviet athletes ... is a victory for the Soviet form of society; it provides irrefutable proof of the superiority of socialist culture over the moribund culture of capitalist states'.[48]

Inevitably, the Soviet model raised serious questions for Britain, where the political and sporting implications attracted serious study in the light of the Soviet Union's achievements at the 1952 Helsinki Olympics (where Britain performed poorly and gained its only gold medal in the final event) and the decisive victories of the Hungarian football team over both England (6–3, 7–1) and Scotland (4–2) during 1953/54. Sport became a far from insignificant element in British relations with Communist bloc states, particularly in the wake of the more outgoing Soviet attitude consequent upon the death of Stalin (March 1953) and the Korean War armistice (July 1953). However, the increased frequency of contacts – which included athletics (e.g. London versus Moscow, October 1954), football (Arsenal's visit to Moscow, October 1954; Moscow Spartak's visit to England, November 1954; England-Hungary games in November 1953 and May 1954; Scotland versus Hungary, December 1954) and table tennis (England versus Hungary, November 1953) – posed serious questions for British governments anxious 'to prevent international sporting events from being used for the purposes of Communist propaganda'.[49] The fundamental question of whether or not to take on Soviet bloc states remained the subject of anguished official debate because of the belief that 'the attitude of the Communist countries to sport is entirely different. To them sport is an extension and an instrument of policy and in dealing with them on a matter of international sport it would be folly to overlook this'.[50]

As happened with Hitler's Germany, the politics of sport were thrust on reluctant British governments, which were unable to prevent matches versus Communist bloc states from acquiring a political dimension in the eyes of the wider world. For instance, in 1954 Arsenal's visit to Moscow, resulting in a humiliating 0–5 defeat by Moscow Dynamo, prompted official regrets about 'indifferent England teams being lured to Moscow and slaughtered in order to enable the Soviets to enlarge upon their sporting prowess'.[51] Television excerpts compounded the impact of press reports on the unfortunate impression given about the declining quality of British football and sportsmanship. For the Foreign Office, this match did 'nothing to enhance British prestige in the field of sport … its main effect was to minister to Russian self-satisfaction and to their conviction of their complete superiority over us even in fields in which we are traditionally expert'.[52] Even so, the constant temptation to intervene for the protection of British *political interests*, including national prestige, had to be balanced against the risks of unwelcome publicity establishing official interference in sport. British governments, though fundamentally opposed to Anglo-Communist sporting links, deemed it *politically unwise* to block them, for 'any attempt to rig up our own Curtain would be inconsistent with our liberal ideas and our general line of propaganda'.[53] In the meantime, the Foreign Office, recalling extensive national soul-searching following British disappointment at the Helsinki Olympics and England's defeats by Hungary, anticipated that the basic problem might resolve itself through other means; thus, it was hoped that media and public demands to arrest British decline would prompt appropriate urgent action by sporting bodies.

A similar ambiguity about sport's autonomy characterized the British media, which also liked to believe that British sport was still relatively untainted by political pressures as compared to the Communist bloc; thus, Peter Wilson of the best-selling *Daily Mirror* reminded readers that such countries 'regard a sporting triumph as justification for their "superior" way of life'.[54] In this vein, a few days later, the *Daily Mirror* informed readers of the way in which the Hungarian press presented Hungary's 6–3 victory over England as the product of 'constructive work in a socialist country'.[55] But politics and sport were never quite as divorced from each other in the British press as journalists liked to think (and wanted readers to believe). British achievements in major sports were invariably presented, at least implicitly, as a reflection and reinforcement of national prestige and values. For example, in May 1954 Bob Ferrier, previewing England's return match with Hungary for the *Daily Mirror*, pointed to the fixture's extra-sporting relevance, including its cold war dimension: 'Our football, a grossly commercialised business, is on trial against their football, a science, a culture and an art at one and the same time. The contrast is as stark as that between the Sovietised State and the eternal freedom of Britain, and only here can one experience the deepest sincerities of all things British.'[56] Four days later, *The Times*, acknowledging yet another crushing defeat by Hungary on the football field, lamented that 'such defeats as we received at Budapest do our prestige no good whatsoever abroad'.[57]

Nor should such repeated sporting setbacks be viewed in isolation from the broader international political context, where Britain was struggling to maintain power and influence vis à vis the two superpowers in order – to quote Sir Roger Makins, a senior diplomat – 'to avoid sinking to the level of a second or third class Power'.[58] As Anthony Eden, the Foreign Secretary (1951–55), conceded, 'once the prestige of a country has started to slide there is no knowing where it will stop'.[59] However, despite lengthy agonizing and the reluctant scaling-down of commitments, it took the 1956 Suez Crisis to force the British government, media and people to face up to the international realities of the post-1945 world, including Britain's economic and fiscal weaknesses and consequent inability to act independently of the USA government.[60] For Guy Millard, Eden's private secretary, among others, Suez was 'a political defeat of the first magnitude'.[61] For many Britons, disappointing Olympic performances and international footballing defeats were treated as sporting setbacks of a similar 'magnitude'. Admittedly, there were occasional successes, most notably the 1953 Ashes victory in cricket and Roger Bannister's 1954 first sub-four minute mile, but these triumphs failed to alter the basic picture of decline. However, it is worth noting the government's attempt to exploit such isolated successes; thus within a week of setting the record Bannister was sent to the USA 'at the direction of the Foreign Office' to fly the flag for the British Information Services (BIS)!62 The BIS also produced a film of Bannister's run for distribution in the USA and around the world.

During this period Britain's long-standing status as a major world force in both the international political and sporting spheres seemed to rest largely upon inertia and past glories rather than upon current strengths and achievements. British governments and people faced the harsh realities of the post-1945 world involving the loss of traditional hegemony, the appearance of strong rivals, most notably in the Communist bloc, and the need for a radical change of course across a range of political, military, economic and *sporting* fronts. Naturally, the Suez crisis took centre stage, but perhaps for the man in the street the apparent loss of leadership in the world of sport was equally, if not more, worrying. Certainly, the state of British sport aroused widespread media and popular interest, as demonstrated by the extensive post-mortems following both the Helsinki Olympics and the Hungary matches; for example, a *Daily Mirror* cartoon implied that '1953 and all that' was destined 'to go down in our history book' alongside 1066: '1066 the Normans, 1953 the Hungarians'.[63] Typically, Peter Wilson used past glories as a reference point when reporting England's loss to Hungary to the *Daily Mirror*'s readers in a front-page article entitled 'The Twilight of the (Soccer) Gods'.[64]

Discussions in the British media at the time, typified by a 'Why Russia Beats Us at Our Games' article written by an MP for the *News of the World* following a parliamentary delegation's visit to the Soviet Union, praised how things were done in the Communist bloc, warned about the political and sporting consequences of inaction and identified aspects for improvement and action in Britain, including facilities, coaching and training techniques.[65] Reporting Bannister's mile record as a rare British success, the *New York Herald Tribune* offered a perceptive commentary:

You can scarcely imagine with what appalling seriousness the Britons view the playground. This is doubly so where international competition is involved, and here England has been forced to eat cold mutton for a good many years. ... Their international triumphs have been few and short-lived. ... In column after column, the tune has been the same; 'Lo, all our pomp of yesterday is one with Nineveh and Tyre'. Now here comes Bannister. ... Roar, Lion, Roar![66]

Actual responses by sporting and official bodies go beyond the scope of this chapter, but the increasingly professional approach adopted by British sport towards training and coaching, among other developments, was complemented by a series of political moves including Noel-Baker's creation of an all-party Parliamentary Sports Committee, composed of members 'with an interest in international sport' (1952); sport's identification in political party manifestos as a legitimate governmental responsibility (e.g. the Labour Party's *Leisure for Living*, 1959), the publication of the wide-ranging Wolfenden Report on Sport and the Community (1960), the appointment of a Minister for Sport (1962), and the creation of the Sports Council (1965).[67] Throughout the period, external developments, most notably the success of the Soviet model, provided both a spur and example for progress.

British sport in today's world

Today, cultural diplomacy has become multifaceted and increasingly operates through a complex web of cross-border contacts. Within this context, Britain has much to offer the world in terms of not only opera, drama and other high arts but also sport, whose national projection potential has often been underrated. In this regard, advice forwarded soon after the Second World War by the British legation at Berne possesses a contemporary resonance. The legation, comparing visits made by musicians and others sent by the British Council, claimed that visiting British footballers 'make a stirring appeal to the Swiss heart, the effect of which far outweighs the effect of propaganda directed at the Swiss head'.[68]

In June 1999 Kofi Annan, the UN Secretary-General, used his meeting with Joseph Blatter, the President of FIFA, to stress that sport was simultaneously a defining characteristic of nationhood and a global force acting as a 'common language' extending across racial, religious, social and other boundaries.[69] Sport fits in perfectly with the emerging global, multi-identity, consumer-driven televisual world, for it provides strong images and high drama based upon an irresistible blend of predictability and surprise reaching directly out to the feelings and emotions of spectators and television viewers, whether watching in London, Paris, Berlin, Rome, Athens, New York, Beijing or Tokyo. Nor are words required to enable people to follow the storyline.

In many respects, Britain has a head start in exploiting sport's propaganda potential in today's world, given that its sporting heritage means that – to employ a phrase beloved of politicians and commentators – Britain is expected to punch, or rather perform, above its weight and already possesses a range of global brand names in most sports, including football (e.g. Arsenal, Manchester United), golf (St Andrews), rowing (Henley) and tennis (Wimbledon). *Potentially*, sport is able to project favourable images of *any nation* to a large and receptive global audience, particularly young people. These images include leadership and distinctive performance in the world's major sports, national sporting skills and values (e.g. dynamism, fair play, team spirit, ethnic integration, gender equality), modernity (e.g. new stadiums) and the ability to stage successfully major world events. At the same time, British sport, having re-packaged and re-invented itself during the 1990s to exploit effectively expanding commercial and media possibilities, came to be viewed as an invaluable instrument to challenge outmoded stereotypes of the UK abroad. From this image-building perspective, success remains the best form of propaganda, as recognized by the Foreign and Commonwealth Office (1987): 'Britain has potential influence, though our reputation waxes and wanes with the performance of our national teams … the government has an interest in the performance of British athletes on the field (*which tends to reflect on the image of Britain as a whole*) [author's emphasis] and in the performance of British fans off the field'.[70] The final phrase, emphasizing the additional need for good spectator conduct, reminds us of the double-edged nature of national projection through sport. Thus Sir John Burgh, the British Council's director general, recalled that during the mid-1980s overseas images of Britain were dominated by 'football hooligans, decline, racial friction and archaic traditions'.[71] Contemporary descriptors of British football as 'a slum sport played in slum stadiums watched by slum people' were far from helpful.[72]

During the 1990s both Conservative and Labour governments adopted a more activist approach towards sport, partly because of widespread concern about the adverse impacts upon British prestige of a series of disappointing international sporting performances. Once again, the relative success of other countries was to the fore, with British politicians and the media using the Australian Institute of Sport (AIS) at Canberra as perhaps the prime reference point for the growing focus upon elite sport and international performance. In 1995 John Major, both impressed and depressed by the bowling of Shane Warne, an AIS product, promoted the idea of a similar elitist institution in Britain in his *Raising the Game* initiative: 'The government wants to see established a British Academy of Sport. While it is not for the Government to set up and run such an Academy, this Policy Statement lays down the challenge to the sports world and points the way forward.'[73] Soon afterwards, in 1996, 'the British team returned from the Atlanta Olympics with a medal haul that barely showed up on the airport metal detectors'.[74] By contrast, the AIS, dubbed the 'Gold Medal Factory' because three-quarters of Australia's medal-winners had passed through the institute, became even more attractive to the Major government, which modelled the proposed British Academy of Sport (BAS) on the AIS. Subsequently, the Blair government imparted its own gloss on Major's initiative; thus in 1997 the BAS was renamed the United Kingdom Sports Institute (UKSI) and restructured to operate regionally rather than centrally. Meanwhile, individual sports sought to benefit from foreign, most notably Australian, expertise. Although the FA appointed a Swede as the new coach of England, Australians have taken up a range of high profile posts, including the head of the English cricket academy (Rodney Marsh), national performance director of British swimming (Bill Sweetenham), chief executive of 'Sport England' (David Moffett) and national director of the English Institute of Sport (Wilma Shakespear).[75]

Moreover, during the late 1990s the British Council, having largely ignored sport since the late 1930s, decided to incorporate sport into its work to 'help Britain improve its international standing and build relationships' as well as to help dispel outdated negative images.[76] In part, this initiative, based upon the premise that 'Britain is particularly strongly placed to use sport as a means of communicating messages about itself', represented a response both to critiques of the council's failure to exploit what many saw as a major British asset and to feedback based upon recent surveys of foreigners' attitudes towards Britain (*Through Other Eyes*, 1999–2000).[77] However, the move should also be seen in the context of the Blair government's process of re-branding Britain during a period when the perceived power of branding means that 'image and reputation are becoming essential parts of the state's strategic equity'.[78] Thus, 'Panel 2000', a government initiative looking at new ways of promoting Britain overseas, strongly endorsed sport's use as an instrument of 'public diplomacy' (the FCO's information department was recently renamed the 'public diplomacy department') capable of reaching the British Council's target audience.[79]

Conclusion

Modern sport represents a major political, economic, social and cultural force in today's world. Certainly, British governments and, somewhat belatedly, the British Council have became more alert to the propaganda potential of sport, which has emerged as a subtle but significant part of the British propaganda apparatus, a form of soft power perceived to be capable of achieving substantial impacts in today's globalized society. However, the two archival-based case studies discussed here establish that, contrary to carefully cultivated public images, before the 1990s British governments often acted privately in a manner that blurred, if not ignored, the line supposedly separating politics and sport. In turn, these episodes, characterized by the impact of foreign models, provided a foundation for the more overt interventionist policies adopted towards sport during the past decade by the Major and Blair governments. This transformation was also facilitated by the fact that British sporting bodies, having previously jealously guarded their non-governmental status, lobbied the government for a ministry of sport to spearhead a drive for British international sporting success.[80] In the event, the government's sports strategy, published as *A Sporting Future For All* in April 2000, failed to go this far, even if there were references to a 'new deal' between government and sport's governing bodies, the need to enhance the prospects for 'more success for our top competitors and teams in international competition' and the urgent 'need to learn the lessons of our competitor nations': 'Government cannot and should not dictate. But Government can and should ensure that the opportunities are there for those who wish to seize them.'[81]

Within this context, Blair's government has repeatedly articulated support for sport, most notably the desire to stage major international sporting events; indeed, the Labour Party's 2001 election manifesto promised that 'we will maintain the elite funding we put in place for individual athletes [*sic*], with a first-class athletics stadium for the World Athletics Championships in 2005'.[82] However, events soon began not only to raise questions about the Blair government's preparedness and ability to translate rhetoric into reality but also to exert adverse impacts upon British prestige. To some, disappointment consequent upon the abortive British bid for the 2006 World Cup was countered by the award to London of the 2005 World Athletics Championships. However, despite its election manifesto commitment and attempt to use sport for national projection, in October 2001 the Blair government decided against proceeding with a new athletics stadium at Pickett's Lock and announced that the event could no longer be staged in London. The displeasure of Lamine Diack, the president of the IAAF (International Association of Athletics Federations), was compounded by strong criticism from politicians and the media. Tim Yeo, the Shadow Cabinet's spokesman for culture, summed up the situation well: 'Britain has suffered a severe blow to its international prestige … the international sporting community feels very let down.'[83] Moreover, the episode, viewed in conjunction with the fiasco regarding the rebuilding of Wembley as a national football stadium, was adjudged to have seriously damaged British prospects of bidding successfully for the 2012 Olympics or the 2014 World Cup. The Blair government appeared guilty of reneging on both election manifesto and ministerial promises as well as of displaying a distinct lack of feel for the politics of international sport. Certainly, the apparent gap between government rhetoric and events suggested a distinct lack of 'joined up government', both within government as well as between it and sporting bodies. As one editorial observed, 'unless the Government matches its rhetoric with commitment, we risk being ranked in international sporting terms alongside the likes of Colombia'.[84] Within days, Jacques Rogge, the president of the International Olympic Committee (IOC), implied that these problems had inflicted irreparable damage upon any bid by London to host the 2012 Olympics: 'United Kingdom and Great Britain was [sic] the cradle of modern sports. ... I think they have to reflect and think very seriously whether they, as a society, including the government, are doing enough to play a leading role in the world of sport. But the Pickett's Lock issue, after the Wembley issue, is definitely not a good sign.'[85] The extent to which Manchester's successful staging of the 2002 Commonwealth Games redressed the situation remains debatable, particularly given the IOC's apparent belief that any Olympic bid must be based on London.[86]

The period since John Major announced his *Raising the Game* initiative has witnessed a more active and overt governmental role towards sport, with a strong focus on elite sport for propaganda reasons. Even allowing for the fact that any benefits will become apparent only in the long term, hitherto actual achievements have proved rather limited. Progress on what commenced as the NAS, and is now the UKSI, has been extremely slow and tortuous, while attempts to win the right to host major sporting occasions have done little to enhance British sporting prestige. Britain's 2006 World Cup bid was not only mishandled but also attracted few votes from FIFA members. Admittedly, Britain gained the 2005 World Athletics Championships, but then failed to fulfil promises made to both the British people and the IAAF, thereby leaving 'England's reputation as a capable host of sporting events ... in tatters'.[87] As the FCO acknowledged, sport impacts upon British prestige, but not always in a positive sense. Meanwhile, we await the results of the Blair government's decision, announced in May 2003, to support a British bid for the 2012 Olympics.

Following Major and Blair, 'sport matters' and has a new significance, but this has yet to be reflected in either British policy outcomes or the teaching and research of most historians and international relations specialists. Hitherto, even histories of British propaganda have done little to take account of sport's role in projecting Britain in the wider world or to evaluate why Britain's international sporting performance has proved a significant criterion impacting on national prestige.[88] Certainly, there exists scope for studies investigating what correlation exists between kicking a football between three wooden posts more times than one's opponents, or for having people who can run 100 metres faster than their counterparts, and acquiring national prestige. The contemporary emphasis placed upon re-branding Britain, including the focus upon public diplomacy and communication in a globalized society, provides a suitable framework for contextualizing such studies, most notably the fact that assertions about national prestige need to be viewed alongside broader policy objectives.

6

A changing discourse?
British diplomacy and the
Olympic movement

AARON BEACOM

Introduction

Writing on the history of diplomacy is dominated by description of a move
away from 'old' patterns of inter-state diplomatic activity and towards 'new'
more complex forms that involve a range of state and non-state actors, gener-
ating a broader diplomatic agenda.[1] In this context, international sport,
involving a complex of non-state actors, is viewed as an increasingly appropriate subject of diplomatic discourse.[2] Yet the evidence of diplomatic
activity as it relates to the modern Olympic movement contrasts with such
perceptions of the linear progression of sport from the periphery to the centre
of the international agenda. There has rather been significant fluctuation in
the level and nature of such activity, throughout the history of the modern
Games. For example, British and American diplomatic activity surrounding
the 1936 Berlin Olympic Games was particularly intense when compared
with a number of more recent Games.[3] Furthermore, contrary to the view that
non-governmental organizations (NGOs) have only recently become players
in international diplomacy, the diplomatic activities of the International
Olympic Committee (IOC) are evident as early as the 1920s.

Many of the complexities of modern diplomacy are not new. Even in the
case of diplomacy relating to the Olympic Games, there has long been
evidence of multi-layered diplomacy involving state, regional and municipal
level political administrations as well as commercial interests, surrounding
the bidding for the Games. Such evidence highlights limitations to realist
interpretations of diplomacy in international sport, with its pre-occupation
with the interaction of states.[4] It suggests that a more pluralist perspective
would be helpful not only in contributing to an understanding of the nature
of diplomacy relating to sport in contemporary society, but also when investigating diplomacy throughout the history of modern sport.

This chapter confines itself to considering the characteristics of diplomacy through three themes in Olympic politics. The first reflects on

aspirations of the IOC to play a part in international diplomacy and the power of state-centred interests to limit such aspirations. The second looks, from a British perspective, at the long-running debate regarding the role of the state in the Olympic boycott. In particular, contrasts and similarities between the experiences of 1936 and 1980, are explored. The third considers, again from a British perspective, diplomatic activity as it relates to the process of bidding for the Olympic Games. In all three themes, the chapter is concerned with indications of continuity as well as change, in the nature of related diplomatic discourse.

Certain aspects of diplomatic activity as it relates to the Olympic Games, are universal to diplomacy relating to other international sporting events, for instance the soccer World Cup and the world athletics championships. The agents of diplomatic activity are similar in terms of the government departments involved and the role of national and international sports agencies. The diplomatic activities are also broadly similar in terms of their links to cultural and commercial relations and the requirement for consular support. Nevertheless there are important differences in the sense that the broader representation of states and the international profile of the Games have led to the perception that they are indeed a microcosm of international society. It is these unique characteristics, suggesting a particular significance attached to diplomacy as it relates to the Olympic movement, which underpins the claim that such an investigation can provide insights into the nature of diplomacy.

While it is not the intention here to engage in the conceptual debate as to what constitutes diplomacy, it is noteworthy that the term is generally used to describe the management of relations between states and is historically presented as integral to the emergence of the nation state.[5]

The sense of 'change' also, however, permeates much of the literature, with the term 'new' frequently appearing as an appendage. In particular it has been used when referring to discourse resulting from institutional and cultural changes to diplomacy, which reputedly took place in the wake of the First World War.[6]

While acknowledging that change in the nature of diplomatic discourse has taken place, historical evidence calls into question the level of change and highlights the continuous and recurring elements evident in such discourse.

The Olympic movement and diplomacy

The idea that 'sporting' activities could perform a mediating role in the interaction of 'territories' has a long history. Archaeological and anthropological evidence would indeed suggest that such activities have been used in a number of cultures to mediate between the natural and spiritual 'worlds'.[7] Historians of medieval Europe have referred to the role of the tourney in regulating relations between feudal entities.[8] In these historical contexts, the contest is not so much a conduit for related acts of mediation; rather it becomes an act of mediation itself. The same may be said of the modern Olympic Games in the sense that while they act as a forum for formal diplomatic exchanges between participating nations, they also perform a mediating role in their own right. This role is central to the aspirations of the International Olympic Committee (IOC) to become a player in international diplomacy. The ideal of the games providing a forum for the 'communion' of athletes from across the world is articulated through their organization as festivals with their own 'sovereign' identity. Within these festivals, even the most senior of the diplomatic corps find themselves playing by a different set of rules.[9] These rules have been conceived and developed by a body of individuals distinct from, though sharing much in common with, those involved in mainstream diplomacy.

The IOC: diplomatic aspirations

The modern Olympic movement has, from its inception, been in many respects highly politicized.[10] The distinct universe of discourse of the modern Olympic movement in the inter-war years clearly reflected the main tenets of the internationalist aspirations evident in much of inter-war diplomacy. The spirit of that period, the search for a formula to avoid the total conflict witnessed in the First World War, had been the basis for the development of thinking on international diplomacy. Whether or not for purely opportunistic reasons, de Coubertin acknowledged and related to the aspirations of the League of Nations.[11] Kanin notes how de Coubertin 'jumped on the band-wagon of Wilsonian (neo-Kantian) ideology'.[12] He cites a letter from de Coubertin to the president of the League shortly after the 1920 Antwerp Olympics, which outlined the similarities between the aspirations of the League and those of the IOC:

> Twenty six years ago our committee introduced and applied, as regards sporting activities, the very principles upon which the League was organized and by means of their Olympiads they brought into existence an international collaboration which is getting closer and more effective. After the triumphal celebration of the seventh Olympiad held in Antwerp, you must be personally aware, Mr President, of the power attained by the Olympic movement and you know how much it is bringing together the youth of every country.[13]

Kanin goes on to note that the decline of the League of Nations system brought to an end efforts to develop a role for the Olympic movement in the wider political arena. It encouraged re-focusing on the original aspiration of sport as a function in the moral development of youth internationally. Yet there continued an inherent tension in the activities of the Olympic movement, as indeed there were in the aspirations of de Coubertin himself, between a celebration of national prowess and a nurturing of a belief in internationalism. This is poignantly expressed in part of a speech written by de Coubertin for the closing of the Berlin Games, but which he was not asked to deliver: 'The swaying and struggles of history will continue but little by little knowledge will replace dangerous ignorance, mutual under-standing will soften unthinking hatreds. ... May the German people and their head be thanked for what they have just accomplished.'[14] The struggle between 'Kantian' idealism and the sort of 'Machiavellian' realism that won such a conclusive victory at the 1936 Games was brought into sharp relief. Indeed it may be argued that the journey of Olympism during the inter-war years reflects the journey of internationalist thought from hopefulness, through disillusionment, to eventual defeat.

Notwithstanding these early difficulties encountered, internationalist aspirations have re-emerged as integral to the philosophy of the Olympic movement. These have been reflected recently in collaboration between the IOC and the United Nations (UN). The UN-sponsored 'International Year for a Culture of Peace', celebrated throughout 2000, included collaboration between the IOC and the United Nations Educational Social and Cultural Organization (UNESCO) in the setting up of a World Conference on Education and Sport for a Culture of Peace (held in Paris, July 1999).[15] Such activity may indeed form an important dimension of the internationalist rehabilitation of the movement. An exploration of the language of the IOC provides an indication of its continued diplomatic aspirations – it provides identity cards and flies the Olympic flag as an indication of its territorial sovereignty over the chosen site for the duration of the Games. The recent proposals concerning the restructuring of the Games contained the plan to nominate Olympic 'attachés' from individual national Olympic committees (NOCs) to provide a link between these NOCs and the organizing commit-tee for the Olympic Games.[16]

The revival of the notion of the 'Olympic truce', associated with the ancient Greek Olympics, is of particular significance in relation to the language of conciliatory internationalism in the Olympic movement. The first project was launched in 1992 following the break-up of the Federal Republic of Yugoslavia, where the stated objective of the IOC was to 'defend the interests of the athletes, protect the Olympic Games and consol-idate the unity of the Olympic movement'.[17] Potential conflict with UN Security Council Resolution 757 of 1992, in which sport was included for the first time as a recognized element within sanctions policy, quickly became apparent. 'A compromise was reached as the UN Security Council Sanctions Committee accepted the IOC's proposal that the athletes of Yugoslavia be allowed to participate in the Barcelona Games as individu-als'.[18] The idea of a revived Olympic truce was given public support outside the Olympic movement, first from the Organization for African Unity (OAU) in June 1993 and the UN General Assembly (October 1993).

The symbolic launch of the truce on 24 January 1994, to cover the period of the Lillehammer winter games, involved a still more impressive line-up of NGOs, including the World Health Organization (WHO), the United Nations Children's Fund (UNICEF) and the Red Cross. Of particular significance was the continuing conflict in Yugoslavia. Somewhat ironically, the IOC was assisted by the UN High Commissioner for Refugees and by the Norwegian government in 'facilitating the evacuation of the NOC's leaders and athletes from Sarajevo so that they could go to Lillehammer and take part in the Games'.[19] Thereafter, an item on the Olympic truce is permanently on the agenda of the UN General Assembly in the year prior to the Olympic Games. Concerning the Sydney Olympic Games, the 54th session of the UN General Assembly adopted a resolution entitled 'Building a Better World Through Sport and the Olympic Ideal' on 24 November 1999. On a symbolic note, the UN flag now flies at all competition sites of the Olympic Games.

Diplomatic activity between the IOC and other organizations broadly defined as NGOs – in particular the UN and UNESCO – has recently manifested itself in other ways. The staging of a 'World Conference on Education and Sport for a Culture of Peace', jointly organized by UNESCO and the IOC as part of the build-up to the UN International Year for a Culture of Peace, is noteworthy in this respect.[20] In relation to the Sydney Games, the role of the IOC in bringing together the two Koreas within the opening ceremony will doubtless be presented in the future as an example of the continued influence of the organization on the international stage. Such experiences suggest the need for a more pluralist interpretation of international diplomacy in relation to the Olympic movement, paying more than just lip-service to the influence of sports NGOs in the process. At the same time it is necessary to acknowledge the limitations of pluralism given the continuing central role of the state in setting the parameters for diplomatic discourse.

The Olympic movement: diplomatic limitations

The increasing significance of sport as an aspect of the domestic and international political agenda has created the conditions in which national sports organizations can potentially play a more proactive role in policy-making and implementation. If a pluralist perspective to international relations is an accurate interpretation of the international environment, it should be possible to identify increasing numbers of situations in which such sporting organizations are actively engaged in international politics. Certainly in relation to the UK, sports organizations are consulted on a range of politically sensitive issues such as drug misuse, and recently there has been liaison between the Home Office and the Football Association on the issue of soccer violence. Their influence outside a narrow range of issues does however, appear to remain marginal.[21] In addition, revelations concerning corruption in the bidding process for successive Olympic Games have had a negative impact on the capacity of the IOC to influence international policy issues. Such revelations have been used to justify increasing political involvement in sports issues and have resulted in the real and threatened loss of valuable commercial support.[22]

The influence of state-centred political interests is certainly apparent when considering the international response to controversy surrounding the awarding of the 2002 winter games to Salt Lake City. The scandal had implications not only for the IOC membership, but also for the organizing committee for the games.[23] On 2 March 1999, Senator George Mitchell, head of the US Olympic Committee (USOC)'s special commission into the Salt Lake City scandal, called for an independent audit of the IOC's finances and a ban on gifts and other expenses for IOC and USOC officials.[24] In June 1999, since the IOC 2000 Commission – created in response to widely publicized allegations of corruption within the IOC – was still considering proposals for the re-constitution of the IOC – interim rules were agreed and used in order to reach a decision for the hosting of the 2006 Winter Olympic Games.[25] These rules limited the amount of contact that IOC members could have with the organizing committees of the proposed sites. Also in June, the 109th session of the IOC in Seoul, the first to be televised, reflected the tensions building up in the movement at that time. There was reportedly conflict between the IOC and the Sydney Games organizing committee concerning its decision to cut perks normally expected by the IOC members. Michael Knight, chief executive of the committee, apparently upset some of the IOC membership by lecturing them on the need for reform and on the reasoning behind the decision to reduce the budget for IOC expenses.[26] Political pressure was building on the IOC from all sides. There were indeed fears that a number of IOC members may be arrested as a result of evidence from the Salt Lake City inquiry and subsequent inquiries by the police and the FBI into bribery allegations.[27] Allegations were also being made concerning corruption relating to the selection of Nagano for the 1998 winter Games and of Sydney for the 2000 summer Games, although they were not of the same magnitude as in the case of Salt Lake City. Here was an opportunity for the state to impose parameters on the activities of a sports NGO.

The IOC has however, survived these crises and is taking the initiative in reconstituting itself to ensure its future acceptance in the international community. Perhaps the legacy of the recent difficulties will be the shifting of influence between, rather than away from, sports organizations. In this context a *Financial Times* leader article in January 1999 argued that the responsibility for reform of the Olympic movement lay within the movement itself.[28]

Olympic diplomacy and the boycott debate

Much of 'realist' writing on politics and the Olympic movement presents sport as a 'political tool' being 'used' by states to further political objectives.[29] This writing has frequently focused on sports diplomacy as an addition to traditional diplomatic practices, for example reinforcing the government position on the diplomatic recognition of states, or indicating dissatisfaction with the behaviour of the host state. The argument as to whether or not withdrawal from the Games should be included as an element of the diplomatic portfolio is particularly controversial since it challenges directly the principle of political autonomy upon which the Olympic movement attempts to base its affairs at both national and international level. Nevertheless, a variety of pressures can be, and have been, brought to bear on NOCs and IOC representatives, to support the 'foreign policy line'.[30]

This issue was brought into sharp relief three decades ago in the comprehensively documented conflict surrounding international recognition of the People's Republic of China (PRC). PRC recognition entered a critical period in the lead up to the Montreal Games in 1976. Essentially this centred around conflict between the Canadian government and the IOC over whether or not the Taiwanese Olympic team could be recognized as the official team representing China at the same time as Canada had instituted a 'one China' policy. Espy notes that 'Canada recognized only the PRC as the legitimate representative for all of China. Canada felt it would compromise that policy if it allowed the athletes from Taiwan to compete as representatives of the Republic of China.'[31] The fact that Taiwan was a member of the IOC, and had previously competed as the 'Republic of China' and that the PRC was not a member, brought the Canadian government into direct conflict with the IOC. A compromise was suggested by the IOC, which would enable the Taiwanese team to enter the games as 'Taiwan-ROC'. This was however, rejected by the Taiwanese, who wished to march and compete under their own flag and name – the Republic of China. The IOC capitulated on the eve of the Games, under pressure from the Canadian government's determination to stick to its 'one China' policy. Espy further comments that the executive board 'announced that it would submit a resolution to the full session of the IOC that Taiwan should compete as Taiwan under the Olympic banner'. In the event, neither the Taiwanese nor mainland China competed in the Games.[32]

The controversy surrounding participation of Taiwan and China is generally supportive of a realist perception of sports boycotting as an aspect of international relations. It suggests the 'use' of sport as a political tool, the ascendancy of the state over non-state interests and the view of state interests as essentially 'coherent'. A closer investigation of British diplomacy relating to possible boycotts of the Games, does however, suggest that this 'realist' perspective also has its limitations.

British diplomacy and Olympic boycotts

Foreign policy, far from being coherent and unambiguous, must frequently attempt to reconcile contrasting interests and aspirations both within and outside government. In relation to the Olympic Games, the issue of whether or not to press for a boycott of the Games becomes problematic as a result of such ambiguity. Further difficulties arise where there is dissension as to what constitutes an appropriate level of government involvement in decisions relating to international sport. Both sets of issues have been apparent in the relationship between the British government and the Olympic movement, in particular concerning the 1936 Berlin Olympics and the 1980 Moscow Games. Additionally, both indicate in their contrasting ways that far from there being a linear increase in diplomatic activity relating to international sport, concentrations of such activity can be found at times of particular international tension.

In relation to the 1936 Games, accounts of one incident – Royal Naval participation in the Olympic regatta in Kiel – highlight the nature of the difficulties faced by policy-makers. In March 1936, the British naval attaché in Berlin informed the Foreign Office of the unofficial request made by the organizing committee of the 1936 Berlin Olympiad for a visit of a British warship to coincide with the Olympic Games. A subsequent inquiry by the Royal Navy as to whether such a visit by one of His Majesty's ships would be politically desirable, resulted in much agonizing. A Foreign Office minute in March commented that unless the Rhineland crisis was solved, such action would be undesirable and that therefore a decision should be deferred.[33] Further correspondence from the Admiralty referred to the fact that the Swedes, Danes and Americans appeared to have decided to send warships, but that 'most countries are waiting for a lead from us'.[34] A Commander Long identified a further complication in that should a warship be sent, a decision would have to be made as to whether or not the Royal Navy would then participate in the international naval sailing races which were to be held at Kiel, the naval rendezvous port. The reply to the Admiralty on 20 March indicated that Eden wanted to defer a decision until 10 April. A minute dated 11 May indicates that Eden believed that the visit should take place, but was still unwilling to make a final decision. Debate continued until the beginning of June when – due to a separation of the warship issue from the naval races issue[35] – it was finally possible for the Royal Navy to extract a ruling from the Foreign Office that it would indeed be in order to send a warship.[36]

On the basis that foreign policy is, of necessity, 'a series of more or less disjointed undertakings … which can rarely if ever be subsumed under a coherent overall strategy',[37] it is hardly surprising that there was dissension as to the most appropriate diplomatic response at that time. However, dissension has emerged not only because of foreign policy differences but also as a result of difference of opinion concerning the appropriateness of diplomatic involvement in sport and, in some cases, from lack of clarity as to the nature of the Olympic movement and the regulatory framework governing various aspects of the Games. The 1936 incident demonstrates this dissension and highlights the ambiguity evident in the responses of British politicians and civil servants when engaged in activities relating to international sport. That elements in the British government considered the invitation to the naval sailing races in Kiel as diplomatically significant is clear. That there was a deep disquiet as to what constituted the most appropriate response is equally clear. It should also be noted that decisions were being taken against the background of considerable pressure-group resistance to British participation at the Berlin Games (as noted in Peter Beck's chapter).

A more recent example of continued 'diplomatic' tensions was the government's position on British participation in the 1980 Moscow Olympic Games. Intense British diplomatic activity at the time reflected the redefined foreign-policy objectives of the new Conservative administration, escalating tensions in East-West relations in the wake of the Soviet invasion of Afghanistan and a growing awareness of the political currency of international sport. The diplomatic activity reflects the ambiguity of a 'non-interventionist' administration determined to use its influence to ensure non-participation of athletes in the Games. Countering this, the collective influence of national and international sports governing bodies had by now reached a significant level in terms of their capacity to influence government policy. While some athletes accepted, apparently on point of principle, that they should not attend the Games, there was sufficient agreement to counter government pressure and eventually to ensure the participation of British athletes.[38] This was not the first time that diplomatic activity relating to the Olympic Games involved government departments other than the Foreign Office. However, interaction between the Foreign and Commonwealth Office (FCO) and the Department of the Environment (DoE), which at that time held the portfolio for the development of sport, does suggest some movement of sport up the political agenda, both domestically and internationally.[39]

In January 1980 Sir Denis Follows, chairman of the British Olympic Association (BOA), confirmed his determination to represent the interests of individual British athletes and their national federations where, he noted, 'at the time of writing not one voice has been raised against participating in the Moscow Olympics'.[40] While he recognized the serious implications of the Soviet invasion, the rights of athletes to participate in the Games must, it was felt, not be compromised.[41] Follows ended his article for the *Daily Express* by emphasizing the importance of decisions relating to sport being made by sporting bodies, as was the case in relation to rugby contacts with South Africa. He hoped that the BOA 'will be accorded a similar privilege'.

Yet pressure both from within and outside the UK and from governmental and non-governmental sources soon began to build on the BOA to follow the US lead and boycott the Games.[42] Suggestions included the possibility of switching the Games to an alternative venue with the financial support of a number of pro-boycott governments. Follows, having pointed out the difficulties of attempting to influence a change of venue so close to the Games, received a further letter signed by the Prime Minister, dated 19 February (BOA Archives). This acknowledged grave misgivings concerning suggested

change of venue, but commented that 'as you will have seen from my statement in the House of Commons on 14 February, the Government has decided
that its advice to British athletes must be not to go to the Games in Moscow
next summer'.

In response to this letter, Dennis Howell, a Labour MP active in the
Birmingham Olympic bid, circulated a memorandum to governing bodies,
copied to Follows, which indicated that the government's advice, 'is not
shared by HM opposition'.[43] He went on to point out the rights of athletes in
democratic countries to travel and participate in the Games. In the memorandum he noted the apparently contradictory decision to support economic,
and in one instance sporting, contacts with the Soviet Union, while at the
same time calling for a boycott of the Games. He challenged the Prime
Minister's statement at question time that the Moscow Olympics would
repeat the dangers of the 1936 Berlin Olympics and would be used for
propaganda, arguing that the time to object was in 1974 during the bidding
process. He went on to remind the government that:

> In any case, the games do not belong to Moscow, the Soviet Union or any
> other country. They are the property of the IOC. This fact was recognised
> by the Council of Europe Sports Ministers who resolved to protect the
> integrity and independence of the IOC and successfully fought to prevent
> the Olympics becoming a subsidiary of UNESCO. It is sad that
> Governments who took that stand are now prepared to depart from it.[44]

Before the full debate on the proposed boycott of the Moscow Olympics in
the House of Commons, the Foreign Affairs Committee discussed the implications in some detail and prepared a briefing report.[45] The report began by
identifying the government's official position as set out in an FCO
memorandum circulated in February 1980. Section 12 of the report noted
that 'the Government considers that the gravity of the Russian action has
made it impossible to dissociate attendance at the Olympic Games in
Moscow from official approval of Soviet behaviour: for the Russians, the
Olympic Games will be a major political event'.[46]

The FCO was not the only government department with an interest in the
outcome of the boycott debate. The Department of the Environment at that
time had responsibility for the provision of sport in the UK. In a memorandum submitted by the DoE on 22 February, support is again given to the
ideals of the Olympic movement in relation to the separation of sport from
politics. The argument that NOCs should operate free from 'pressures of any
kind whatsoever, whether of a political, religious or economic nature' is
referred to as a 'noble' ideal. However, it notes that 'politics in the wider
sense affect sport in every country to a greater or lesser degree, ranging from
financial assistance by governments benefiting the whole sport movement to
total direction for political ends in more totalitarian regimes'.[47] On that basis
it argues that sportsmen and women had the same rights and responsibilities

as all UK citizens, and they could not expect to go about their 'sporting business' in isolation from what is going on around them.

Apart from government and the BOA however, there were other actors in the debate. The ambiguous position of the Sports Council in relation to the debates about attendance of British athletes does cast some light on the relationship between the organization and government. Parliamentary Under-Secretary of State for the Environment Hector Monro drew attention to the clause in the Sports Council charter that noted that the council shall 'have regard to any general statements on policy of our government that may from time to time be issued to it by our Secretary of State'. Monro therefore argued that under the terms of the royal charter by which the Sports Council was created, it should accept the advice of the Secretary of State on political matters. While he noted that the Council had been created to deal with the administration of sport, getting it 'out of the hair of government', when issues relating to international affairs arose, it was right that the government should take the lead. The Sports Council had, in a memorandum dated 15 February 1980, commented that it 'did not subscribe to the naive view held by some, that politics can be apart from sport'.[48] In that sense it accepted that it would have to take seriously any government suggestion of a change of venue since there may be 'significant factors' leading to such a request that it was not fully aware of. The situation was however being accepted 'with regret' since 'never again can our country protest that sport is not an instrument of foreign policy'. It goes on to point out that the consequences of such a policy could mean that 'the Olympics would be wrecked beyond recall' and that the British influence in international sporting federations 'would be severely curtailed'.[49]

In relation to the actors involved at this time it is also noteworthy that the influence of athletes, both as individuals and as a collective, was evident during the debates. The International Athletes Club had on 3 March sent a letter, signed by 78 athletes, to Mrs Thatcher affirming their right to take part in the Moscow Games (BOA Archives). The Foreign Affairs Committee noted that:

> They did not accept that their presence there would indicate support for Soviet policies and expressed willingness to demonstrate their disapproval by refusing to take part in the ceremonies. The covering letter also gave notice that the Athletes Club intended to approach the IOC for permission to send a team to Moscow if the BOA acted in breach of Rule 24c of the Olympic Charter, that is, if it responded to political pressure. (BOA Archives)

The committee also referred to a letter of 26 February from Adrian Metcalfe and Liz Ferris expressing the views of athletes. It noted their comments that the price of the short-term embarrassment of the Soviet Union if the Games are boycotted may be the 'total destruction of the Olympic Movement'.[50]

In the event, the collective influence of the sports organizations and the dominant sports personalities carried the day and Britain was represented at the Games. The failure of the Thatcher administration to halt the participation of British athletes, together with its apparent lack of resolve over the issue of sanctions against Iran in the wake of the American hostage crisis, created tension in the so-called 'special relationship' with the USA.[51] The episode further serves to illustrate the capacity of sports non-governmental organizations to challenge the position of the state, using its relative autonomy from government to its advantage.

The debate concerning the appropriateness of sports boycotts being used as a political tool continues, as recently witnessed in relation to the 2003 cricket World Cup.[52] Regarding the Olympic Games specifically however, it is noteworthy that in an era when, under the auspices of the UN, the use of collective sanctions as a diplomatic tool is increasing in frequency, there have been a decrease in incidences of sanctions relating to the Olympic Games. This challenges arguments presented by writers on the politics of sport, concerning its increased politicization. It remains to be seen however, whether Olympic boycotts re-emerge given current international tensions and despite continued efforts by the IOC to avoid such developments.

Multi-layered diplomacy and the Olympic movement: The challenge of bidding for the Games

The diplomatic significance of the bidding process has long been recognized. Since the onset of the modern Olympic Games, the process has engaged the diplomatic machinery, both formal and informal, of those countries hoping to host the Games. The traveller and writer Theodore Cooke argued that the decision to award the 1908 Games to London was greatly influenced by the fact that the King and Queen of England were present with the Prince and Princess of Wales for the 1906 Olympic Games in Athens.[53] He noted that the official British representative at the Athens Games was not only a member of the fencing team but also the president of what was known at that time as the British Olympic Council.

The bidding process also demonstrates diplomacy beyond the level of the state, with the requirement for interface between international organizations and local as well as national political administrations. The scale of the modern Olympic Games and the level of economic activity generated around them have, particularly after the financial success of the 1984 Games, ensured that bidding for the opportunity to host the games has become an increasingly competitive event in its own right. That a city rather than a country hosts the Games results in the focus of international attention on that city, although the region and country involved have a considerable stake in ensuring the success of the ensuing festival. There is clear evidence – to be discussed later – of the activities of the Foreign Office in relation to British bids. In addition, municipal authorities and local business interests, which have so much to gain from hosting the Games, become locked into intense diplomatic activity.

As with many aspects of diplomacy related to the Olympic Games, while 'municipal diplomacy' may have become more prominent and formalized in recent decades, it is evident in records of bidding throughout the twentieth century. Such municipal diplomacy is evidenced in relation to the British bid for the 1940 Games – subsequently withdrawn on Foreign Office advice in the light of the favoured Tokyo bid and then cancelled in response to the outbreak of war.[54] The interest of the municipal authority, City of London, was maintained when the focus of an investigation committee, under Lord Portal, switched to the 1944 Games. A representative of the Lord Mayor of London was invited to the inaugural meeting to comment on the views of the civic authorities. The range of activities which the authorities had engaged in were noted in relation to the 1908 Games, and Portal commented that 'nothing can be done without the help and full cooperation of the City of London'.[55] A further indication of the nature of organizations involved in the bidding process is given by reference to the attendance at the meeting, which included a representative of the Travel and Industrial Development Association of Great Britain and Ireland, 'because I [Portal] believe that they can also give us valuable help by telling us how best to publicize the Games so that foreign visitors may be induced to visit England and swell the number of spectators'.[56]

With the onset of war the issue of hosting an Olympic Games was off the agenda for the BOA. The possibility of submitting a bid re-emerged, as far as evidenced from official records, at a meeting held in the offices of the Amateur Athletic Association on 5 November 1945.[57] Lord Portal had already agreed to preliminary arrangements being made for a bid to host the 1948 games. It was also confirmed that the Lord Mayor of London was supportive of the idea of hosting the 1948 Games. While there was opposition to hosting the games in a city that was still clearly affected by the war, equally it was argued that the Games could provide a catalyst for economic development of the city.[58] Generally, then, the interest and involvement in the 'diplomacy' of bidding for the Olympic Games, by a range of actors below the level of the state, had been apparent for some time. The role of the municipal authorities in particular, as actors in diplomatic discourse, is however brought into sharp relief in relation to Manchester's bids for the 1996 and 2000 Olympic Games.

The diplomacy of bidding for the Olympics: The Manchester experience

The effort to secure the 1992 Olympic Games for Birmingham had met with a very low level of support in the IOC voting rounds in 1986. Hill argues that:

> Birmingham is thought to have done badly because most of its team were unused to the corridors of international power.... The bid was not

endorsed with any great enthusiasm by the British government, which was represented at the final vote only be the low-ranking Minister for Sport, Richard Tracey, who in any case arrived too late to have much time for last-minute lobbying.[59]

With the failure of attempts to secure the 1992 Games, attention turned to 1996. It was at this stage that Manchester made its first serious move. Hill argues that the leader of the group forwarding the Manchester bid, Bob (later Sir Robert) Scott, identified the key weakness in the Birmingham effort as lack of serious government involvement.[60] He noted, for instance, the active support of Jacques Chirac for the (eventually second placed) Paris bid. Howell's securing of the 97th IOC session for Birmingham did little to assist the fortunes of a revived bid by Birmingham for the 1996 Games and the BOA threw its weight behind the Manchester package. Hill also argues that the Manchester team was fairly satisfied with the progress of its relations with government, but that it would perhaps have performed more effectively if Britain's minister for sport had not been so junior in the hierarchy.

The British Prime Minister Margaret Thatcher intervened in November, writing a letter in support of the Manchester bid to Juan Antonio Samaranch, the president of the IOC. This was followed by a visit to England by Samaranch during which he was entertained by members of the royal household. In terms of government representation at the IOC session in Tokyo, where the final decision concerning the 1996 Games was taken, this time a more senior minister, Chris Patten, the Secretary of State for the Environment, was in attendance.[61] The efforts were again unsuccessful, however, with Atlanta being awarded the 1996 Games. Shortly after this announcement, London and Manchester entered the initial stages of the bidding process to host the 2000 Games.

The London efforts represent a particularly clear example of diplomatic activity across local, regional and central government as well as national and international sports organizations and business interests. The process triggered initially three separate groups wishing to assemble the London bid. The presence of Sebastian Coe, by then the prospective Conservative parliamentary candidate for Falmouth, as a key figure in one of these, was particularly noteworthy.

Debate concerning the awarding of the 2000 Games was ongoing at the time of the 1992 Barcelona Olympics and the presence there of the Princess Royal, an IOC member, and Prime Minister John Major should perhaps be seen in this context. In an exchange in the House of Commons early in July, David Mellor, then Secretary of State for the Department of National Heritage, commented that:

> We stand one hundred per cent behind Manchester's bid. My Right Hon. Friend the Under-Secretary of State will be going to Barcelona next week as will a number of other ministers, to ensure that it is made

clear to the IOC that the British Government fully support Manchester and will make sure, if it is successful, the Olympics are run superbly well.[62]

This clear government involvement is in contrast to the sentiments expressed in a separate exchange two weeks earlier. Foreign Minister Douglas Hurd argued in response to a question on whether a sports boycott should be reinstated against South Africa given the slow rate of regime change, that generally more patience was needed and that 'a sports boycott would not be a good idea. It is for sporting bodies to decide and not governments, but to start down that weary road would give entirely the wrong signal.'[63] The apparent ambivalence between these interventionist and non-interventionist approaches is noteworthy, particularly when considered in the context of the 1980 Moscow Games. It simply marks a more recent stage in a pattern of contradictory stances taken by ministers throughout the history of Olympic diplomacy. A leading article in *The Times* stressed the commitment required to ensure a successful bid. It argued that 'London's Olympic bid for 2000 collapsed precisely because that level of commitment was nowhere on sight. Clearly the British case for 2000 will not be heeded if government and people are seen to begrudge the effort and investment'.[64] The ambiguity of government towards sport was apparently ongoing.

In terms of the impact of local government organization on the bidding process, *The Times* had identified the collaboration of the Manchester group with the Greater Manchester Council as a key element in its efforts to secure the Games. This could be compared with the situation in London, where the authority generally charged with strategic planning, the Greater London Council, was no longer in existence. The BOA was demanding that cities should obtain signed statements of support from their civic authorities, but the Corporation of London had said that it would not be prepared to contribute financially to staging the Olympics in London – 'Nor would it be prepared to sign the agreement'.[65]

While the Manchester bid was unsuccessful, the experience did have a lasting impact on the city, revitalizing it and ensuring a base of skills existed that could be utilized in future negotiations for international events. It provided a clear illustration to politicians of the immensity of the international sports circuit and the level of commitment necessary to secure a successful bid. The success of the bid for the 2002 Commonwealth Games owed much to the lessons learned during that process.

British diplomacy and future British Olympic bids: The Wembley controversy

There appears in recent years to have been a growing awareness that the image of the UK internationally and the protection of its international interests is increasingly linked to sport both in terms of performance of athletes and in terms of the capacity to host major events. This is evidenced by a number of government initiatives including the FCO 'Panel 2000' consultation exercise with its objective of contributing to policies capable of enhancing 'perceptions of Britain abroad'.[66] In terms of government support for bids to stage international sports events in the UK, a 1999 report by the Select Committee on Culture, Media and Sport called for a more collaborative approach to such activity, noting that 'the government cannot be expected to throw its weight behind bids and events over which it has no say'.[67] Nevertheless, despite such government initiatives and despite new sources of funding in the form of the National Lottery, it would appear that ambiguity and conflicting messages from ministers continue to be the reality. Perhaps nowhere is this clearer than in the controversy surrounding the proposals to develop a new international stadium on the Wembley site.

Initial proposals to develop the Wembley site were made by the then English Sports Council in 1995 as it was generally recognized that the existing stadium was 'nearing the end of its viable life'. It was envisaged that a facility capable of hosting major international sports events was central to the drive to enhance the profile of Britain in international sport. From the onset, the project attracted criticism; particularly the lack of consultation with key sports agencies such as the BOA and UK Athletics. In the 1999 report to the select committee, it was noted that the new English National Stadium at Wembley 'is at the centre of our plans to host major international sporting events like the World Cup in 2006, the Olympic Games and the World Athletics Championships'.[68] The select committee expressed grave concerns as to the 'apparent lack of strategic thinking in the approach to the project by the English Sports Council and the government'.[69] It noted the slippage of the timescale for completion of the event and considered that serious questions remained to be answered regarding the feasibility of a multi-activity venue. It requested that as a matter of urgency a 'Minister for Events' should take overall responsibility for the project, with serious consideration given to direct government assistance for the project.

In a memorandum submitted by the BOA to the select committee in January 2000, the organization expressed particular concern about the direction of the project and the lack of serious consultation that had accompanied it. This lack of consultation had led it to rely on press reports that Wembley would form a central part of further bids to host the Olympic Games. Working from this assumption and from subsequent assurances given by the English Sports Council – now known as 'Sport England' – the BOA had based an 18-month feasibility study on a bid for the Olympic Games on the principle that the Wembley site would be the focal point of such an event. A range of concerns centred round the seating capacity of the proposed development. The memorandum noted that the BOA had not been aware of early decisions concerning the requirements of the stadium, nor had they even been aware of the existence of a National Stadium Monitoring Committee. They were reliant on the English Sports Council to put the case for a stadium capable of hosting the Olympics – even though, crucially, the BOA was the agency with responsibility for determining the appropriateness of an Olympic bid.[70] Due to continuing concerns as to the effectiveness of this method of lobbying, Simon Clegg, the chief executive of the BOA, attempted to open communications directly with the Department of Culture, Media and Sport (DCMS). Initially his overtures met with no response. Only after six months did the department respond by requesting that Sport England provide the BOA with a full briefing. While this initially allayed its fears, concerns over the design of a new Wembley stadium re-emerged and the BOA continued throughout 1999 to oppose the provision of what it considered to be an inappropriate development, given the aspirations to host an Olympic Games in the future.

By December 2000 the media were reporting that the project was running into further problems. A report in the *Independent* argued that 'there appears to be a conspicuous lack of leadership at government level'.[71] Since the proposals for a running track had been removed completely, the stadium could no longer act as the focus for a future Olympic bid. Recriminations continued throughout 2001. The findings of a select committee set up to investigate the difficulties were published during the week beginning 19 November. Chris Smith – the DCMS Secretary – was the focus of particular criticism with, among other comments, his 'scandalously inept treatment of public money'.[72] On the basis of the experiences of Wembley, the select committee argued for the creation of a ministerial position with responsibility for major events. The rationale was that 'someone with authority to cut through the complex structures and vested interests of a myriad of sporting organizations was needed if Britain is to contemplate hosting a major world sporting event'.[73] It was noted by MPs on the committee that the government had to be much clearer regarding its attitude to high-profile sports events such as the Olympics. The report stated that 'we believe that the Government must decide, and state clearly, whether or not it wishes the UK to be a host for larger sporting events'.[74]

Controversy continued throughout 2002. Finally in October the plans for the new stadium at Wembley were unveiled. It appeared that thinking had gone 'full circle' with the inclusion of a removable running track for athletics events. The logistics of installing the track and its limitations meant however that serious questions remained concerning the notion of a truly multi-use 'national stadium'. The project, described by the Secretary of State at the DCMS, Tessa Jowell, as 'a long and at times painful journey', is estimated to cost around £757 million with expected completion in 2006.[75]

It is generally acknowledged that the project was poorly managed from the outset and that something of this scale needed careful co-ordination by government. Again however, the recurring problem of lack of clarity concerning the parameters of government responsibility for such a venture, added to the problems of finding a consensus among the many shareholders. From the perspective of public diplomacy, the Wembley project did create a negative impression of British capability to deliver in international events. The success of the Commonwealth Games in Manchester in August 2002 and the initially positive assessment of the impact of hosting the Games on the economy of Manchester went some way to countering this impression. Nevertheless questions do remain concerning the responsibilities of government in such projects.

Understanding diplomacy through Olympic sport

In his investigation of 'Thatcher's Diplomacy', Sharp reduces to one line British diplomatic activity relating to the 1980 Olympic Games in Moscow.[76] Such is the significance attached to sport in the study of international relations. Yet this activity was central to the British government's response to the Soviet invasion of Afghanistan. Writers on international relations have, with their focus on so-called 'high politics', tended to exclude the ludic aspect of human existence as a subject not worthy of serious investigation. Outside a small body of scholars involved in the study of sport, there continues to be an unwillingness to accept any notion of sport as integral to economic, political and social development. By reference to the 'mediating' dimension of sport, the link between Olympism and internationalist thought and the ambiguous though often pivotal role of Olympic diplomacy in support of foreign policy objectives, the relevance of investigating diplomacy through the prism of the Olympic movement becomes apparent.

The assessment of diplomatic activity as it relates to the Olympic movement does indicate an 'opening up' of the diplomatic process and the existence of a wider range of interests – both within and outside government – with a stake in the process. At the same time it indicates a number of consistent themes in such diplomatic activity. These are worthy of consideration as they raise questions concerning the general development of diplomacy and the need for a more interpretive approach to understanding the nature of such discourse.

That non-governmental sports organizations demonstrate aspirations to become players in international diplomacy is not new. Such aspirations were evident in the activities of the IOC in its early years. At the same time there remain important limitations to such aspirations. As developments following revelations of corruption relating to the Salt Lake City bid for the 2002 winter Games demonstrate, actors representing state interests have the capacity to set limitations on the activities of Olympic organizations – in particular the IOC and organizing committees for the Olympic Games – concerning their activities relating to the bidding process.

With regard to Britain, the state has continued to demonstrate ambiguity concerning how it perceives the relationship between sport and politics. This is reflected in its attitude towards diplomacy in sport and the extent of its willingness to support provision for international sport. This ambiguity has at times, over the period of the last century, perhaps been advantageous from a diplomatic perspective. In the lead-up to the 1936 Berlin Olympics, apparent confusion over the remit of government in relation to international sport did buy precious time, which enabled the administration to gauge the response of the international community and indeed to decide on its own best course of action.[77] In contrast, in 1980, while the government took a clear line in calling for a boycott of the Moscow Games, the BOA's long tradition of autonomy from government was fully and successfully exploited by itself and a number of sports federations. This, together with a high level of media support, enabled it to overcome pressure from government and send a team to Moscow.

The adoption of a more pluralist approach is important when investigating diplomacy as it relates to the bidding process for the Olympic Games. Again, such diplomatic activity has been in evidence for some time. Even in 1906 a range of governmental and non-governmental organizations was engaged in arrangements for the 1908 Games. This has been demonstrated in relation to the 1940, 1944 and 1948 bids, as well as the more recent bids for the 1992, 1996 and 2000 Games and the opening stages of bidding for the 2012 Games. Throughout, there have been mixed messages from government regarding its remit in the process. Even in terms of the 2000 Manchester bid, while a relatively high level of government support was provided, this support came late in the process, too late to make a significant difference. In addition, its justification was presented in terms of the contribution it made to the infrastructure of Manchester, rather than the development of international sport as an end in itself.

It appears from recent developments that lessons concerning the need for a coordinated campaign with leadership provided by government have not been learned. The difficulties surrounding the Wembley project illustrate a significant lack of communication between government and key sports agencies, in particular the BOA, which has ultimate control over the submission of a British bid for the hosting of the Olympic Games. This made it difficult to 'sell' diplomatically abroad. It remains to be seen whether or not such shortcomings will be overcome in the process of bidding for the 2012 Olympic Games. In relation to public diplomacy, such domestic developments do matter.

7

Moving the goalposts:
The governance and political
economy of world football

SIMON LEE[1]

Introduction

This chapter explores the relationship between sport and international relations through a case study of the governance and political economy of professional football. Governance provides the central theme because the debate surrounding its nature and practice, paralleling the globalization debate, has been central to the increasing importance of political economy in the development of IR. However, while generally associated with political power and authority, governance has remained an essentially contested concept.[2] For political economy, the governance debate has primarily concerned the relationship between sources of political authority and the market. As private actors, most notably trans-national corporations and non-governmental organizations, have grown in importance, allowing for a more society-centred approach to policy-making and the governance of markets, so the increasing complexity of the relationship between a greater number of public and private actors has challenged the political and institutional capacity of the state to steer the policy choices affecting society and the economy.

Sport is not immune to the conflicts between public regulation and private power that lie at the heart of the governance debate, and football, the world's single most popular sport, expresses them particularly clearly. No other professional sport generates so much commercial revenue or popular allegiance, at either club or international level. At the same time, the sudden and huge inflow of income which football attracted during the 1990s created major problems of governance for a sport traditionally run by private and largely amateur associations. In particular, important questions have been raised concerning the distribution of wealth and the ownership and control of major sporting institutions by the tendency of private corporate interests to displace or supplant the traditional associational pattern of football's governance.

After an initial analysis of the nature of governance of sport in general, the chapter focuses upon three different levels of governance and three aspects of the governance of football: first, at the global and international level, developments in the relationship between FIFA (the Fédération Internationale de Football Association) and UEFA (the Union des Associations Européennes de Football); second, at the national level, the issues surrounding the distribution of income in the English Premier League; third, at club level, the corporate governance of Manchester United plc. In all three aspects, a pattern of increasing corporate power over the governance of football during the 1990s emerges, as a huge and rapid commercialization has transformed it into a major global business. Understanding the nature and implications of this rapidly evolving relationship between sources of public and private power at a variety of levels of governance has therefore become an important challenge for IR.

The governance of sport

A key characteristic of IR during the 1990s has been the increasing contribution made to it by the discipline of international political economy (IPE) and, more recently, global political economy (GPE), driven by two key discourses.[3] First, discourse over the nature of the constraints that globalization places upon national sovereignty in policy-making between the 'hyperglobalizers', for whom globalization has rendered national policy largely redundant, the 'sceptics', for whom the notion of the powerless state has been exaggerated to the point of mythology, and the 'transformationalists', for whom globalization has unleashed an unprecedented period of social change upon states and societies alike.[4] A second discourse concerns the transition from government to governance in the relationship between the public and private domains, between the state and market, at various levels from the local to the global. While its widespread usage in IR both belies and reflects its essentially contested nature, the concept of governance has been associated with attempts to influence policy through the exercise of political power and authority over a number of public and private actors.[5]

Although core executives and other key sources of political authority retain the desire to steer from the centre and assert control over policy, resources, priorities and outcomes, they have had to confront the reality of both their own institutional fragmentation and unintended outcomes and consequences arising during and from policy implementation. Rhodes, for example, has noted how governance is 'the product of the hollowing out of the state from above (for example, by international interdependencies), from below (for instance, by special-purpose bodies), and sideways (for example, by agencies)'.[6] This pattern is especially applicable to the governance of sport, where the administration of both professional and amateur sports has traditionally remained predominantly private, founded upon a system of national and international federations, which have zealously guarded their autonomy from the public sphere while simultaneously lobbying for public funding of their physical and human infrastructures. Thus the European

Council declared, after its Nice summit, that the European Commission neither wished, nor was in a position, to impose any given model of organization upon sports federations. Sports organizations would continue to have the right to organize themselves, albeit with due regard for national and community legislation.[7] Some have seen this as an abdication of political responsibility for protecting football from the inherent uncertainty and instability of market forces.[8]

A system of private governance in sport, in which the principles of transparency and accountability to players, spectators and administrators alike have tended to be honoured as often in their breach as in their observance, has provided an environment in which representatives of governing hierarchies have frequently been accused of bribery and corruption. In particular, during the presidencies of Juan Antonio Samaranch at the IOC and Dr João Havelange at FIFA, these institutions have tended to appear as autocratic structures dominated by personalized relations around key individuals.[9] For example, when evidence emerged of 'a culture of improper gift-giving' by representatives of Salt Lake City bidding to host the 2002 Winter Olympics, ten IOC members eventually resigned. Furthermore, an ethics inquiry conducted by the US Olympic Committee, headed by Senator George Mitchell, concluded that 'ethical governance has not kept pace with the rapid expansion of the Olympic movement' and that 'the IOC's lack of accountability has directly contributed to the gift-giving culture'.[10] With the expansion of international competition, the weakening of distinctions between professional and amateur sportsmen/women and the general commercialization of sport, the governance of sport has become an increasingly salient political issue for both national governments and institutions beyond the nation-state, notably the EU and trans-national corporations.

Sport's governing bodies have been questioned over their capacity to act simultaneously as regulatory institutions and as commercial entities in the negotiation of sponsorship and broadcasting rights. In global terms, sport is a rapidly growing industry, accounting for around 3 per cent of world trade, of which the US maintains a 42 per cent, and Europe a 36 per cent, share. Sports sponsorship alone generates an estimated $15 billion per annum, while the sale of television rights and tickets generates $42 billion and $50 billion per annum respectively.[11] The 1998 World Cup tournament in France generated sales of FIFA World Cup branded merchandise worth $1.2 billion, and the recently completed 2002 World Cup was expected to see this income rise to $1.5 billion. Individual athletes have also benefited – in Major League Baseball, Alex Rodriguez has signed a ten-year contract worth $252 million (£175 million) in a league where, following the protracted 1996 players' strike, the average salary is $1.8 million. However, as the Sydney Olympics and 1998 World Cup vividly demonstrated, and as other chapters in this book illustrate, the importance of major global sporting events has extended far beyond the purely economic and commercial to embrace key political issues, including the conception and expression of national identity and the role of trans-national corporate interests in the governance of inter-national sport. Furthermore, as the controversy surrounding Formula One motor racing supremo Bernie Ecclestone's £1 million donation to the British Labour Party (subsequently returned) highlighted, sport can penetrate to the very heart of the domestic political agenda and destabilize governments.

As such revenues have increased, the top clubs in major sports have frequently questioned not only the right of sporting associations to negotiate on their behalf but also the distribution of revenue where that does not reflect their greater market power. Furthermore, because sports depend upon a competitive balance in their league structures, increasing inequalities in income, and top clubs' pursuit of European 'super-leagues' (for example, in association football and rugby union), have threatened to undermine the viability of existing leagues. Competitive balance has also been threatened by trans-national multimedia companies (notably Canal Plus, BSkyB and NTL) owning, or having major stakes in, more than one club participating in the same national or international competition.[12] Consequently, a key challenge for those governing sport has been to reconcile conflicts of interest between players, clubs, leagues, spectators, sponsors, broadcasters and their respective representative associations, while maintaining both a competitive balance in sporting competitions and income streams commensurate with the continuing prosperity and further expansion of professional and amateur sports.

The governance of professional football

As mentioned above, football remains the world's single most popular sport, commercially or via allegiance, and has more than 200 million registered players. The 1998 World Cup finals had a record 32 participating nations, compared to only 16 in 1992, and the total television audience for the tournament was estimated at 37 billion, an average of 578 million per game, with the final itself attracting around two billion viewers. Indeed, it was estimated that the 2002 World Cup would generate $26.8 billion or 0.6 per cent of GNP for Japan and $8.8 billion or 2.2 per cent for South Korea.[13] The investment bank HSBC has calculated that shares in the countries hosting the previous ten World Cups outperformed those in the rest of the world by an average of 8.8 per cent in the six months prior to the finals, although host-country stock markets fell by an average of 6.4 per cent in the subsequent six, suggesting that football generates only a short-term financial feel-good factor.[14] Football can also have a detrimental impact on national economic performance: up to £3.2 billion was expected to be lost from GNP due to workers' 'sickness' during England's matches in the 2002 World Cup finals.[15] In fact, manufacturing production fell by 5.3 per cent in June, compared with the previous month, the largest monthly decline in 23 years.[16]

The governance of world football is complicated by the fact, as Szymanski and Kuypers have noted, that 'football is a game, but it is also a business' with an estimated worldwide turnover of £150 billion. Lying 'somewhere between war and economics', football combines fierce competition and the motivation to win on the one hand, and cooperation and exchange within league and cup structures and according to established laws and regulations on the other.[17] But 'if the gap between the dominant and lagging clubs in the league becomes too large then a significant number of league matches become too predictable and the absence of strong competition leads to unexciting games that attract few spectators'.[18] The governance of football must therefore attempt to reconcile individual clubs' drive to maximize competitive and commercial success with the maintenance of a successful league structure.

The governance of football has been further complicated during the 1990s by the entrance of significant new private actors seeking greater influence over the distribution of football's rapidly growing income and wealth. For example, at club level, in 1991, 20 of England's elite clubs broke away from their established representative body, the Football League, and created their own body, the Premier League. This change in the governance of English football has enabled the Premier League clubs to negotiate separate broadcasting contracts, such that in the 2000/1 season they received £267 million, over 93 per cent of the £286 million paid by television companies to English professional clubs.[19] This pattern was repeated across Europe seven years later, when an elite group of 14 prestigious clubs were persuaded by Media Partners, the Milan-based company owned by Silvio Berlusconi, later Italian Prime Minister, to form the G14[20] in order to 'maximize television revenue from the Champions League'.[21] The proposed 16-team European Super League, guaranteeing each member club a £23 million per season income, has given the G14 the leverage to force European football's governing association, UEFA, into major concessions, notably over the distribution of television revenues. Thus, in 2000/1 the UEFA Champions League's 32 participating clubs received €490 million, 73 per cent of the €670 million the competition generated.

This leverage has also been used to insure the elite clubs against radically reduced revenue from football broadcasting rights across Europe. ITV Digital's £315 million contract with the English Football League has been cancelled; Germany's Kirch media group, which had promised to pay €721 million for broadcasting rights for seasons 2002/3 and 2003/4, has collapsed; and eight of Italy's Serie A clubs, which negotiate broadcasting rights individually, have failed to secure €10 million deals from the two pay-TV companies, who have offered only €4.5 million. The result has been an intensification of elite clubs' demands on national and European football's governing associations for a further redistribution of income in their favour, and on national governments for subsidies to rescue financially stricken leagues. In Germany, for example, both the federal and state authorities have explored the potential for a €200 million financial bail-out for the 36 clubs in the top two professional leagues.[22] In Italy, Serie A's top clubs postponed the start of the 2002/3 season by two weeks, embarrassing Prime Minister Silvio Berlusconi – who, as honorary chairman of AC Milan, owner of the largest commercial broadcaster, Mediaset, and, by virtue of being leader of the parliamentary majority, controller of the state broadcaster RAI, faces a major conflict of interests when confronted with demands for his intervention and mediation, all at a time when a new conflict-of-interests law had yet to negotiate its passage through the Italian parliament.[23]

The new elite, then, driven by commercial interests, has established structures to increasingly rival the long-established national, international and supranational associations that have governed twentieth-century football. Yet its demands upon government when faced with financial difficulties demonstrate the limitations of private governance rather than public government of professional football. Indeed, the expansion of FIFA's membership – from eight national associations in 1904 to 203 in 2000 – and among FIFA's six constituent continental federations and confederations (UEFA's membership rose from 25 national associations in 1954 to 51 by 2000), coupled with the increased revenues generated by world football, has focused attention upon the transparency and probity of the world football's governance structures.

As the percentage of associations in FIFA from Asia, Oceania and Africa has increased, and teams from these countries have improved their performance during recent World Cups, the demand has grown for greater representativeness and support for developing nations' interests from world football's governing institutions. For example, Issa Hayatou, president of the Confederation of African Football (CAF), has called for Africa's allocation of five of the 32 places at the 2002 World Cup to be increased, to reflect the fact that, with 51 member associations, CAF provides one-quarter of FIFA's total membership.[24] In response, FIFA president Joseph Blatter repeatedly promised, before his re-election at the 53rd Ordinary FIFA Congress in Seoul in May 2002, that Africa will stage the 2010 World Cup.[25]

During the late 1990s, the governance of world football was also characterized by an increasing rift between its two major governing bodies, FIFA and UEFA, fomented by three key conflicts between two of world football's principal powerbrokers. First, the failure in the June 1998 election for the FIFA presidency of UEFA's president, Lennart Johansson, to defeat his bitter rival, Sepp Blatter. Second, Blatter's January 1999 proposal for a biennial World Cup, whose inaugural event would coincide with UEFA's own Euro 2004 in Portugal. Third, South Africa's failure in July 2001 to win the contest to host the 2006 World Cup. Germany, Johansson's preferred choice, was chosen instead, thereby reviving memories of Blatter's 1998 FIFA presidential campaign, allegedly successful due to promises, ultimately broken, to deliver the World Cup to an African nation.

Underlying FIFA-UEFA antagonism has been a rift over the probity of their respective approaches to football's governance. FIFA prefers a pyramidal structure, at the base of which lie the fans, players and then the clubs.

Lying above these stakeholders are the national associations and six continental associations (Europe, South America, North/Central America, Asia, Africa and Oceania).[26] At the apex lies FIFA, whose claims to be 'truly democratic' in its internal governance have been based upon a presidential election process in which every member association has one vote, irrespective of size and past contribution to world football. Furthermore, FIFA's code of conduct, its 'ten golden rules', include the rejection of 'corruption, drugs, racism, violence and other dangers to sport'.[27] Yet UEFA's chief executive, Gerard Aigner, has joined Johansson in repeatedly challenging Blatter's claim to transparent, democratic governance.

The dispute came to a head over the bankruptcy of the sports marketing group ISMM/ISL, FIFA's long-standing marketing partner, and one of only two companies to be given broadcasting rights for the 2002 World Cup. The withdrawal of insurance company AXA as underwriter for the 2002 World Cup only served to exacerbate the dispute. Blatter has conceded that the demise of ISMM/ISL will cost FIFA up to SFr100 million.[28] Indeed, at FIFA's July 2001 extraordinary congress in Buenos Aires, Blatter confessed that FIFA had been 'forced to take out bridging loans of around £150 million to help offset the ISL deficit but I guarantee I will wipe that out before next year's World Cup'.[29] Dissatisfied with Blatter's explanation, UEFA requested no fewer than 25 written answers from Blatter concerning ISL's demise, the creation of FIFA's own marketing agency, FIFA Marketing AG, the failure of the Traffic Marketing Group to sell any television and marketing rights for the suddenly aborted World Club Championship, and the financing of the 2001 Confederations Cup. UEFA also raised a number of more minor but nonetheless significant issues affecting FIFA's governance, including the request for a detailed organizational chart of FIFA's own administration, incorporating a complete inventory of the identity, cost, role and job specifications of Blatter's presidential advisors, the new staffing structure within FIFA Marketing AG and its relationship to FIFA's administration.[30]

In response to this implicit yet withering critique of the governance of football under his presidency, Blatter announced a complete audit of FIFA's finances. Once completed, Blatter claimed that KPMG's audit would be presented to FIFA's constituent associations, federations and confederations 'to show there is transparency and the figures given are not rumours'.[31] However, Blatter opposed the establishment of FIFA's own internal audit committee (IAC) in March 2002, and then ended its work on 11 April, leading 11 members of the 24-man FIFA executive to threaten legal action against Blatter in the Swiss courts for 'misuse of funds'.[32] On the eve of the FIFA presidential election, in which Issa Hayatou challenged Blatter, David Will, a FIFA vice-president who had been conducting an inquiry into FIFA's finances, wrote to all national football associations that FIFA had lost £215 million from 1999 to 2002. FIFA had disguised the loss by borrowing £313 million against anticipated profits from the 2002 and 2006 World Cups. When Will attempted to disclose these findings to the May 2002 FIFA

Congress, countering FIFA finance director Urs Linsi's claim that FIFA was actually £400 million in credit, Blatter denied him a platform and was consequently roundly jeered.[33] Michel Zen-Ruffinen, FIFA's general secretary, had produced his own damning report three weeks earlier, claiming that FIFA had lost up to 800 million Swiss francs (£366 million) during Blatter's tenure and that Blatter had made unauthorized secret payments from FIFA funds. Blatter then barred Zen-Ruffinen from any future involvement in FIFA's finances.

Despite the disharmony in FIFA's ranks and widespread allegations of corruption, Blatter was re-elected as president by 139 votes to Hayatou's 56. No fewer than 117 of the 202 FIFA federations eligible to vote had been the recipients of £275,000 payments from FIFA's 'GOAL' programme, which Blatter had projected as his personal funds.[34] Once re-elected, Blatter immediately asserted his authority by securing the removal of Zen-Ruffinen as FIFA general secretary and Keith Cooper as communications director and the withdrawal of the legal action by the 11 FIFA executive members. Furthermore, Blatter has proposed the restructuring of the governance of FIFA by its transformation from an association into a company. Blatter's opponents, however, see this as an attempt to make FIFA's governance even less transparent and accountable, as Blatter would enjoy the right to appoint the company's board of directors and thereby bypass FIFA's executive committee.[35]

The frequency of corruption allegations at FIFA in recent years demonstrates the extent to which traditional patterns of governance in football's governing associations, dependent upon opaque organizational hierarchies and the patronage of key individuals, is no longer tenable. This is particularly evident when such governance structures can only be sustained by major borrowing against projected income, thereby mortgaging the sport's future and risking the loss of confidence among sponsors. The rapid increase in commercial revenue, which saw UEFA's own income spiral from SFr66.7 million in 1994/5 to SFr389.3 million in 1998 (both World Cup years)[36] has demanded new standards of transparency in football's governance structures, not least because of the demands of potential sponsors and the capacity of clubs and their owners to create alternative sources of political authority within the sport.

In this regard, and confronted by the challenge that the G14 group and other leading European clubs pose to the political authority of football's established associations, UEFA plans to introduce a club licensing system for the 2004/5 season. Launched in February 2001, the system has been piloted in eight UEFA associations (England, Luxembourg, Netherlands, Norway, Slovenia, Spain, Sweden and Scotland). However, in seeking to raise standards of governance at club level by proposing to licence only those clubs which can demonstrate rigorous controls on their financial, sporting, coaching, legal and administrative infrastructures, UEFA has discovered that reforming the governance of major sporting institutions is far from straightforward. Indeed, the launch of the licensing system has had to be postponed by one year owing to the complexities arising from compiling the licensing manual.[37]

Both FIFA and UEFA's experience demonstrates that to achieve a more transparent governance is far from a technocratic exercise but involves difficult negotiation with a plethora of private and public actors at a variety of levels of governance. While football associations have traditionally zealously guarded their autonomy from governments, their rapidly expanding incomes and involvement with politically sensitive regulatory issues surrounding media ownership, broadcasting rights and labour markets have inevitably attracted the intervention of government. The decisions of the European Commission to endorse UEFA's rule banning a company or individual from having direct or indirect control of more than one club competing in a UEFA club competition, while allowing the central marketing of certain 'core' commercial rights so as to maintain the solidarity in European football,[38] are but two recent examples.

Football at the national level: The conservatism of private governance

Problems of governance, including the reconciliation of the interests of new and wealthy market entrants with those of longer-standing stakeholders in the sport, notably supporters, have also arisen at the national level. This can be seen most vividly in England, the home of both the oldest governing association, the Football Association (FA), founded in 1863, and the world's most affluent professional football league – the only one able to achieve an income of more than £1 billion.[39] England's dual status as the spiritual home of professional football and the world's most commercially dynamic league is also reflected in the contrast between, on the one hand, a pattern of governance by private association which has only recently begun to come to terms with the demands of rapid commercial expansion, and, on the other, the challenge posed to the political authority of the sport's traditional governance structures by a breakaway Premier League, whose clubs are increasingly owned by trans-national media corporations.

To understand English football's failure to modernize its governance structure until the 1990s, we must acknowledge its development in the earlier decades of the twentieth century. During the inter-war period, English football's governing bodies were highly conservative, exemplified in the FA's failure to participate in the development of the global game. The FA withdrew from FIFA in 1920 and 1932 over disputes concerning fixtures with the defeated powers, and so England did not participate in the 1930 and 1938 World Cups. Furthermore, despite having 150,000 affiliated members by 1934, the National Federation of Football Supporters' Clubs and ordinary supporters had little influence over the governance of English football – either in its embryonic stages or during its halcyon days.[40]

The problems of conservatism in English football governance, and the underlying tensions between clubs and their governing associations, was demonstrated in 1960 when a £47,000 deal to show 26 live Football League games collapsed after clubs objected to a deal negotiated without their involvement.[41] At the same time, the question of the abolition of the maximum wage had become a matter of dispute with the Professional Footballers' Association (PFA) in June 1960 and remained unresolved until a June 1963 court ruling that it constituted 'an unjustifiable restraint of trade'.[42] Football's conservatism was also reflected in the failure to act upon the Football League's 1961 *Pattern for Football* or the 1968 Chester Report,[43] both advocating wholesale restructuring.[44]

The conservatism and complacency of English football's governing elites, which hindered modernization of the game's physical and human infrastructures, meant that football was vulnerable before a new commercially driven corporate elite committed to the commodification of the English game for private profit. The recent problems surrounding the governance of English football have reflected a departure from the earlier balance between commercial needs and the central spirit of the game. Indeed, the FA-sanctioned creation of the Premier League in 1992 has been aptly depicted as 'a betrayal of a century of the traditional structure'.[45] Before the era of stock-market flotations, English football was governed according to a set of principles that had helped maintain a degree of equality between the professional clubs. In particular, rule 34 of the FA's regulations meant that club directors could not draw a salary; nor could anyone derive a major income from owning football club shares because dividend payments were limited to 5 per cent of nominal face value. Furthermore, if a club had to be wound up, it was protected against possible asset-stripping by the regulation that surplus assets must be distributed to sporting benevolent funds or other local sporting institutions.[46] Once rule 34 could be circumnavigated, the rapidly expanding assets of English football were vulnerable to market agents whose shareholders' interests would not necessarily coincide with either the maintenance of competitive balance or the redistributive principles which had hitherto informed football's governance.

Two key failures in the governance of modern English football have arisen from, and accentuated, growing commodification. The first came in 1983 when, against the backdrop of a threatened elite breakaway league, Tottenham Hotspur became the first English football club to launch a stock-market flotation. Rule 34, previously a barrier to such transactions, was surmounted by the football club and its assets becoming a subsidiary of a holding company, Tottenham Hotspur plc, which henceforth could act without the constraint of the FA's rules, allowing for opportunistic company directors to cream off a windfall dividend from football's dramatically rising income stream from broadcasting and sponsorship. The second key failure arose in the aftermath of the 15 April 1989 Hillsborough Stadium disaster, itself testimony to the crumbling infrastructure of English football. In his final report into the disaster, Lord Justice Taylor identified five factors responsible for 'a general malaise or blight over the game'.[47] Four of these (hooliganism, poor facilities, old grounds and excessive drinking) were substantially remedied during the 1990s through legislation[48] and over £500 million of long-overdue stadium investment. The fifth, poor leadership of the English game, has remained unattended to because of the failure of football's governing bodies to undertake 'the fullest reassessment of policy for the game'[49] recommended by Taylor.

Governing the trickle down of poverty

English football appears now to be drowning in affluence. In a recent global league table of world football's richest 20 clubs, the Premier League had the largest presence with eight, ahead of Italy (six) and Spain, Scotland and Germany (two each).[50] Additionally, Manchester United plc (*sic!*) is the world football's richest club, its annual results for 2000/1 reporting a 30 per cent rise in pre-tax profits to £21.79 million on a turnover up 12 per cent to a record £129.6 million.[51] The financial significance of English Premier League football has been further highlighted by Deloitte and Touche's analyses of football finance and England's Premier League clubs.[52] They calculate that over the five years to summer 1999, the clubs in the Premiership in 1998/9 had an income of £2.32 billion, paid £1.22 billion in total wages, made operating profits (before transfers) of £316 million and paid out £477 million net in player transfer fees.

Accompanying this affluence, however, are increasing inequalities between richer and poorer clubs, both within the Premier League and between it and its poorer relation, the Football League. In 1999/2000, the 20 Premier League clubs generated £587 million more revenue than their Division One counterparts which meant that the average Premiership club income of £38.6 million was five times greater than the First Division average of £7.7 million. Furthermore, Deloitte and Touche predicted that the average income gap between Premier League and First Division clubs would further widen to £60 million for the 2002/3 season. Income inequality is also evident in the lower divisions. The average income gap between First and Second Division clubs is predicted to rise from £5 million in 1999/2000 to £8.1 million in 2002/3, and that between Second and Third Division clubs is expected to increase from £2 million to £2.7 million.[53]

These inequalities have exposed a major weakness in the governance of English football. Traditionally, English professional football's four divisions have operated upon the principle of significant income redistribution from richer to poorer clubs. This was accomplished by both an equitable formula for distributing revenue from gate receipts and television broadcasting rights and via poorer clubs' sale of promising home-grown players to the elite clubs. There is now little evidence of a 'trickle down' of affluence from the Premier League to the remainder of English football. The Premier League remains characterized by rampant wage inflation, with total wages and salary costs rising 30.4 per cent in 1999/2000 to £471 million, resulting in an overall Premier League wages/turnover ratio of 61 per cent. Indeed, it is estimated that Premier League players' wages rose by 266 per cent, or 30 per cent annually, between 1993/4 and 1998/9. In the First Division, the wages/turnover ratio has risen from 76 per cent in 1995/6 to 95 per cent in 1999/2000. Although the Football League clubs received a welcome £27 million income from net total transfer payments from the Premier League clubs in 1999/2000 (up from a meagre £1.5 million in 1997/8), this was less than one-fifth of the £182 million of transfer fees paid to overseas clubs, itself amounting to no less than 53 per cent of the £340 million invested in new players by English clubs during 1999/2000. The overall result was that in 1999/2000 the Premier League recorded a pre-tax loss of £34.5 million (compared to a loss of £13.5 million in 1998/1999) and the Football League a massive loss of £110.1 million (equivalent to 36 per cent of its total income and up from £75.3 million in 1998/9).[54]

With its growing inequalities in income and wealth, overseas trade deficit and dependence on foreign labour to make good skills shortages both on and off the field, English football can be regarded as an appropriate metaphor for the broader political economy of English society.[55] The demise of major clubs such as Nottingham Forest, Queen's Park Rangers and Sheffield Wednesday,[56] all crippled by millions of pounds of debt and unable to return to the Premier League, appears to demand urgent action from football's governing associations to redistribute income from the rich elite to the impoverished majority in order to nurture the sport's traditional grassroots. Thus far, little remedial action has been forthcoming. The Premier League has committed itself to devoting 5 per cent of its income from the sale of television rights to the Football Foundation, a new institution launched at 10 Downing Street in July 2000, whose rationale is the provision of 'a new generation of modern facilities in parks, local leagues and schools through-out the country to promote education, recreation and community development'.[57] However, demands for further redistribution, in the form of a continuation of the customary 5 per cent allocation of television revenue to the PFA to pay for players' welfare and education,[58] resulted in a protracted dispute and threatened players' strike in late 2001 which demonstrated the growing rift between the self-interest of clubs, players, players' agents and broadcasters and the general good of the sport.[59]

Although strike action was eventually called off when the parties negotiated a deal guaranteeing the PFA £17.4 million of television revenue annually for three years, the conduct of the dispute demonstrated the increasing influence of corporate interests over English football.[60] The backdrop to the threat of strike action was a dramatic decline in major clubs' quoted share prices[61] and a significant fall in television audiences and advertising revenue – calling into question not only the sums broadcasters paid for existing terrestrial and satellite television rights[62] and minority shareholdings in many Premier League clubs[63] but also the likely size of the next television deal.[64] In these circumstances, some Premier League clubs could not afford to leave unchallenged the PFA's claim to a greater share of revenue and influence over English football's governance than the Premier and Football Leagues were prepared to sanction. Fearing an imminent squeeze in football's income, among the most vocal opponents of the PFA were those chairmen of Premier League clubs with the greatest financial interest in ensuring their retention of the maximum share and control over football's income and wealth. For example, both Peter Ridsdale (Leeds United) and Peter Hill-Wood (Arsenal) claimed that striking players would be in breach of their contracts with their respective clubs.[65] Their vanguard position among those challenging the PFA was not unconnected with the financial challenges confronting both clubs. Despite its most successful run in the European Champions League, and a resulting increase in turnover from £52.4 million in 1999/2000 to £86.25 million in 2000/1, Leeds United nevertheless reported a £4.03 million pre-tax loss for 2000/1, at a time when it was seeking to finance a move to a new stadium.[66] Similarly, Arsenal also faced the prospect of having to finance the £250 million projected cost of its planned move from Highbury to a new stadium at Ashburton Grove. The legitimacy of the PFA claim to a significant share of revenue and a major stake in the governance of professional football had therefore, in their view, to be contested.

The PFA actually had the strongest claims to being the most transparent among English football's governing structures and the most philanthropic in furthering the development of English football. Not only did the 1992 Trade Union and Labour Relations Act require it to publish an annual return with the Certification Office for Trade Unions and Employers, more extensive than the annual accounts produced for the stock market by listed football clubs, but the PFA had also long assumed the role of the UK's largest sports charity, donating no less than £10.5 million of its total income of £13 million in 2000 to charitable purposes.[67] Premier League clubs have therefore faced the dilemma that in questioning the legitimacy of other actors to a role in the governance of English football, they may paradoxically focus greater attention upon the legitimacy of their own role.[68]

FC to plc: the corporate governance of Manchester United

Many of the key issues in the governance of professional football globally are writ large in the political economy of Manchester United plc, world football's biggest club The £623.4 million attempted takeover of United by BSkyB, and Secretary of State for Trade and Industry Stephen Byers's April 1999 decision to block the takeover on competition and broader public interest grounds, brought into focus trans-national broadcasting businesses' role in accentuating income inequalities and threatening football's competitive balance.[69] However, United's recent negotiation of a £302.9 million 13-year deal with Nike, the high-profile trans-national sportswear corporation, under which Nike enjoy exclusive sponsorship, merchandising and licensing rights from 1 August 2002, has brought trans-national capital's role in world football into even sharper focus. Nike has the right to terminate the agreement in July 2008, while only £133.4 million will be paid to United over the first six years of the deal. Beyond the sponsorship and licensing revenues, Nike's net profits from licensing, retailing and merchandising will be divided 50/50. If United fails to finish in the top half of the Premier League or to qualify for European cup competitions, the amounts payable by Nike will be reduced under the terms of the contract. Therefore United's ability to capitalize upon its commercial dividend from Nike may be offset by the fear that underperformance on the field may lead to a further collapse in its faltering share price.

The political sensitivity of the Nike contract was highlighted on 15 October 2000 when the BBC current affairs series *Panorama* identified that child labour was being used in Cambodian factories manufacturing Nike products.[70] Nike had previously become embroiled in allegations concerning the use of child labour to manufacture footballs in Pakistan in 1995. At the same time, the deal between United and Nike had been negotiated when the lower house of the Brazilian Parliament had been investigating the ten-year deal between Nike and the Brazilian Football Confederation. A number of controversies surrounded this deal: first, it coincided with a particularly lean period for the Brazilian national side; second, the precise destination of the revenue arising from the deal had become a matter of uncertainty; third, the question of whether the deal with Nike, an American multinational, constituted an unacceptable infringement of Brazilian sovereignty had arisen: it has been alleged that the corporation placed pressure upon Ronaldo, the central figure in Nike's 1998 advertising campaign, to play in the 1998 World Cup final, despite his pre-match convulsions.[71] These matters have been given additional spice by the fact that the current chairman of the Brazilian Football Confederation is the former son-in-law of João Havelange, the Brazilian who, previously head of Brazilian football, was FIFA president for 24 years.[72]

Long before the Nike negotiation, Manchester United supporters had experienced the malign impact of corporate interests when the club badge was re-branded by removing the letters 'FC' (denoting 'Football Club'), thereby transforming it into a global corporate brand. Supporters' suspicions had been further aroused by the failure of David Gill, the plc's deputy chief executive, to confirm that the revenue from the Nike contract will be used to purchase new players or improve existing players' contracts. Gill has stated that the Nike deal was 'part of our overall business model going forward, but it doesn't incrementally change the wages structure'.[73] The announcement of the deal 21 months before the end of the existing sponsorship deal with Umbro had in any case so angered Umbro that it was reported to be contemplating legal action. Its temper will not have been helped by the fact that Peter Kenyon, ex-Chief Executive of Manchester United Plc, had been an Umbro executive prior to his arrival at United.

Shareholders United, the influential representative of Manchester United supporters' shareholdings, also saw the Nike deal as dubious, since it appeared to contravene the club's new customer charter, which specified that the club would not deal with any companies using child labour.[74] At its 17 November 2000 annual general meeting (AGM), Manchester United plc board members refused to discuss the Nike deal, despite its importance for the plc's corporate governance and interest for supporters' organizations, on the grounds that legal advice precluded the contract's discussion, a somewhat paradoxical position since the club had already announced the contract. Oliver Houston, Shareholders United spokesman, described the meeting as 'a sham' suggesting that 'it made a mockery of the supposed new openness and accountability at Old Trafford'.

The practical problems of the current model of corporate governance in major football clubs are evident in the relationship between Manchester United plc and Shareholders United. The latter's own shareholding in the plc amounts to only two million shares among its more than 700 members. However, the influence of this shareholding may be disproportionate to its size if other and larger shareholders can be persuaded to support Shareholders United's resolutions at shareholders' meetings. For example, at the 1999 AGM, Shareholders United was able to attract the votes exercised on behalf of more than 10 per cent of the total shareholding in the plc. The key problem confronting Shareholders United concerns the distribution of the shareholdings in the plc. According to Shareholders United's own estimates before the November 2000 shareholders' AGM, while individuals (30,328 people), constituting 99.56 per cent of the total number of shareholders, held 19.78 per cent of 260 million shares, seven club directors and financial institutions held 9.29 per cent and 70.93 per cent of the shares respectively.[75] Under British company law, if the directors of a football club are presented with a course of action, e.g. the BSkyB offer for Manchester United, that is held to be in the interests of the parent company but not the football club, then 'they would be legally obliged to adopt the course of action that was in the interests of the parent company of which they were directors. The interests of the football club, and their fans, would have to be sacrificed'.[76] In effect, this form of corporate governance ensures that financial institutions' interests will always prevail over those of supporters and other key stakeholders in the game, not least when major shareholders' and supporters' interests diverge.

Given the ease with which powerful corporate media interests have outmanoeuvred football's governing institutions, there have been demands for an end to the secretive, unaccountable and private governance of football and the search for alternative modes of governance which would allow greater involvement of key stakeholders in the game, notably supporters, managers and players. Two possibilities have been identified for a third way in the governance of football clubs. First, the principal of mutualization might be extended to football clubs, so that supporters would actually own the club itself. The principal practical obstacles here would be the need to buy out existing share capital – many hundreds of millions of pounds in Manchester United's case. Second, football clubs could adopt trust status, under which shares in the club would be held in trust and no dividends would be paid. Although, trust status has been successfully introduced at Northampton Town,[77] and appears, at the time of writing, to offer a genuine alternative for smaller clubs, at larger clubs the key obstacle would again be the cost of buying out existing institutional shareholders. The Department of Culture, Media and Sport has sponsored an initiative, 'Supporters Direct', to assist supporters to buy shares in their football clubs. Chris Smith, the then Culture Secretary, announced in 2000 that the government would finance the start-up costs of Supporters Direct but that thereafter the organization would arrange loans through the Cooperative Bank for fans wishing to invest in their clubs.[78] At the launch of Supporters Direct, Smith acknowledged that 'there is an increasing danger in these days of high finance that clubs can become separated from their fans'.[79] Unfortunately, the Blair government's tepid response to the recommendations of the Football Task Force's December 1999 report, *Football: Commercial Issues*, suggests little prospect of a radical overhaul of the governance (corporate or otherwise) of English football clubs.[80] If the governance of the richest and most widely broadcast league does not offer a progressive role model, there is little prospect of best practice in governance being diffused among world football's poorer national leagues and associations.

Conclusion

From this analysis of the governance of football, three conclusions, all with implications for the relationship between IR and sport, may be drawn. First, that private corporate interests are increasingly influencing the governance of professional football at all levels. In the case of UEFA, the introduction of a club-licensing scheme has been motivated partly by a desire to distance itself from FIFA by being seen to have a more transparent approach to the governance of European football. Second, that corporate interests' increasing role in the governance of football has focused attention upon the willingness of political authorities at the national, international and supranational levels to intervene in the governance of sport in general.

Only states and major political institutions, most notably the EU, possess the necessary power and resources to provide a framework for corporate governance and social responsibility that will ensure that the pursuit of private self-interest does not undermine the broader interests of sport as a whole. However, the willingness of political authorities to intervene in football's governance has not been consistent. At the national level, for example, in the UK, the Blair government was prepared to intervene to block the BSkyB takeover of Manchester United. Having suffered major political embarrassment as a consequence of its stewardship of the Millennium Dome project, the government has been more reluctant to assume responsibility for managing the redevelopment of Wembley, England's national stadium. This is despite the fact that not only does the project involve £120 million of National Lottery funding but also the repeated delays in the project have led indirectly to the embarrassing inability of London to host the 2005 World Athletics Championship (as outlined by Aaron Beacom in Chapter 6) because of the absence of a suitable alternative venue during Wembley's redevelopment. The prospects of successful future British bids for the World Cup and Olympic Games have consequently receded.

At the supranational level of governance, the EU has demonstrated a greater willingness to intervene in the governance of European football. The landmark European Court of Justice judgment in December 1995, on the case bought by Jean-Marc Bosman, a Belgian professional footballer, concerning the freedom of movement of workers in the European single market, has led to an active role for the European Commission in the negotiation of a new set of rules to govern football's labour markets with a FIFA/UEFA task force. At the same time, in recognition of the fact that one-third of the population of the EU member states regularly engage in sporting activity and the EU's 600,000 sports club constitute the largest social network in Europe, the European Commission has concluded that it, together with the EU's member states and sporting federations, can make 'an effective contribution to the promotion in Europe of sport that is true to its social role, while ensuring that the organizational aspects assimilate the new economic order'.[81] However, the EU's capacity to play a more proactive role in the governance of sport in general will continue to be constrained by the fact that none of its member states has made special provision for sport in its respective national legislation or has, at best, only granted special provisions on a case-by-case basis.[82]

Our third conclusion is that the governance of sport demonstrates that the challenge for IR in general and IPE in particular is to develop conceptual frameworks and research methodologies that will enable the development of a better understanding of the role of private actors in the transition from government to governance. The multi-level governance of professional football illustrates the extent to which political authority over sport is much more diffused between football associations, clubs, league representatives and corporate interests, notably those who now control broadcasting rights and increasingly own major football clubs. Nor can the governance of sport be entrusted primarily to corporate interests. This is because the arenas of politics and markets are not necessarily characterized by the same principles of social organization, and the morality of the market and the private interests of corporations may not coincide with either the morality of politics or the general interest of sport as a whole.[83]

Epilogue

ROGAN TAYLOR

To someone such as myself writing from outside the IR discipline, it should be obvious that sport has a considerable impact on international affairs. Sport as a 'fan-experience' is essentially about relationships, and those sports that send their taproots deep into communities and nations have always been felt as strong promoters of an acute sense of identity. The dealings between Australia and Britain for example are conducted (in the public mind) almost solely on the fields of various sports. Who knows of what the dialogue between the *governments* of these two nations consists? Do we care? But when it comes to producing a rugby or cricket team capable of beating the Aussies, millions of Brits really do care. They want to know how the Australians have learnt consistently to produce such great players; how they organize their sport and what we can learn from them.

Perhaps we should not be too surprised, though, by the apparent absence of academic analysis of sport's impact on international relations (a lacuna this volume has attempted to fill). Even the disciplines most clearly relevant for the study of sport and society – history and sociology – took a century to take sport seriously, especially a sport like association football which was deemed (despite its high-born origins) to 'belong' to the working class and, therefore, somehow to be unworthy of such considerations.

Yet football was – and remains – one of the most powerful prisms through which relations of many kinds can be refracted and seen more clearly. As Simon Lee points out to good effect in his chapter on governance, the metaphorical power of football to illustrate the 'political economy of English society' is potent: growing gaps between rich and poor in football over the past decade and a half mirror what has happened in Britain over the same period. If you look at issues such as nationalism, gender, race, class, ownership and local and national politics, sport in general, and football in particular, is a useful microcosm of its host society. But it is in the field of *identity-formation* that some sports seem to occupy positions of most significance; and here football appears – at least throughout most of the world – pre-eminent. As all human relations proceed from a sense of 'self' (experienced individually or as a group), the power of football to contribute, both positively and negatively, to the formation of that sense for many millions of people is surely worthy of our best academic efforts.

One of the most fascinating aspects of sport's, especially football's, impact on perceptions of identity is its ability to operate on so many levels. It seems to 'work' from the most local to the national levels with consummate ease. Football teams that represent a pub, a street, a school or a district of a small town can stimulate the most passionate emotions and identifications. In these examples, football may only affect small numbers of people in each case, but the intensity of feeling it generates can equal – even surpass – that which exists among much larger numbers when a team representing the nation as a whole runs out onto the pitch. It matters little whether the 'sense of community' and one's identity with it is 'real' in easily measurable ways. Benedict Anderson's 'imagined communities' are what count here. Communities are constructed in realms other than the concrete; the living sense of community exists, in part, as an act of imagination and in an emotional ether. Its realm is partly 'ethereal' and – in accordance with a very long tradition of all human society – it is constructed through distinctive myths and dramas, tales of heroes and villains, and the collective and contrasting experiences of joy and pain. Rather like a football match.

That football promotes a sense of nationhood where nothing else seems to is a commonplace observation today. They say 'Italy' only really exists as a nation (as opposed to a bunch of rival city-states and regions) when the *Azzurri* run onto a football field, and that is true of a number of more recently (and artificially) constructed nations, especially in Africa where colonial powers drew boundaries without any recognition of the real 'borders', defined by common language and culture. Yet football can just as easily *divide* a nation (as when a club from the north of Italy plays one from the south), illustrating football's promiscuity in the identification process. Football will serve any master, as many politicians have discovered.

Football's ability to help construct senses of identity and communal solidarity would undoubtedly 'work' at levels higher than the national. Those politicians keen to promote a sense of community in the European Union, for example, probably hanker after an 'EU United' team as the most effective means of putting the 'Community' on Europe's emotional map. Inter-continental football matches – Africa v South America; Asia v Europe – would surely trigger strong identity-support among otherwise very disparate peoples within a continent. And if we could find football-playing space creatures out there, the Earth v Planet Zog match would be huge, as the entire human race got behind 'our boys', regardless of which nation or continent they came from.

The sense of identity and solidarity that sport can promote, at national or other levels, can serve just as easily as a form of resistance to political norms. Sport may have been used in the old Soviet bloc for undisguised propagandist purposes, as Peter Beck indicates in his chapter, but it also worked against those prevailing values. For example, almost any form of nationalism among the satellite nations within the post-war Soviet bloc was viewed with deep suspicion in Moscow. Yet the peoples of Czechoslovakia,

Poland, Hungary and so on felt the victories of their own teams as an expression of the superiority of their own nations (not of socialism). Victories over the Soviets themselves were, of course, sweetest of all.

The great Hungarian football team of the post-war period, with its tremendous run of victories (losing but one match in the six years from 1950 to 1956), brought untold joy to their compatriots, not as an example of 'socialist organization' but as an expression of 'Magyar magic'. The sorrow inflicted by that one loss (in the World Cup Final of 1954) not only triggered street riots and disorder at home but also became a prelude to the great Hungarian uprising 18 months later.

One of the few remaining countries still dominated by a form of Stalinism, North Korea, has been considerably affected by the part-hosting of World Cup 2002 by its 'other half', the Republic of South Korea. The late bid to host 2002 by the republic (against a Japan that had assumed victory with the support of then FIFA President, João Havelange) was given added romantic power by KFA President Dr Chung Mong Joon's stated aim to use the World Cup as a way of re-uniting the two Koreas. In the end, of course, 2002 was shared between Japan and Korea, but that did not prevent the South Korean government from offering to play some matches in North Korea and – though such proposals were eventually dismissed – the offer itself was highly significant.

Despite strong censorship by the North Korean state, news of the World Cup (and of South Korea's tremendous success in reaching the semi-finals) could not be kept from large numbers of the population in the North. Illegal broadcasts of matches on radio and TV – and broadcasts by the state TV channel (which tried to block out the stadium advertisements so it wasn't obvious the matches were being played in South Korea!) – prevented a complete blackout. At the end of the World Cup, Dr Chung duly received congratulations from his counterpart in the North and – as a direct result – the '2002 South-North Unification football match' was played in Seoul in early September. The stadium was sold out; no national flags were allowed in order to avoid embarrassment and only a 0–0 draw marred the occasion. North Korea decided to send a delegation of athletes and officials to the South (the first time in half a century) to take part in the Asian Games in Busan at the end of September. Even TV crews from Europe and China are finding their way into the North to interview the Koreans who performed so well in the 1966 World Cup (when North Korea beat Italy) and talk to athletes.

Clearly football and sport in general can't work miracles in the field of international relations. Even though, at the time of writing there appears to be an impasse, here are many profound reasons why North Korea has sought to end its isolation, not least the almost complete collapse of its economy and widespread starvation among its people. Nor should one overlook the importance of the *personal* ambitions of individual politicians like Dr Chung, who reportedly sees himself as the first president of a unified Korea. But football has been used very effectively as the driver in accomplishing a transition across considerable diplomatic impasse; and athletics is another 'field' on which the new relationship can be prosecuted. Sport in international relations is like sex for separated couples: it can provide the *ground* on which relations can be resumed under the stimulus of desire.

It can also, of course, lead to divorce. The current crisis at FIFA and the long-standing friction between the world footballing body and UEFA are potential sources of a major rift in 'international relations' (and potentially profitable areas for further IR analysis). The situation at FIFA is not unlike the state of play in England in the late 1980s. The oldest 'football family' in the business – the Football League – was about to fall apart. The big clubs were unhappy with the league's 'democracy' which ensured that the money they were largely responsible for delivering was distributed among every member. FIFA President Blatter has been accused of ensuring his position by buying the votes of numerous 'small' footballing nations through various FIFA schemes to redistribute its money. But where does that money come from? The 'big' football countries, most of which are in Europe and whose presence in the World Cup guarantees the hugely valuable TV rights revenue from which FIFA derives most of its income.

What is to stop UEFA – or a group of countries within UEFA –inviting Brazil, Argentina and a couple of the leading African nations to join them in a 'premier' World Cup? President Blatter wouldn't have much money left to shore up his position with the TV rights revenues from a'Rest of the World' competition. And what would his position be worth in terms of power?

The possibility of 'divorce' in world football is currently largely unspoken but when the tail seeks to wag the dog too often, the dog *usually* bites it off; many sports have seen the collapse of central organizing bodies and their 'championships'. The same 'market forces' and drives for power that forced the emergence of the English Premier League already operate in an increasingly neo-liberal 'globalized' world order and could operate in the international sporting arena. Just as 'globalization' coexists with a simultaneous fragmentation, expressed in, *inter alia*, the rise of religious fundamentalisms, nationalism, regionalism and economic regression in many parts of the world, so the existing unevenness and inequality in international sport would intensify.[1] The consequence for international relations of the potential atrophy of sporting links, reinforcing a wider fragmentation, could be a very serious destabilization and even, *in extremis*, disaster.

Notes

NOTES TO SERIES EDITOR'S FOREWORD

1. J.A. Mangan (ed.), *Sport in Europe: Politics, Class, Gender* (London: Frank Cass, 1999), Prologue, p.vii.
2. Ibid.
3. Ibid.
4. Ibid.

NOTES TO PROLOGUE

1. See Osvaldo Croci, 'Taking the Field: The EC and the Governance of European Football', paper presented at the 7th biannual EUSA International Conference, Madison, Wisconsin, 31 May–2 June 2001.
2. Peter J. Beck, 'For World Footballing Honours: England versus Italy, 1933, 1934 and 1939', in J.A. Mangan (ed.), *Europe, Sport, World: Shaping Global Society – European Sports History Review*, 3 (London: Frank Cass, 2001).
3. Antonio Missiroli, 'European Football Cultures and their Integration: The "Short" Twentieth Century', *Culture, Sport, Society*, 5, 1 (Spring 2002).

NOTES TO INTRODUCTION

1. Such criticism has also been extended to political science. In 1998 Lincoln Allison wrote that 'Political science lags behind social history and sociological theory in its contributions to the academic understanding of sport'. See L. Allison, 'Sport and Civil Society', *Political Studies*, 46, 4 (1998), p.709.
2. T. Taylor, 'Sport and International Relations', in L. Allison (ed.), *The Politics of Sport* (Manchester: Manchester University Press, 1986), p.29.
3. R. Levermore, review of J. Coakley and E. Dunning (eds), *Handbook of Sports Studies* (London: Sage, 2000), *Millennium: Journal of International Studies*, 30, 2 (2001).
4. A number of articles have been published in other languages on sport and IR. For example, in France, P. Arnaud and A. Wahl (eds), *Sports et relations internationales* (Metz: Centre de Recherche, 1994); in Poland, G. Mtodzikowski, 'Sport we wepolczesnych stosunkach miedzynarodowych' [Sport in contemporary international relations], *Sprawy miedzynarodowe*, 26, 4 (April 1973).
5. B. Lowe, *Sport and International Relations* (Champaign, IL: Stipes Publishing Co, 1978).
6. B. Houlihan, *Sport and International Politics* (Hemel Hempstead: Harvester Wheatsheaf, 1994).
7. M. Shapiro, 'Representing World Politics: The Sport/War Intertext', in M. Shapiro and J. Der Derian (eds), *International/Intertextual Relations – Postmodern Readings of World Politics* (Lexington, MA: D.C. Heath, 1989).
8. J. Riordan and A. Krüger, *The International Politics of Sport in the 20th Century* (London and New York: E. & F.N. Spon, 1999).
9. M. Szczepaniak, 'The Role of Sports in International Relations', *Indian Journal of Politics*, XV, 1 & 2 (1981).
10. H. Kyröläinen and T. Varis, 'Approaches to the Study of Sports in International Relations',

Current Research on Peace and Violence, 1 (1981).

11. J. Galtung, 'Sport as a Carrier of Deep Culture and Structure', *Current Research on Peace and Violence*, 5, 2 & 3 (1982).

12. C.R. Hill, 'Keeping Politics in Sport', *The World Today*, July 1996.

13. P. Boniface, 'Football as a Factor (and a Reflection) of International Politics', *The International Spectator*, XXXIII, 4 (1998).

14. L. Allison and T. Monnington, 'Sport, Prestige and International Relations', *Government and Opposition*, 37, 1 (Winter 2002).

15. Lowe, *Sport and International Relations*, p.v.

16. Szczepaniak, 'The Role of Sports in International Relations', p.248.

17. Allison and Monnington, 'Sport, Prestige and International Relations', p.106.

18. B. Keys, 'Sport and International Relations: A Research Guide', *The SHARF Newsletter*, March 2002, p.7.

19. J. Rosenau, *Linkage Politics* (New York: The Free Press, 1969).

20. R. Keohane and J. Nye, *Power and Interdependence*, 2nd edn (New York: HarperCollins, 1989), p.4.

21. Ibid., p.25.

22. R.W. Cox (ed.), *The New Realism: Perspectives on Multilateralism and World Order* (London: Macmillan, 1997), p.xvi.

23. For the pioneering application of Gramsci's thought to IR, see R.W. Cox, 'Social Forces, States, and World Orders: Beyond International Relations Theory', *Millennium: Journal of International Studies*, 10, 2 (Summer 1981).

24. The idea of a transnationalism has been developed in the neo-Gramscian tradition, and especially by members of the 'Amsterdam School'. Key writers here are Henk Overbeek, Kees van der Pijl, Bastian van Apeldoorn, Magnus Ryner and Otto Holman.

25. Leslie Sklair captures the abiding, but circumscribed, importance of states when he writes of his 'attempt to transcend the contradictions of a state-centrism that fails to recognize the global, and a globalism that fails to recognize the persistence of states': *Globalization. Capitalism and its Alternatives*, 3rd edn (Oxford: Oxford University Press, 2002), p.7.

26. A. Giddens, *The Consequences of Modernity* (Cambridge: Polity, 1990), p.64; D. Harvey, *The Condition of Postmodernity* (Oxford: Blackwell, 1989).

27. Sklair, *Globalization, Capitalism and its Alternatives*, p.9.

28. J. Maguire, *Global Sport. Identities, Societies, Civilizations* (Cambridge: Polity, 1999).

29. K. Ohmae, *The Borderless World* (London: 1990).

30. H. Patomäki, *After International Relations: Critical Realism and the (Re)construction of World Politics* (London: Routledge, 2002), pp.4–5.

31. S. Smith, 'Is the truth out there? Eight questions about international order', in T.V. Paul and J.A. Hall (eds), *International Order and the Future of World Politics* (Cambridge: Cambridge University Press, 1999), p.99.

32. See A. Sayer, *Realism and Social Science* (London: Sage, 2002), especially chapter 2.

33. See C. Enloe, *Maneuvers: The International Politics of Militarizing Women's Lives* (Berkeley, CA: University of California Press, 1999); C. Enloe, *Bananas, Beaches and Bases* (Berkeley, CA: University of California Press, 1990); C. Enloe, *The Morning After: Sexual Politics at the End of the Cold War* (Berkeley, CA: University of California Press, 1993); R.B.J. Walker, 'Gender and Critique in the Theory of International Relations', in V. Spike Peterson (ed.), *Gendered States: Feminist (Re)Visions of International Relations Theory* (Boulder, CO and London: Lynne Rienner, 1992); A. Jones, 'Does "Gender" Make the World Go Round? Feminist Critiques of International Relations', *Review of International Studies*, 22, 4 (1996); and A. Jones, 'Engendering Debate', *Review of International Studies*, 24, 2 (1998).

34. A. Callinicos, *Against the Third Way* (Cambridge: Polity, 2001), p.93.

35. See, for example, Cox, *The New Realism*. This contains a useful list of other publications under the MUNS programme.

36. K. Blanchard, 'The Anthropology of Sport', in Coakley and Dunning, *Handbook of Sports Studies*, p.151.

NOTES TO CHAPTER 1

1. This chapter is based in part on a paper presented to the 'Sport and IR 2' panel at the Annual

Conference of the British International Studies Association (BISA), University of Bradford, 19 December 2000. I would like to express my gratitude to Stephen Essex, Mike Pugh, Neil Cooper, Ian Bailey (all University of Plymouth) and Costas Constantinou (University of Keele) for their comments.

2. It is recognized that these terms are notoriously difficult to define. However, for the purpose of this chapter nation is defined as a group of people believing they belong to the same group, which may (or not) co-exist within state boundaries. A nation-state is a territorial entity that usually includes more than one national community. The primary form of global political interaction is between state units and is therefore termed inter-state rather than international.

3. C. Weber, *Simulating Sovereignty – Intervention, the State and Symbolic Exchange* (Cambridge: Cambridge University Press, 1995), p.1.

4. K. Waltz, *Theory of International Relations* (New York: McGraw-Hill, 1979), p.95.

5. J. Mayall, *Nationalism and International Society* (Cambridge: Cambridge University Press, 1990), pp.7–8.

6. For a detailed discussion of the reading and justification of relating the contemporary world to ancient Greece, see Mayall, *Nationalism and International Society*, pp.8–9. For instance, Hinsley asserts that the modern attributes of the ancient Greek system of diplomacy operated the same balance of power system as the contemporary inter-state structure: F.H. Hinsley, *Nationalism and the International System* (London: Hodder & Stoughton, 1973), pp.67–72.

7. M. Norman, 'Imagine There's No Racism', *London Evening Standard*, 12 Oct. 2000, p.15.

8. For a more comprehensive discussion see E.J Hobsbawm, 'Inventing Traditions', *The Invention of Tradition* (Cambridge: Cambridge University Press, 1983).

9. J.R. Llobera, *The God of Modernity – The Development of Nationalism in Western Europe* (Oxford: Berg, 1994), p.ix.

10. As quoted in S. Redhead, *Post-Fandom and the Millennial Blues – The Transformation of Soccer Culture* (London: Routledge, 1997), p.42.

11. A. Linklater, 'The Achievements of Critical Theory', in S. Smith et al. (eds), *International Theory: Positivism and Beyond* (Cambridge: Cambridge University Press, 1996), pp.282–4.

12. P. de Coubertin, *The Olympic Idea: Discourses and Essays* (Stuttgart: Verlag Karl Hoffman, 1967). De Coubertin is known as the founder of the modern Olympic movement.

13. J. Galtung, 'Sport as a Carrier of Deep Culture and Structure', *Current Research on Peace and Violence*, 5 (1982), p.143.

14. BBC online, 'Wargames: when sport gets serious', http://news.bbc.co.uk/hi/english/special_report/1999/02/99/e-cycolpedia/ne.../363381.st, posted 8 June 1999, accessed 18 March 2001.

15. Quoted in H. Kyröläinen and T. Varis, 'Approaches to the Study of Sports in International Relations', *Current Research on Peace and Violence*, 4, 1 (1981), pp.72–3.

16. Translated from Liberation, printed in the *Independent*, 2 July 1998, p.23.

17. Quoted from www.easports.com/98/fifa/index.html, accessed 10 July 1998.

18. Sample of a 'hooligan' website, quoted from D. Campbell, 'England fans pour in for trouble', *Observer*, 11 June 2000, p.5.

19. 'Football's coming home, whatever that may be', *Guardian*, 19 June 2000, p.18.

20. 'Sunsport Message to Kevin Keegan', *Sun*, 17 June 2000, p.104. This headline had a double meaning, playing on England manager Kevin Keegan's comments made in the mid-1990s, referring to his desire for Newcastle United to defeat Manchester United when he managed Newcastle.

21. O. Holt, 'Hooligans bring England to brink', *The Times*, 19 June 2000, p.5.

22. An example of this took place in Tavistock, Devon, where a house where a German woman lived was attacked. See C. Morton, 'Thugs target German woman', *Plymouth Evening Herald*, 20 June 2000, p.1.

23. This is not so say that the existence of boundaries does not have very real consequences or that boundaries are not treated as being 'real'.

24. B. Wedemeyer, 'Sport and Terrorism', in J. Riordan and A. Krüger (eds), *International Politics of Sport in the Twentieth Century* (London: E. & F.N. Spon, 1999), p.220.

25. J. Sugden and A. Tomlinson, *FIFA and the Contest for World Football – Who Rules the Peoples Game?* (Cambridge: Polity, 1998), p.9.

26. P.N. Nkwi and B. Vidacs, 'Football: Politics and Power in Cameroon', in G. Armstrong and R. Giulianotti, *Entering the Field: New Perspectives on World Football* (Oxford: Berg, 1997), p.128.

27. Sugden and Tomlinson, *FIFA and the Contest for World Football*, p.9.

28. S. O'Brien, *Planet Football*, Channel 4 television (UK), 1 June 1998.

29. Elias's theory is discussed in detail in N. Elias and E. Dunning, *Quest For Excitement: Sport and Leisure in the Civilizing Process* (Oxford: Basil Blackwell, 1986), pp.16–21.
30. Sugden and Tomlinson, *FIFA and the Contest for World Football*, p 7.
31. *Independent*, 7 July 1998.
32. Over a report by A. Martin, *Independent*, 14 July 1998.
33. *Independent*, 10 July 1998.
34. R. Lloyd Parry, 'Arriverderci, Italy: Koreans revel in a golden moment', *Independent*, 19 June 2002, p.5. B. Reade also argued that the official slogan of the 2002 World Cup should be 'two enemies, two World Cups', *Daily Mirror*, 1 June 2002.
35. G. Moore, 'The world tunes in for Mali's showcase', *Independent*, 18 Jan. 2002, p.22.
36. C. White, 'Durkin is ready to toe FIFA's tough line', *Independent*, 9 June 1998, p.29.
37. R. Boyes, 'Germany's turn to confront its shame', *The Times*, 23 June 1998, p.1.
38. Ibid., p.1.
39. De Coubertin, *The Olympic Idea*, p 131.
40. Armstrong and Giulianotti, *Entering the Field*, p.30.
41. G. Moore reported that it was the 'biggest celebration since the Allied liberation' ('Zidane is inspiration as France claim place in history', *Independent*, 13 July 1998, p.28).
42. Quoted in M. Walker, 'Fighting lovers out for revenge', *Guardian*, 4 July 1998, p.4.
43. J. Cowley, 'A long history of dignity in defeat', *The Times*, 2 July 1998, p.23.
44. These headlines and reports were analysed and shown by the BBC2 programme, *World Cup – What the Papers Say*, 4 July 1998.
45. Although many media outlets, including broadsheet 'quality' newspapers, were guilty of such rants, the *Sun* provided the most frequent examples of 'Argie-bashing'. The day after England defeated Argentina, the *Sun* (June 8 2002) devoted at least 17 pages to the victory. Headlines included 'Up Yours Senors', 'We wanted revenge... boy did we get it', and a cartoon (p.8) suggested that the victory would be used as justification for the Argentinian government to declare war over the Falkland Islands. Furthermore, there were reports of Diego Maradona's picture being burnt around the UK.
46. Kyröläinen and Varis, 'Approaches to the Study of Sports in International Relations', p.67.
47. S. Scharenberg,, 'Religion and sport', in Riordan and Krüger, *The International Politics of Sport in the Twentieth Century*, p.91.
48. J. MacClancy, 'Sport, Identity and Ethnicity', in J. MacClancy (ed.), *Sport, Identity, and Ethnicity* (Oxford: Berg, 1996), pp.1–20.
49. B. Anderson, *Imagined Communities* (London: Verso, 1992), p.104.
50. For a full discussion of these accounts see R. Falk, *The Promise of World Order* (London: Harvester Wheatsheaf, 1987); J.W. Burton, *World Society* (Cambridge: Cambridge University Press, 1972). A basic account of Mitrany's functionalism is provided by C. Brown, who asserts that 'Functionalism as a theory offers an account of international functional cooperation which attempts to transcend the state, and create a new global order, as does its offshoot, the world society approach': C. Brown, *Understanding International Relations* (Basingstoke: Macmillan, 1997), p.128.
51. Such as Linklater, 'The Achievements of Critical Theory'.
52. R. Jackson, 'Juridical Statehood in Sub-Saharan Africa', *Journal of International Affairs*, 46, 1 (Summer 1992).
53. O. Stuart, 'The Lions Stir: Football in African Society', in S. Wagg (ed.), *Giving the Game Away* (London: Leicester University Press, 1995), p.34.
54. J. Riordan, 'The Worker Sports Movement', in Riordan and Krüger, *The International Politics of Sport in the Twentieth Century*, p.106.
55. Sugden and Tomlinson, *FIFA and the Contest for World Football*, p.9.
56. Quoted from A Fan's *Guide to Euro 2000* (Nyon: UEFA, 2000).
57. Quoted in *Independent*, 30 Oct. 2000.
58. R. Giulianotti, 'Scotland's Tartan Army in Italy: The Case for the Carnivalesque', *The Sociological Review*, 39, 3 (1991).
59. See for instance J. Borneman and N. Fowler, 'Europeanization', *Annual Review of Anthropology*, 26 (1997).
60. L. Allison, 'Sport and Nationalism', in J. Coakley and E. Dunning (eds), *Handbook of Sports Studies*, London: Sage, 2000), p.348.
61. S. Kuper, *Football Against the Enemy* (London: Orion, 1994).
62. K. Clark, 'Soccer stretches Taleban rules', http://news.bbc.co.uk', 12 Aug. 2000, accessed 15

March 2001.
63. C. Bromberger, 'A third half for Iranian football', *Le Monde Diplomatique*, April 1998.
64. H. Pearson, 'Fifteen Days in FIFA-land: Harry Pearson's World Cup Travels', *When Saturday Comes Supplement*, Aug. 1998.
65. *Guardian*, 19 June 2000.
66. Translation from editorial in the French newspaper *Le Figaro*, published in *Independent*, 16 June 1998.
67. Editorial, *Guardian*, 11 July 1998.

NOTES TO CHAPTER 2

1. The ideas in this chapter were first explored in A. Budd, 'Capitalism, Sport and Resistance: Reflections', *Culture, Sport, Society*, 4, 1 (2001). That article was, in turn, stimulated by C. Bambery, 'Marxism and Sport', *International Socialism*, 73 (1996).
2. R. W. Cox, 'Social Forces, States, and World Orders', in R. W. Cox and T. Sinclair, *Approaches to World Order* (Cambridge: Cambridge University Press, 1996), p.100.
3. See J. Maguire, *Global Sport. Identities, Societies, Civilizations* (Cambridge: Polity, 1999), p.79.
4. Towards the end of 2001, Britain's footballers prepared for strike action over their union's share from television contracts, used to provide education and enhance non-sporting skills for the three-quarters of trainees that clubs discard, frequently with no alternative skills, before the age of 21. Class distinctions in football may be obscured by the high wages of the elite, but they persist.
5. For a discussion around these ideas see S. Meikle, *Essentialism in the Thought of Karl Marx* (London: Duckworth, 1985).
6. J. Rosenberg, *The Empire of Civil Society. A Critique of the Realist Theory of International Relations* (London: Verso, 1994), p.4.
7. E. Cashmore, *Making Sense of Sport* (London: Routledge, 1990), p.42.
8. J. Hoberman, 'Sport and ideology in the post-Communist age', in L. Allison (ed.), *The Changing Politics of Sport* (Manchester: Manchester University Press, 1993), p.17.
9. H. Vanderzwaag, *Toward a Philosophy of Sport* (London: Addison-Wesley, 1972), p.56.
10. K. Marx, *Capital Volume 1* (Moscow: Foreign Languages Publishers, 1954), pp.183–4.
11. K. Marx, *Grundrisse. Foundation of the Critique of Political Economy* (Harmondsworth: Penguin, 1973), p.507.
12. K. Marx, *Early Writings* (Harmondsworth: Penguin, 1975), p.326.
13. K. Marx and F. Engels, 'Manifesto of the Communist Party', in *Karl Marx. Selected Works, Volume 1* (London: Lawrence & Wishart, 1942), pp.208–9.
14. See J. Holloway, 'Global Capital and the National State', in W. Bonefeld and J. Holloway (eds), *Global Capital, National State and the Politics of Money* (London: Macmillan, 1996).
15. C. Harman, 'The State and Capitalism Today', *International Socialism*, 51 (1991).
16. On the relationship between capitalism and democracy, see E. M. Wood, *Democracy Against Capitalism. Renewing Historical Materialism* (Cambridge: Cambridge University Press, 1995). On the evacuation of parliamentary power in Britain see P. Gowan, 'T[RTF bookmark start: _Hlt529627111][RTF bookmark end: _Hlt529627111]he Origins of the Administrative Elite', *New Left Review*, 162 (March/April 1987).
17. B. Anderson, *Imagined Communities: Reflections on the Origin and Spread of Nationalism* (London: Verso, 1983); I. Wallerstein, *Utopistics. Or, Historical Choices for the Twenty-first Century* (New York: The New Press, 1998), p.21. T. Magdalinski, 'Organised Memories: The Construction of Sporting Traditions in the German Democratic Republic', in J.A. Mangan (ed.), *Sport in Europe. Politics, Class, Gender* (London and Portland, OR: Frank Cass, 1999), p.144, refers to the state-orchestrated 'organisation of forgetting and remembering' in her analysis of identity formation through sport in post-war East Germany. Exclusionary attempts to mask class antagonisms led Lenin, for example, to demand citizenship rights for immigrants, for fear that international solidarity would otherwise be weakened.
18. M. Chamberlain, *The New Imperialism* (London: The Historical Association, 1970), p.38.
19. N. Bukharin, *Imperialism and World Economy* (London: Merlin, 1987), p.62.
20. J. Hargreaves, 'Sport, Culture and Ideology', in J. Hargreaves (ed.), *Sport, Culture and Ideology* (London: Routledge & Kegan Paul, 1982), p.41.
21. On the exploitation of sportswear workers in Asian sweatshops see J. Pilger, *The New Rulers of the World: A Special Report* (ITV, 18 July 2001), and J. Pilger, 'Spoils of a Massacre', *Guardian*

weekend magazine, 14 July 2001.
22. See S. Greenfield and G. Osborn, *Regulating Football. Commodification, Consumption and the Law* (London: Pluto, 2001), p.195.
23. J. Maguire, *Global Sport,* p.148.
24. See D. Smith, 'The Mysterious Shadow of the Ronaldo Affair', *Independent,* 7 Aug. 1998.
25. J. Ryan, *Little Girls in Pretty Boxes: The Making and Breaking of Elite Gymnasts and Figure Skaters* (London: Women's Press, 1996), pp.3–4. Catherine Louveau, 'Golden, But Still Girls', *Le Monde Diplomatique* (English edition), Oct. 2000, makes a number of important points about the position of women in contemporary sport.
26. H. Braverman, *Labour and Monopoly Capitalism* (New York: Monthly Review Press, 1974).
27. Cashmore, *Making Sense of Sport,* p.62.
28. Braverman, *Labour and Monopoly Capitalism,* p.278.
29. Milan and Genoa's football teams still go by their English names; Argentina, whose first Football Association president in 1893 was a British businessman named Alexander Watson Hutton, has a team called Newell's Old Boys; Juventus's strip is reputed to be a copy of that of Notts County and Athletic Bilbao's of Sunderland; and the forerunner of Moscow Dynamo, Orekhovo Sports Club, was established by two Blackburn entrepreneur brothers – Dynamo still plays in Blackburn's colours. British workers introduced football to Romania, to Russia via St Petersburg, to Uruguay in the Penarol rail yards and so on.
30. W. Vamplew, 'Sport and Industrialization: An Economic Interpretation of the Changes in Popular Sport in Nineteenth-Century England', in J.A. Mangan (ed.) *Pleasure, Profit and Proselytism* (London and Portland, OR: Frank Cass, 1988), p.12.
31. C. Mercer, 'A Poverty of Desire: Pleasure and Popular Politics', *Formations of Pleasure* (London: Routledge & Kegan Paul, 1983), p.89.
32. A. Harvey, 'Football's Missing Link: The Real Story of the Evolution of Modern Football', in Mangan, *Sport in Europe*; R.W. Lewis, '"Touched Pitch and Been Shockingly Defiled": Football, Class, Social Darwinism and Decadence in England, 1880–1914', in Mangan, *Sport in Europe.*
33. See M. Weber, *Gesammelte politische Schriften* (Munich, 1921), pp.140–2, discussed in G. Lukacs, *History and Class Consciousness* (London: Merlin, 1971) pp.95–6.
34. Cashmore, *Making Sense of Sport,* p.59.
35. The so-called socialist states – USSR, China, those in eastern Europe and so on – were also located within this capitalist world system. They were not hermetically sealed from external processes and while their competition with the West was not chiefly of a commodity form, the military competition that shaped East-West relations imparted to these states a similar imperative to exploit workers and accumulate. Industry was not owned as personal property, although effective economic control was in the hands of a tiny percentage of the population, but from the standpoint of a global mode of production it was private property in the sense that it was demarcated and differentiated from property owned outside the states concerned. Thus these states are best understood as state-capitalist.
36. Lewis, '"Touched Pitch and Been Shockingly Defiled"', p.118.
37. E. Hobsbawm, 'Mass-producing Traditions: Europe, 1870–1914', in E. Hobsbawm and T. Ranger (eds), *The Invention of Tradition* (Cambridge: Cambridge University Press), p.298.
38. Cashmore, *Making Sense of Sport,* p.171.
39. The American Communist Party led an attempted boycott of the Berlin Olympics. Avery Brundage, president of the US Olympic Committee and later of the IOC, argued that 'certain Jews must now understand that they cannot use these Games as a weapon in their boycott against the Nazis' (quoted in P. Hain, 'The Politics of Sport and Apartheid', in Hargreaves, *Sport, Culture and Ideology,* p.233). That the Nazis used the Olympic Games to assert Aryan supremacy did not cause him such concern.
40. Quoted in J. Rees, *The Algebra of Revolution. The Dialectic and the Classical Marxist Tradition* (London: Routledge, 1998), p.221.
41. Marx, *Capital Volume 1,* p.171.
42. N. Geras, *Marx and Human Nature. Refutation of a Legend* (London: Verso, 1983), p.96.
43. G. Williams, 'The Concept of "Egemonia" in the Thought of Antonio Gramsci', *Journal of the History of Ideas,* 21 (1960), p.587.
44. J. A. Mangan and C. Hickey, 'English Elementary Education Revisited and Revised: Drill and Athleticism in Tandem', in Mangan, *Sport in Europe,* p.63.
45. K. Marx, 'The Eighteenth Brumaire of Louis Bonaparte', in *Karl Marx. Selected Works, Volume 2* (London: Lawrence & Wishart, 1942), p.315. Marx's ideas on religion can also be applied to

sport. For consumers of sport it can appear as a new religion, a distraction from social grievances and an 'opium of the people' which helps cement class rule. But Marx did not conceive religion simply as a form of ideological duping. For 'religious suffering is at one and the same time the expression of real suffering and a protest against real suffering. Religion is the sigh of the oppressed creature, the heart of a heartless world and the soul of soulless conditions. It is the opium of the people.' That the exploited and the oppressed sometimes require an opiate and 'illusions about their condition' is because they experience a 'condition that requires illusions' (K. Marx, 'A Contribution to the Critique of Hegel's Philosophy of Right. Introduction', in *Early Writings* (Harmondsworth: Penguin, 1975) p.244. The alienation, exploitation and oppression of the majority of humanity produces not only openness to soothing illusions about its conditions but also resistance.

46. D. Robins, 'Sport and Youth Culture', in Hargreaves, *Sport, Culture and Ideology*, p.145.
47. The ideas on resistance in this section derive in part from the analysis of agency in P. Anderson, *Arguments Within English Marxism* (London: Verso, 1980), ch.2
48. S. Kuper, *Football Against the Enemy* (London: Phoenix, 1994), pp.43–4.
49. Quoted in A. Tomlinson and G. Whannel (eds), *Five Ring Circus: Money, Power and Politics at the Olympic Games* (London: Pluto, 1984), p.28.
50. J. Wilson, *Politics and Leisure* (London: Allen & Unwin, 1988), p.23.
51. Saldanha argued 'I don't choose the President's ministry, and he can't choose my forward line'. Quoted in Kuper, *Football Against the Enemy*, p.201.
52. Ibid., p.198.
53. 'Modernization' is now well established. The 1990 manager Sebastiao Lazaroni argued that Brazil 'must become less playful' (quoted in Kuper, *Football Against the Enemy*, p.203). Capitalist development has not eradicated the shanties but has reduced the space available for play. Today the clubs recruit more heavily from schools and sports clubs and therefore from middle-class white kids.
54. See Kuper, *Football Against the Enemy*, p.175.
55. O. Bayer, *Futbol Argentino* (Buenos Aires: Editorial Sudamericano, 1990), quoted in Kuper, *Football Against the Enemy*, p.178. Reaction to enforced silence has been used to explain the widespread use of psychotherapy in Argentina.
56. N. Elias and E. Dunning, *Quest for Excitement: Sport and Leisure in the Civilizing Process* (Oxford: Blackwell, 1986).
57. Geras, *Marx and Human Nature*, p.108.
58. J. Wilson, *Politics and Leisure*, p.17.

NOTES TO CHAPTER 3

1. See, for example, A. Bairner, *Sport, Nationalism and Globalization* (Albany, NY: SUNY Press, 2001); R. Brookes, *Representing Sport* (London: Arnold, 2002); J. Maguire, *Global Sport* (Cambridge: Polity, 1999).
2. See, for example, G. Armstrong. and R. Giulianotti (eds), *Fear and Loathing in World Football* (Oxford: Berg, 2001); J. Sugden and A. Tomlinson, *FIFA and the Contest for World Football* (Cambridge: Polity, 1998); S. Wagg (ed.), *Giving the Game Away* (London: Leicester University Press, 1995).
3. D. Stevenson, 'Women, Sport and Globalization; Competing Discourses of Sexuality and Nation', *Journal of Sport and Social Issues*, 26, 2 (2002).
4. R.W. Connell, *Masculinities* (Berkeley, CA: University of California Press, 1995).
5. R.W. Connell, *Gender and Power* (London: Polity Press, 1987), p.183.
6. M. Mac an Ghail (ed.), *Understanding Masculinities* (Buckingham: Open University Press, 1996), p.105.
7. B. Humberstone, 'Femininity, Masculinity and Difference: What's Wrong with a Sarong?', in A. Laker (ed.), *The Sociology of Sport and Physical Education* (London: Routledge, 2002).
8. Connell, *Masculinities*, p.77.
9. R.W. Connell, 'An Iron Man: The Body and Some Contradictions of Hegemonic Masculinity', in M. Messner and D. Sabo (eds), *Sport, Men and the Gender Order: Critical Feminist Perspectives* (Champaign, IL: Human Kinetics, 1990), p.94.
10. See ibid.; Connell, *Masculinities*.
11. L. Bryson, 'Challenges to Male Hegemony in Sport', in Messner and Sabo, *Sport, Men and the*

Gender Order, p.173.

12. J.A. Mangan (ed.), *Making European Masculinities: Sport, Europe, Gender* (London and Portland, OR: Frank Cass, 2000), p.186 (emphasis in original).

13. See J.A. Mangan (ed.), *Shaping the Superman: Fascist Body as Political Icon – Aryan Fascism* (London and Portland, OR: Frank Cass, 1999); J.A. Mangan (ed.), *Superman Supreme: Fascist Body as Political Icon – Global Fascism* (London and Portland, OR: Frank Cass, 2000); J.A. Mangan, R. Holt and P. Lanfranchi (eds), *European Heroes: Myth, Identity, Sport* (London and Portland, OR: Frank Cass, 1996).

14. S. Lopez, *Women on the Ball: A Guide to Women's Football* (London: Scarlet Press, 1997), p.4.

15. J. Maguire, 'More Than a Sporting Touchdown: The Making of American Football in England, 1982–90', *Sociology of Sport Journal*, 7, 3 (1990).

16. M. Messner, 'Sport and Male Domination: The Female Athlete as Contested Ideological Terrain', *Sociology of Sport Journal*, 5, 3 (1988); M. Messner, *Power at Play: Sport and the Problem of Masculinity* (Boston, MA: Beacon Press, 1992); D. Sabo and J. Panepinto, 'Football Ritual and the Social Reproduction of Masculinity', in Messner and Sabo, *Sport, Men and the Gender Order*.

17. N. Christopherson, M. Janning and E. McConnel, 'Two Kicks Forward, One Kick Back: A Content Analysis of Media Discourses on the 1999 Women's World Cup Soccer Championship', *Sociology of Sport Journal*, 19, 2 (2002).

18. Lopez, *Women on the Ball*, p.111.

19. P. Hastie, 'Perceptions of Girls About Their Participation in Aussie Footy', *Women in Sport and Physical Activity Journal*, 2, 1 (1991).

20. See K. Pedersen, 'Friluftsliv Viewed from the Top of Europe', in P. Higgins and B. Humberstone (eds), *Celebrating Diversity: Learning by Sharing Cultural Differences* (Buckinghamshire: European Institute for Outdoor Adventure Education and Experiential Learning, 1998); B. Humberstone and P. Pedersen, 'Gender, Class and Outdoor Traditions in the UK and Norway', *Sport, Education and Society*, 6, 1 (2001).

21. J. Riordan, 'Chinese Women and Sport: Success, Sexuality and Suspicion' (unpublished paper, University of Surrey, 1996).

22. Brownwell (1995), 'Training the Body for China: Sports in the Moral Order of the People's Republic', cited in Riordan, 'Chinese Women and Sport', p.14.

23. See S. Ichimura and R. Naul, 'Cross-cultural Assessments and Attribution to Female Soccer: Japan and West Germany', in J. Standeven, K. Hardman and D. Fisher (eds), *Sport for All: Into the 90s: Proceedings of the 7th International Symposium for Physical Education* (Aachen: Germany: Meyer & Meyer Verlag, 1992) p. 220.

24. J. Lever, *Soccer Madness* (Chicago, IL: University of Chicago Press, 1983).

25. Lopez, *Women On the Ball*; Ichimura and Naul, 'Cross-cultural Assessments'.

26. L. Andersson, 'Women of Substance', *When Saturday Comes*, August 1995, p.12.

27. J. Williams and J. Woodhouse, 'Can Play, Will Play: Women and Football in Britain', in J. Williams and S. Wagg (eds), *British Football and Social Change: Getting into Europe* (London: Leicester University Press, 1991).

28. S. Shaw and J. Amis, 'Image and Investment: Sponsorship and Women's Sport', *Journal of Sport Management*, 15, 3 (2001).

29. J. Harris, 'Defending Like Women: An Interpretive Sociological Study of Female Collegiate Football Players' (unpublished Ph.D. thesis, Buckinghamshire Chilterns University College, Brunel University, 1998); J. Harris, 'Playing the man's game: sites of resistance and incorporation in women's football', *World Leisure*, 43, 4, 2001.

30. B. Cox and S. Thompson, 'Multiple Bodies: Sportswomen, Soccer and Sexuality', *International Review for the Sociology of Sport*, 35, 1 (2000).

31. S. Scraton, K. Fasting, G. Phister and A. Bunuel, 'It's Still a Man's Game? The Experience of Top Level Women Footballers in England, Germany, Norway and Spain', *International Review for the Sociology of Sport*, 34, 2 (1999).

32. Cox and Thompson, 'Multiple Bodies'; Harris, 'Defending like Women'.

33. J. Nauright and T.J.L. Chandler (eds), *Making Men: Rugby and Masculine Identity* (London and Portland, OR: Frank Cass, 1996), cited in J. Wright and G. Clarke, 'Sport, the Media and the Construction of Compulsory Heterosexuality: A Case Study of Women's Rugby Union', *International Review for the Sociology of Sport*, 34, 3 (1999), p.229.

34. Wright and Clarke, 'Sport, the Media and the Construction of Compulsory Heterosexuality'.

35. Cox and Thompson, 'Multiple Bodies'.

36. M. Kimmel, 'Series Editor's Foreword' in J. McKay, M. Messner and D. Sabo (eds),

Masculinities, Gender Relations and Sport (Thousand Oaks, CA: Sage) p.xiii. See also Christopherson, Janning and McConnel, 'Two Kicks Forward'.

37. Brookes, *Representing Sport*, p.138.

38. See for example, D. Davis, 'Portrayals of Women in Prime-network Television: Some Demographic Characteristics', *Sex Roles*, 23, 5/6 (1990); B. Luebke, 'Out of Focus: Images of Women and Men in Newspaper Photographs', *Sex Roles*, 20, 3/4 (1989); L. Vande Berg and D. Streckfuss, 'Profile: Prime-time Television's Portrayal of Women in the World of Work: A Demographic Profile', *Journal of Broadcasting and Electronic Media*, 36 (Spring 1992).

39. M. Duncan, 'Sports Photographs and Sexual Difference: Images of Women and Men in the 1984 and 1988 Olympic Games', *Sociology of Sport Journal*, 7, 1 (1990); M. Duncan and M. Messner, 'The Media Image of Sport and Gender', in L. Wenner (ed.), *Mediasport* (London: Routledge, 1998); M. Kane and H. Lenskyj, 'Media Treatment of Female Athletes: Issues of Gender and Sexualities', in Wenner, *Mediasport*.

40. A. Chisholm, 'Defending the Nation: National Bodies, US Borders, and the 1996 US Women's Gymnastics Team', *Journal of Sport and Social Issues*, 23, 2 (1999); J. Harris, 'Lie Back and Think of England: The Women of Euro 96', *Journal of Sport and Social Issues*, 23, 1 (1999); J. Harris and B. Clayton, 'Femininity, Masculinity, Physicality and the English Tabloid Press: The Case of Anna Kournikova', *International Review for the Sociology of Sport*, 37, 3-4 (2002), pp.397–414.

41. See for example, J. Hargreaves, *Sporting Females* (London: Routledge, 1994); R. Pirinen, 'Catching Up with Men? Finnish Newspapers' Coverage of Women's Entry into Traditionally Male Sports', *International Review for the Sociology of Sport*, 32, 3 (1997).

42. S. Billings, 'In search of Women Athletes: ESPN's List of the Top 100 Athletes of the Century', *Journal of Sport and Social Issues*, 24, 4 (2000).

43. B. Humberstone (ed.), *Her Outdoors: Risk, Challenge and Adventure in Gendered Open Spaces* (Eastbourne: Leisure Studies Association, 2000).

44. D. Rowe, J. McKay and T. Miller, 'Come Together: Sport, Nationalism and the Media Image', in Wenner, *Mediasport*.

45. R. Boyle and R. Haynes, *Power Play: Sport, the Media and Popular Culture* (London: Longman, 2000).

46. Stevenson, 'Women, Sport and Globalization'.

47. D. Hand, 'Football, Cultural Identities and the Media: A Research Agenda', www.leisure-tourism.com/ReviewsReports/Revi.../HandRvw.htm, accessed 25 June 2002; Harris, 'Lie Back and Think of England'.

48. S. Jansen and D. Sabo, 'The Sport/War Metaphor: Hegemonic Masculinity, the Persian Gulf War, and the New World Order', *Sociology of Sport Journal*, 11, 1 (1994).

49. L. Crolley, D. Hand and R. Jeutter, 'Playing the Identity Card: Stereotypes in European football', *Soccer and Society*, 1, 2 (2000).

50. Harris and Clayton, 'Femininity, Masculinity, Physicality and the English Tabloid Press'.

51. Hand, 'Football, Cultural Identities and the Media'.

52. Christopherson, Janning and McConnel, 'Two Kicks Forward', p.170.

53. B. Anderson, *Imagined Communities* (London: Verso, 1983).

54. E. Hobsbawm, *Nations and Nationalism since 1780* (Cambridge: Cambridge University Press, 1990).

55. Stevenson, 'Women, Sport and Globalization'.

56. J. Hargreaves, 'Outsiders in the Nation: Sport and Women on the Margins', paper presented at 'Sport and Nation' conference, Brunel University, June 2001.

57. H. Zaman, 'Islam, Well-being and Physical Activity: Perceptions of Muslim Young Women', in G. Clarke and B. Humberstone (eds), *Researching Women and Sport* (London: Macmillan, 1997).

58. Hargreaves, 'Outsiders in the Nation'.

NOTES TO CHAPTER 4

1. S. Krasner, 'Structural Causes and Regime Consequences: Regimes as Intervening Variables', in S. Krasner (ed.), *International Regimes* (Ithaca, NY: Cornell University Press, 1983), p.2.

2. See, for example, B. Houlihan, 'Anti-doping Policy in Sport: The Politics of International Policy Co-ordination', *Public Administration*, 77, 2 (1999); and B. Houlihan, 'Policy Harmonization: The Example of Global Anti-doping Policy', *Journal of Sport Management*, 13, 3 (1999).

3. W.W. Franke and B. Berendonk, 'Hormonal Doping and Androgenization of Athletes: A Secret Programme of the German Democratic Republic', *Clinical Chemistry*, 43 (1997).

4. B. Houlihan, *Dying to Win: Doping in Sport and the Development of Anti-doping Policy* (Strasbourg: Council of Europe Publishing, 1999).

5. Australian Senate, Senate Standing Committee on the Environment, Recreation and the Arts, *Drugs in Sport* (interim report) (Canberra: Australian Government Publishing Service, 1989).

6. Dubin Inquiry, *Commission of Inquiry into the Use of Drugs and Banned Practices Intended to Increase Athletic Performance* (Ottawa: Canadian Government Publishing Centre, 1990).

7. Ibid.

8. O.R. Young and G. Osherenko, 'Testing Theories of Regime Formation: Findings from a Large Collaborative Research Project', in V. Rittberger and P. Mayer (eds), *Regime Theory and International Relations* (Oxford: Clarendon Press, 1993), p.249.

9. A. Hasenclever, P. Mayer and V. Rittberger, *Theories of International Relations* (Cambridge: Cambridge University Press, 1997), p.26.

10. R.O. Keohane, *After Hegemony: Co-operation and Discord in the World Political Economy* (Princeton, NJ: Princeton University Press, 1984); R.O. Keohane, *International Institutions and State Power: Essays in International Relations Theory* (Boulder, CO: Westview Press, 1989).

11. S. Krasner, 'Sovereignty, Regimes and Human Rights', in V. Rittberger and P. Mayer (eds.), *Regime Theory and International Relations*.

12. Hasenclever, Mayer and Rittberger, *Theories of International Relations*, p.36.

13. S. Haggard and B.A. Simmons, 'Theories of International Regimes', *International Organisation*, 41, 3 (1983). See also M.A. Levy, R.O. Keohane and P.M. Haas, 'Improving the Effectiveness of International Environmental Institutions', in P.M. Haas, R.O. Keohane and M.A. Levy (eds), *Institutions for the Earth: Sources of Effective International Environmental Protection* (Cambridge, MA: MIT Press, 1993), and O.R. Young and G. Osherenko (eds), *The Politics of International Regime Formation: Lessons from Arctic Cases* (Ithaca, NY: Cornell University Press, 1993).

14. See, for example, V. Peppard and J. Riordan, *Playing Politics: Soviet Sport Diplomacy to 1992* (Greenwich, CT: JAI Press, 1993); B. Houlihan, *Sport and International Politics* (Hemel Hempstead: Harvester-Wheatsheaf, 1994); A. Strenk, 'Diplomats in Tracksuits: Linkages Between Sports and Foreign Policy in the GDR', *Journal of Sport and Social Issues*, 4, 1 (1980); D. Macintosh and D. Black, *Sport and Canadian Diplomacy* (Toronto: McGill-Queen's University Press, 1994).

15. H. Preuss, *Economics of the Olympic Games: Hosting the Games from 1972 to 2000* (Sydney: Walla Walla Press, 2000).

16. A. Moravcsik, 'The Origins of Human Rights Regimes: Democratic Delegation in Postwar Europe', *International Organization*, 54, 2 (2000).

17. B. Hughes, *Continuity and Change in World Politics: Competing Perspectives* (Upper Saddle River, NJ: Prentice Hall, 2000).

18. J.M. Grieco, 'Anarchy and the Limits of Co-operation: A Realist Critique of the Newest Liberal Institutionalism', *International Organization*, 42, 3 (1988); J.M. Grieco, *Co-operation Among Nations: Europe, America, and Non-tariff Barriers to Trade* (Ithaca, NY: Cornell University Press, 1990).

19. A. Wendt, *Social Theory of International Relations* (Cambridge: Cambridge University Press, 1999).

20. E.A. Nadelmann, 'Global Prohibition Regimes: The Evolution of Norms in International Society', *International Organisation*, 44, 4 (1990), p.480.

21. Ibid.

22. P.M. Haas, 'Introduction: Epistemic Communities and International Policy Co-ordination', *International Organisation*, 46, 1 (1992), p.3.

23. B. Houlihan, 'Anti-doping Policy in Sport'.

24. R.O. Keohane, P.M. Haas and M.A. Levy, 'The Effectiveness of International Environmental Institutions', in Haas, Keohane and Levy, *Institutions for the Earth*, p.24.

NOTES TO CHAPTER 5

1. 'President Nelson Mandela: UK-South Africa Sports Initiative Reception, Lancaster House', Sports Council press release, 11 July 1996.

2. N. Macfarlane (with M. Herd), *Sport and Politics: A World Divided* (London: Willow, 1986), p.7; R. Tracey, 'Today' programme, BBC Radio Four, 23 Sept. 1986.
3. *A Sporting Future For All* (London: Department of Culture, Media and Sport, 2000), p.48.
4. *Ambitions for Britain: Labour's Manifesto 2001* (London: The Labour Party, 2001), p.23.
5. *A Sporting Future For All*, p.2.
6. P. Clarke, *Hope and Glory: Britain 1900–1990* (London: Allen Lane, Penguin Press, 1996), p.53.
7. *A Sporting Future For All*, p.11.
8. J. Major, foreword, in *Sport: Raising The Game* (London: Department of National Heritage, 1995), p.ii.
9. J. Major, *The Autobiography* (London: HarperCollins, 1999), p.404.
10. J. Riordan, 'The Impact of Communism on Sport', in J. Riordan and A. Krüger (eds), *The International Politics of Sport in the 20th Century* (London: E. & F.N. Spon, 1999), p.56; B. Houlihan, *Sport, Policy and Politics: A Comparative Analysis* (London: Routledge 1997), pp.61–6.
11. D. Mackay, 'Australian Moffett lands Sport England job', *Guardian*, 6 Nov. 2001.
12. R.D. Mandell, *The Nazi Olympics* (New York: Macmillan, 1971), pp.165–6, pp.258–70; J. Entine, *Taboo: Why Black Athletes Dominate Sports and Why We Are Afraid to Talk About It* (New York: Public Affairs, 2000), p.186. The 1936 Winter Olympics were also held in Germany, at Garmisch-Partenkirchen.
13. Public Record Office (PRO), Sir Eric Phipps to S. Hoare, Foreign Secretary, 16 Dec. 1935, FO371/18884/C8362; Phipps to Hoare, 7 Dec. 1935, FO371/19647/10611; Hans von Tschammer und Osten, 'German Sport', in *Germany Speaks By 21 Leading Members of Party and State* (London: Thornton Butterworth, 1938), pp.219, 222.
14. A. Natan, 'Sport and Politics', in J.W. Loy, Jr., and G.S. Kenyon (eds.), *Sport, Culture and Society: A Reader on the Sociology of Sport* (New York: Collier-Macmillan, 1969), p.203.
15. B. Malitz, *Die Leibesübungen in der Nationalsozialistischen Idee* (Munich: Verlag Fritz Eher, 1933), translation in Committee on Fair Play in Sports, *Food for Thought* (New York: Committee on Fair Play in Sports, 1935), pp.4–5, 11–12.
16. Quoted, PRO, Phipps to Hoare, 16 Dec. 1935.
17. PRO, Phipps to Hoare, 16 Dec. 1935; minute, R. Vansittart, 31 Dec. 1935, FO371/18884/C8362; *Daily Herald*, 31 Dec. 1935
18. Churchill Archives Centre (CAC), Phipps Papers (PHPP), Phipps's diary, 11 Nov.1935, 14 May 1936, PHPP 10/2, pp.143, 215; PRO, Phipps to Eden, 13 Feb. 1936, FO371/19940/C930; Phipps to Foreign Office, 11 Nov. 1935, FO371/18863/C7600; minute, V. Lawford, 18 May 1936, FO371/19940/C3697; Duff Hart-Davis, *Hitler's Games: The 1936 Olympics* (New York: Harper & Row, 1986), pp.46–9.
19. R. Rhodes James (ed.), *Chips: The Diaries of Sir Henry Channon* (London: Weidenfeld & Nicolson, 1967), pp.105–12.
20. PRO, Phipps to Foreign Office, 1 Aug. 1936, FO371/19940/C5677; B. Newton, Berlin, to Eden, 18 Aug. 1936, FO371/19940/C5983.
21. PRO, Lord Lloyd to A. Eden, 22 Dec.1937, T161/907/S35581.
22. P.J. Beck, *Scoring for Britain: International Football and International Politics, 1900–1939* (London and Portland, OR: Frank Cass, 1999), p.10. See also P. Beck, 'For World Footballing Honours: England versus Italy, 1933, 1934 and 1939', *European Sports History Review*, 3 (2001), pp.245–66.
23. Beck, *Scoring for Britain*, pp.17–22, 225–7.
24. Modern Papers Room, Bodleian Library, Oxford University (BL), Conservative Party Archives (CRD), Chamberlain's Margate speech, 2 Oct. 1936, CRD 1/24/2, p.16.
25. Board of Education, *Physical Education in Germany* (London: National Advisory Council/HMSO, 1937), p.3; T. Mason, *Sport in Britain* (London: Faber & Faber, 1988), p.101; S.G. Jones, 'State Intervention in Sport and Leisure in Britain Between the Wars', *Journal of Contemporary History*, 22 (1987), 166.
26. PRO, Minute, H. Freese-Pennefather,10 Jan. 1946, E. Bevin to Viscount Portal, 15 Jan. 1946, FO371/54785/W454,
27. PRO, N. Brook, Cabinet Office, to Foreign Office, 25 Jan. 1946, FO371/54785/W1170; minutes of informal meeting held at Cabinet Office, 20 Feb. 1946, FO371/54785/W2423; minute, H. Freese-Pennefather, 13 March 1946, FO371/54785/W2926.
28. CAC, Noel-Baker Papers (NBKR), P. Noel-Baker to H. Gaitskell, 4 Nov.1947, NBKR6/2/1. Note that Noel-Baker had supported the British boycott campaign against the Berlin Olympics.

29. Lord Aberdare, 'The Olympiad in Britain', *Everybody's*, 1 June 1946, 5; PRO, N. Curtis Bennett to Attlee, 12 Jan. 1948, PREM 8/897.
30. PRO, Hector McNeil, Foreign Office, to Herbert Morrison, Lord President of the Council, 1 July 1947, FO953/4H/P852.
31. PRO, Minutes, Noel-Baker and Attlee, 22 April 1947, PREM8/897; Morrison, Lord President of the Council, 22 July 1948, Hansard Parliamentary Debates (House of Commons), vol.454, cols.569–570.
32. *Manchester Guardian*, 29 March 1948.
33. PRO, Cabinet, 27 March 1947, meeting 33 (47), CAB128/9; *Sunday Dispatch*, 31 Aug. 1947; *Evening Standard*, 2 Sept. 1947.
34. CAC, Noel-Baker to Morrison, Sept. 1947, NBKR6/6/1.
35. CAC, Noel-Baker to N. Brook, 25 Sept. 1947, NBKR6/6/1.
36. CAC, Noel-Baker to W. Laurie, 25 Sept. 1948, NBKR6/6/1; 'The Olympic Games in Retrospect', BBC Radio broadcast, 17 Aug. 1948, NBKR6/7/1; W.D. Clark, 'Olympiad XIV', *New Statesman*, 21 Aug. 1948.
37. PRO, Minute, Marius Cheke, 3 Aug. 1948, FO370/1593/L1872.
38. *Sunday Times*, 1 Aug. 1948.
39. BL, minute, C. Attlee, 7 July 1948, MS Attlee 72 folio 154; P. Llewellyn-Davies, Commonwealth Relations Office, to P. Beards, 17 July 1948, MS Attlee, folios 193–6.
40. BL, Attlee radio broadcast, 28 July 1948, MS Attlee 72, folio 251.
41. New Zealand submission, quoted in UNESCO, *The Place of Sport in Education: A Comparative Study* (Paris: UNESCO, 1956), p.55.
42. *Background Briefing: Sport in the Soviet Union* (London: Foreign and Commonwealth Office, 1980), p.1.
43. *The Times*, 4 Aug. 1952.
44. A. Strenk, 'Diplomats in Track Suits: The Role of Sports in the Foreign Policy of the German Democratic Republic', *Journal of Sport and Social Issues*, 4, 1 (1980).
45. Riordan, 'The Impact of Communism on Sport', p.48.
46. Entine, *Taboo*, p.311; Steve Kettmann, 'East German Dopers Guilty', *Wired News*, 18 July 2000.
47. J. Riordan, 'The USSR', in J. Riordan (ed.), *Sport under Communism: The USSR, Czechoslovakia, the GDR, Cuba* (London: Hurst, 1978), p.30; *Information Report: Sport behind the Iron Curtain* (London: Foreign Office, Sept. 1955), p.2.
48. Riordan, 'The Impact of Communism on Sport', p.57.
49. PRO, H. Hohler, 21 Feb. 1954, FO371/122750/NR1801; Hohler to Labouchere, 11 Dec. 1954, FO371/111496/NH1052.
50. PRO, minute, Gilchrist, 17 May 1951, FO371/93589/C2231/49. See memo by M. Berenson, n/d. (Feb.1952), FO371/98011/C1801.
51. PRO, minutes, Jellicoe, 30 Oct. 1954, Ward, 5 Nov. 1954, FO371/111792/NS1801.
52. PRO, minutes, Hohler, 4 Nov., J. Ward, 5 Nov., I. Kirkpatrick, 10 Nov. 1954, FO371/111792/NS1801.
53. PRO, Hohler to Saner, Budapest, 9 Oct. 1954, FO371/111496/NH1052; minute, Kirkpatrick, 10 Nov. 1954, FO371/111792/NS1801.
54. P. Wilson, 'Footballers Who Play in a Workers' Paradise', *Daily Mirror*, 24 Nov. 1953.
55. Quoted, *Daily Mirror*, 27 Nov. 1953.
56. B. Ferrier, 'Game's the Same, So Down We Go', *Daily Mirror*, 22 May 1954.
57. *The Times*, 26 May 1954.
58. PRO, memo by Sir Roger Makins, 11 Aug. 1951, FO371/124968/ZP24/2.
59. PRO, memo by Anthony Eden, 15 June 1952, CAB129/53, C (52) 202.
60. PRO, Sir Anthony Eden, 'Thoughts on the general position after Suez', 28 Dec. 1956, PREM 11/1138.
61. Memorandum of relations between United Kingdom, USA and France', 21 Oct. 1957, quoted in D. Dutton, *Anthony Eden: A Life and Reputation* (London: Arnold, 1997), p.452.
62. *The Times*, 13 May 1954. In the event, the trip had mixed results, given the cancellation of appearances on sponsored television programmes because of fears of infringing Bannister's amateur status.
63. J. Dunkley, '1953 and all that', *Daily Mirror*, 26 Nov. 1953.
64. P. Wilson, 'The Twilight of the (Soccer) Gods', *Daily Mirror*, 26 Nov. 1953.
65. E. Burton, 'Why Russia Beats Us at Our Games', *News of the World*, 7 Nov. 1954; CAC, Noel-Baker to S. Elliott, 25 Aug. 1954, NBKR6/12/1. A similar debate occurred in the USA: J.

McGovern, 'We'll Lose the Next Olympics: Unless We Can Combat the Russians' All-out Plan for World Sports Domination', *This Week Magazine*, 16 May 1954, pp.7, 16.

66. 'The Four-Minute Mile', *New York Herald Tribune*, 14 May 1954.
67. Houlihan, *Sport, Policy and politics: a comparative analysis*, pp.92-100.
68. Quoted in Beck, *Scoring for Britain*, p.34.
69. UN press release SG/SM/7036, 18 June 1999; FIFA Media Office, press release, 18 June 1999. See also P. Boniface, 'Football as a Factor (and a Reflection) of International Politics', *International Spectator*, 33, 4 (1998), pp.88–9.
70. *House of Commons Foreign Affairs Committee, Fourth Report 1986–87: Cultural Diplomacy*, Foreign and Commonwealth Office memorandum on Britain's overseas cultural relations, 6 March 1987, p.231.
71. *House of Commons Foreign Affairs Committee, Fourth Report 1986–87: Cultural Diplomacy*, minutes of evidence, 29 Oct. 1986, p.24.
72. Quoted in D. Russell, *Football and the English: a Social History of Association Football in England, 1863–1995* (Preston: Carnegie, 1997), p.208.
73. *Sport: Raising The Game*, p.35.
74. Britain was placed 36th in the medals table: Maurice Chittenden, 'Sports Academy Knocked for Six', *Sunday Times*, 13 Dec. 1998.
75. J. Layton, 'Those Who Think Australian, Play Australian', *Independent*, 31 July 2001; J. Alexander, 'Hussain Sketches Plans for Fresh Start', *Independent*, 3 Oct. 2001; D. Mackay, 'Australian Moffett Lands Sport England Job', *Guardian*, 6 Nov. 2001.
76. *Sprint: A Report on the Relationship Between Sport and Society, Education, the Arts and Gender* (London: The British Council, 1999), p.24, p.28.
77. *Sprint*, p.26; A. Hansen, 'Why Does Sport Matter?', *British Studies Now*, 11 (1999), pp.12–13; P. Beck, 'Britain, Image-building and the World Game: Sport's Potential as British Cultural Propaganda', in A. Chong and J. Valencic (eds), *The Image, the State and International Relations* (London: European Policy Unit, LSE, 2001), pp.58–66; British Council, *Through Other Eyes* (London: British Council, 1999) and British Council, *Through Other Eyes 2* (London: British Council, 2000). Both reports are available at http://www.britishcouncil.org/work/survey/reports. htm. Significantly, given its traditional role in promoting the English language, the British Council's website now includes a section on 'Football English': see http://www.footballculture.net.
78. P. van Haan, 'The Rise of the Brand State: The Postmodern Politics of Image and Reputation', *Foreign Affairs*, 80, 5 (2001), pp.3–4. Typically, this article, though identifying the contribution of, say, design, music and fashion to the 'Cool Britannia' campaign, ignores the role of sport.
79. See 'Dreams and Teams', http://www.britishcouncil.org, accessed 10 Sept. 2001.
80. 'Sport Chiefs Demand Ministry for Success', Yahoo! Headlines, 26 Aug. 1999, http://eur.rd..yahoo.com, accessed 28 Aug. 1999; *Guardian*, 27 Aug. 1999.
81. *A Sporting Future for All*, pp.2–3, 5, 15; press release 73/2000, Dept. for Culture, Media and Sport, 5 April 2000.
82. *Ambitions for Britain*, p.23.
83. *Guardian*, 9 Oct. 2001. See also Department for Culture, Media and Sport, *Staging International Sporting 2000.Events: Government Response to the Third Report from the Culture, Media and Sport Committee*, Cm.5288 (London: HMSO, 2001), pp.3–15.
84. 'We Aren't the Champions', *Daily Telegraph*, 6 Oct. 2001.
85. D. Mackay, 'Picketts Fiasco Harms London 2012 Bid', *Guardian*, 16 Oct. 2001.
86. 'Gold Medal Games: Any Olympic Bid Would Count on Manchester's example' (editorial), *The Times*, 5 Aug. 2002.
87. M. Garrahan, 'Athletics Body Refuses Request to Move Games', *Financial Times*, 6 Oct. 2001; B. Houlihan and A. White, *The Politics of Sport Development: Development of Sport or Development through Sport* (London: Routledge, 2002), pp.54–110.
88. For instance, neither Philip Taylor's *The Projection of Britain: British Overseas Publicity and Propoganda* (Cambridge: Cambridge University Press, 1981) nor Frances Donaldson's *The British Council: The First Fifty Years* (London: Jonathan Cape, 1984) integrate sport into the story.

NOTES TO CHAPTER 6

1. For example see K. Hamilton and R. Langhorne, *Diplomacy: Theory and Practice* (London:

Prentice Hall, 1995).

2. L. Allison (ed.), *The Changing Politics of Sport* (Manchester: Manchester University Press, 1993) pp.5–6, argues that there has been a retreat in the 'myth of autonomy' with the increasing acceptance of sport as integral to society and so part of the political process.

3. This is clearly evidenced in archive material relating to foreign office activity, held at the Public Records Office.

4. This realist perspective was encouraged by the experiences of cold war international sports diplomacy with its focus on the reflection of bi-polar political rivalry in sports competition between the USA and the USSR. The boycotts associated with the 1980 and 1984 Games further encouraged the adoption of this perspective at the expense of others.

5. General texts on diplomacy broadly reflecting this view include: A. Watson, *Diplomacy – The Dialogue between States* (London: Methuen Ltd., 1982) and R. Bartson, *Modern Diplomacy* (Harlow: Longman, 1988). G. Berridge, *Diplomacy – Theory and Practice*, 2nd edn (Basingstoke: Palgrave, 2002), p.1 argues that the chief purpose of diplomacy 'is to enable states to secure objectives of their foreign policies without resort to force, propaganda, or law'.

6. D. Dunn (ed.), *Diplomacy at the Highest Level* (London: Macmillan, 1996). p.1 in his introduction to 'summit diplomacy', described such practice as a 'product of the new diplomacy, that is diplomacy in the democratic age between open and accountable governments'. More recently, reference to public diplomacy – the attempt by diplomatic services to influence directly, public opinion abroad – has been presented as a 'new' phenomenon. See e.g. Berridge, *Diplomacy: Theory and Practice*, 2nd edn, pp.17–18. This despite evidence that the British Council were involved in such activity since its initiation in 1934.

7. The Commonwealth Games have also been the subject of intense diplomatic activity linked to boycott threats and concerns about the nature of regimes hosting the event.

8. A. Guttman, *From Ritual to Record: The Nature of Modern Sports* (New York: Columbia University Press, 1978) pp.22–3. Guttman notes that a study of the archaeological evidence of Greek religions teaches us that one can always please the gods by offering them music, poetry, drama and athletic contests. B. Peiser, 'Western Origins of Sport in Ancient China', *The Sports Historian*, 16 (May 1996). In his consideration of sport in ancient China, Peiser notes that archaeological evidence suggests physical (sportive) activities almost exclusively took place during cultic festivals, showing the immense significance of religion and cult in the origins of sport in China.

9. M. Keen, *Chivalry* (New Haven, CT: Yale University Press, 1984). That the tourney did at times reflect many of the characteristics of war, including significant numbers of casualties, also raises the issue of the relationship between sport and war.

10. See J. Macaloon, *This Great Symbol: Pierre de Courbertin and the Origins of the Modern Olympic Games* (Chicago, IL: University of Chicago Press, 1981). Nevertheless the inter-war years are of particular significance when considering the diplomatic aspirations of the IOC.

11. Even ambassadors do not qualify for the designated status which provides them with open access to the Games, unless they are accompanying their head of state.

12. The connection between de Coubertin's thinking and French nationalism has been widely documented. Perhaps the tension between, on the one hand, nationalistic motives and, on the other, the emotional draw towards internationalism is indeed a reflection of the difficulties in realizing the aspirations of the internationalists in the early inter-war years. J. Hoberman, in *The Olympic Crisis* (New Rochelle, NY: Caratzas Publishing, 1986), comments that 'traumatized, as was his entire generation, by the military disaster of the Franco-Prussian war, Coubertin offered a healthful prescription: "sports can provide the virile formula on which the health of the State can be founded".' (p.33). There were a number of tensions in de Coubertin's writing. His inherent French nationalism (implying nationalism is natural) was somewhat at odds with his evolving internationalist convictions. In the context of sport as a social and political panacea, there was a tension between his belief in its ability to act as a social stimulant and its potential tranquillizing effect. Throughout however, there exists the conviction that an international sports movement could contribute to social and political stability – both nationally and internationally.

13. D. Kanin, *A Political History of the Olympic Games* (Boulder, CO: Westview Press, 1981) p.45.

14. Ibid.

15. Cited by J. Macaloon, *This Great Symbol: Pierre de Courbertin and the Origins of the Modern Olympic Games* (Chicago, IL: University of Chicago Press, 1981) p.5.

16. The UN General Assembly's resolution 52/15 of 20 November 1997 established the principle of the 'International Year for a Culture of Peace'.

17. This is distinct from the Olympic attaché appointed by the Foreign Office, whose role is to provide a link between government and the national Olympic team.
18. www.olympic.org/uk/organisation/missions/truce/index_uk.asp (July 1999).
19. It is noteworthy that the IOC also granted provisional recognition to the NOCs of Bosnia Herzegovina, Croatia, Slovenia and Macedonia and invited them to take part in the Games.
20. www.olympic.org/ioc/e/facts/truce/truce_lillehammer_e.html (July 1999).
21. www.olympic.org/ioc/e/news/worldconf/worldconf_intro_e.html. The International Year for a Culture of Peace was celebrated in 2000. The World Conference on Education and Sport for a Culture of Peace was held in Paris from 5 to 9 July 1999.
22. B. Houlihan, *Sport, and International Politics* (Hemel Hempstead: Harvester Wheatsheaf, 1994) refers to this limitation of influence.
23. The loss of major sponsors from recent Olympic Games – Johnson & Johnson from the 2002 Games and Reebok from the 2000 Games – can been viewed in this context.
24. Of the 115 IOC members, 24 were implicated in the scandal and of these, ten were eventually to resign.
25. http://news.bbc.co.uk/l/hi/sport/288650.stm (2 March 1999).
26. The IOC 2000 commission www.olympic.org/uk/news/media_centre/press_release_uu/asp? release=81 included a number of 'external' members, most notably being Henry Kissinger.
27. It is worth noting the increasing cost of supporting IOC members that has been incurred by organizing committees. Lord Killanin, *My Olympic Years* (London: Secker and Warburg, 1983) remarks: 'I recall from those early years how light were the demands which the IOC made on the Organising Committee as regards its own comfort. In 1952 Helsinki was a small city. IOC members had free passes on buses and all of us, except the president, travelled in this manner to sporting events. Today, all IOC members insist on having their own individual cars during the Games. For some eighty members to have cars places an added burden on the resources of the hosts, who also have to provide transport for the numerous teams, competitors and officials. More recently International Federation heads and NOC heads have also had cars. All these are provided by a national car manufacturer, or agent, which means that the officials of the Olympic Movement are subsidised by commercial advertising' (p.32).
28. http://news.bbc.co.uk/sport/iow/115291.stm (17 June 1999).
29. 'The Olympics depend upon powerful commercial interests: the sponsors, the host cities and the TV networks. The Games exist to serve more than these, but rather the world's population. It is therefore no use looking to the sponsors to reform the system, nor to the cities to renounce bribery. The world's only representative, for better or for worse, is the IOC. It must reform itself' (*Financial Times* leading article, 25 Jan. 1999). The sentiment expressed in this leader was markedly different from that expressed in an article two days previously. In the *Financial Times* (23 Jan. 1999) Patrick Harverson argued that 'Although the IOC President Juan Antonio Samaranch has said he will resist attempts to remove him, the final word on whether he stays or goes may well rest with the Olympic movement's new masters in the corporate world.'
30. Variations of this argument can be found throughout writing on the history and politics of sport. R. Espy, *The Politics of the Olympic Games* (Berkeley, CA: University of California Press, 1979), p.3, comments specifically that 'sport is frequently a tool of diplomacy. By sending delegations of athletes abroad, states can establish a first basis for diplomatic relations or can more effectively maintain such relations. Correspondingly, the cancellation of a proposed sport visit to another nation can be used by a state as a means of voicing displeasure with that specific government or with its policies.' Other writers, including Kanin, *A Political History of the Olympic Games* and Hoberman, *The Olympic Crisis*, also adopt this general perspective.
31. The IOC has historically attempted to counter state influence over the organization by creating a structure where members, while drawn from member states, are required to represent the interests of the IOC in those states rather than becoming 'state representatives' in the IOC. Yet this classic model of nineteenth-century liberal internationalism demonstrably falls as the reality of national interests have repeatedly been reflected in decision-making within the IOC. Indeed, it could be argued that the gulf between the theory and the practice of the Olympic movement is a reflection of the ongoing tension between realist theories of the balance of power and contrasting internationalist theories.
32. Espy, *The Politics of the Olympic Games,* p.152.
33. Ibid., p.153.
34. PRO, FO 371/19940: C 1639/306/18 (11 March 1936).
35. In the case of the Americans, a training ship was sent.

36. It was agreed that the two were not inextricably linked in the sense that the naval races would take place in standard-sized yachts prepared by the Germans for the event and, should the decision be made to compete, the British team could travel overland to Kiel. Why this apparently simple conclusion was not arrived at much earlier is difficult to establish.

37. The Admiralty was constantly seeking governmental guidance as to how it should act in the situation. No indication is found in correspondence that it was actively involved in the policy-making process.

38. J. Frankel, *British Foreign Policy 1945–1973* (Oxford: Oxford University Press, 1975), p.2.

39. The equestrian team decided to support the call for a boycott. It cannot be ignored that the Duke of Edinburgh was a prominent figure in that federation and the embarrassment for the government would have been acute should the team have adopted a position that ran counter to that of the government.

40. The Board of Trade, along with the Foreign Office, had been involved in the lead-up to the 1908 Games. The Colonial Office and the India Office were consulted on a number of issues relating to participation of the colonies and the dominions in the 1912 Games.

41. Copy of 'article for the *Daily Express*' dated 18 Jan. 1980 (BOA archives).

42. Dealing with the apparent contradiction of BOA opposition to British rugby in South Africa, Follows notes in the *Daily Express* article that the general opinion of world sporting bodies is very different in the context of sporting links with South Africa than it is in relation to participation in the Moscow Olympics.

43. The impact of the political pressure to boycott the Games was clearly reflected in added financial pressure on the BOA. Its response was partly to appeal to members of the public over the heads of government. In the supporting documentation which accompanied the 25 March NOC resolution to accept the invitation to compete in Moscow, it is noted that 'we have lost some of our expected funding in recent weeks but we believe that the public will wish to rally round Britain's Olympic Team and help them as much as they can. Financial help from the many sports lovers in this country would go a long way towards ensuring full participation' (BOA archives).

44. The memorandum from Howell to the governing bodies (20 Feb. 1980) notes that '[you will wish to consider] the decision of the President of the USA to allow the US boxing team to proceed to the USSR at the same time as the US Olympic Committee was being urged to boycott the Moscow Olympics' (BOA archives).

45. Since the invasion of Afghanistan did not take place until 1980, Howell's argument suggesting that 1974 was the critical date seems spurious. Concerning his argument that the Games were owned by the IOC and not the host country, it is ironic that a similar argument was forwarded prior to the 1936 Games.

46. The issue of the Moscow Games was discussed by the committee on 20 February, 27 February and 5 March. The report was printed and circulated on 12 March 1980.

47. BOA Archives.

48. The Foreign Affairs Committee questioned the Parliamentary Under-Secretary of State for the Environment Hector Monroe on 27 February, on the division of responsibilities between the FCO and the DoE. In response, Monroe identified the FCO as the 'lead department' – in consultation, however, with the DoE who were involved in the funding of athletes via the Sports Council. He also noted that involvement of the Home Secretary was also likely in the event of a boycott in relation to discussions on broadcasting arrangements.

49. BOA archives. Detailed reference to the Sports Council memorandum is set out in the First Report from the Foreign Affairs Committee 1979–80, entitled *Olympic Games 1980* (FO).

50. Ibid., p.10.

51. Ibid., p.16.

52. *The Times*, 30 Jan. 2003 (p.1 sports section) 'ECB – Plans to Hold Fire over Zimbabwe Fixture'. The article highlights the contrast between the Australian and British governments over their response should the respective governing bodies decide not to attend. It notes the Australian government's decision to provide financial aid should their cricketers withdraw from a scheduled match in Bulawayo on 24 February.

53. P. Sharp, *Thatcher's Diplomacy: The Revival of British Foreign Policy* (London: Macmillan, 1996), p.104.

54. T. Cooke, *The Cruise of the Branwen: Being a Short History of the Modern revival of the Olympic Games, Together with an Account of the Adventures of the English Fencing Team in Athens in 1906* (privately published, 1908; copy supplied by the British Library).

55. M. Polley, 'The British Government and the Olympic Games of the 1930s', *Sports Historian*, 170,

1 (May 1997).
56. BOA archives, minutes of 'Investigation Committee' into feasibility of bidding for the 1944 Games, 5 Dec. 1938.
57. Ibid.
58. BOA archives, minutes of BOA meeting, 5 Nov. 1945. Lord Aberdare notes in his introduction that at the meeting of the executive of the IOC on 21–24 Aug. 1945 that it had been decided the Olympic Games should be resumed in 1948. He noted that requests to host the Games had been received from Lausanne and a number of cities in America. The executive had decided to arrange a postal vote, with London being recommended – 'though Lausanne was not ruled out'.
58. BOA archives. minutes of BOA meeting, 5 Nov. 1945.
60. C. Hill, *Olympic Politics: Athens to Atlanta*, 2nd edn (Manchester: Manchester University Press, 1996) p.98.
61. Ibid. p.99.
62. At this time, responsibility for sport lay with a (junior) minister for sport within the Department of the Environment.
63. Hansard, Vol.211, pp.795/6 (July 1992). Mellor's reply was to an oral question posed by 'Mr Hawkins' asking if he 'was aware of the positive impact the Olympic bid was having on the development of the North West of the country?'.
64. Hansard Vol.210, p.841 (1 July 1992). Douglas Hurd was responding to a question from 'Mr Hanson' concerning the most appropriate method of bringing about more rapid change within South Africa.
65. *The Times*, 10 Aug. 1992, p.11.
66. C. Hill, *Olympic Politics*, p.106.
67. The FCO 'Panel 2000' consultative exercise (1998).
68. Fourth report from the Select Committee on Culture, Media and Sport (May 1999), Section VIII: 'A New Approach by Government' (DCMS)
69. Ibid.
70. Ibid.
71. This is further surprising given the enhanced role attributed to NOCs in the bidding process for the opportunity to host the Olympic Games, recommended by the IOC 2000 Commission.
72. Nick Harris, *Independent* (sports section), 9 Dec. 2000.
73. *Daily Telegraph,* 23 Nov. 2001, p.4.
74. *Leisure News,* 29 Nov.–5 Dec. 2001, p.1.
75. Institute of Leisure and Amenity Management (ILAM), *Leisure News* (3–9 Oct. 2002 p.1), ILAM.
76 Report from Select Committee for Culture Media and Sport (published by the DCMS, November 2001).
77. It could be argued that little has changed in this respect and that the apparent confusion over the position of the government concerning the 2003 cricket World Cup in Zimbabwe fulfilled the same purpose.
78. Sharp, *Thatcher's Diplomacy*, p.104.

NOTES TO CHAPTER 7

1 The author must declare an interest as a Manchester United season ticket holder and member of the Independent Manchester United Supporters' Association.
2. This is explored in A. Prakash and J. Hart (eds), *Globalization and Governance* (London: Routledge, 1999) and J. Pierre (ed.), *Debating Governance: Authority, Steering and Democracy* (Oxford: Oxford University Press, 2000).
3. For an explanation of the distinction between IPE and GPE, and their respective relationships to IR, see R. Palan, 'New Trends in the Global Political Economy', in R. Palan (ed.), *Global Political Economy: Contemporary Theories* (London: Routledge, 2000).
4. This conceptual framework is developed in D. Held, A. McGrew, D. Goldblatt and J. Perraton, *Global Transformations: Politics, Economics and Culture* (Cambridge: Polity Press, 1999). The 'hyperglobalizers' are represented by K. Ohmae, *The End of the Nation State: The Rise of Regional Economies* (London: HarperCollins, 1995); the 'sceptics' by P. Hirst and G. Thompson, *Globalization in Question* (Cambridge: Polity, 1996) and L. Weiss, *The Myth of the Powerless State* (Cambridge: Polity, 1998); and the 'transformationalists' by A. Giddens, *The Third Way* (Cambridge: Polity, 1998).

5. For example, P. Hirst, *From Statism to Pluralism: Democracy, Civil Society and Global Politics,* (London: UCL Press, 1997); J. Rosenau, 'Change, Complexity and Governance in Globalizing Space', in Pierre, *Debating Governance.*

6. R. Rhodes, 'Governance and Public Administration', in Pierre, *Debating Governance,* p.71.

7. European Commission, *Report from the Commission to the European Council to the European Council: with a view to safeguarding current sports structures and maintaining the social function of sport within the community framework. (The Helsinki Report on Sport)* (Brussels: Commission of the European Communities, 1999), COM (1999) 644 final.

8. For example D. Clark, 'The Beautiful Game Needs Protection from the Market', *Guardian,* 15 Aug. 2002.

9. For example, Havelange was FIFA president for 24 years until his succession by Joseph Blatter in 1998. This length of tenure was not unprecedented – Jules Rimet, the architect of FIFA's expansion and the World Cup, was FIFA President for 33 years (1921–54).

10. March 1999. See also Aaron Beacom's chapter in this book, at p.97.

11. European Union, *The Development and Prospects for Community Action in the Field of Sport* (Brussels: European Commission Directorate-General X, 1998).

12. For example, following a case brought by Slavia Prague and AEK Athens, the European Court of Arbitration for Sport ruled in July 1998 that it was unlawful for UEFA to create new rules outlawing participation in the same competition by clubs jointly owned without reasonable prior notification of the change in regulations (CAS 98/200, 17 July 1998 cited in European Union, *The European Model of Sport* (Brussels: European Commission, 1999), p.8).

13. Football Expo, 'The Economic and Social Impact of the First World Cup in Asia', Football Expo press release, 11 Jan. 2002.

14. 'Japan, Korea Stocks May See World Cup Rally', Reuters, 21 Jan. 2002, www.fifaworldcup. yahoo.com/en/020118/1/4v9.html, accessed 20 Aug. 2002.

15. 'Football Fever to Strike Workforce', BBC Sport Online, 18 Jan. 2002, www.news.bbc.co.uk/ sport/hi/en…p_2002/newsid_1767000/1767776.stm, accessed 20 Aug. 2002.

16. 'Manufacturing Slump Hits UK growth', BBC News, 23 August 2002, www.news.bbc.co.uk/ 1/hi/business/2211305.stm, accessed 20 Aug. 2002.

17. S. Szymanski and T. Kuypers, *Winners and Losers: The Business Strategy of Football* (London: Viking, 1999).

18. J. Findlay, W. Holahan and C. Oughton, 'Revenue-sharing from Broadcasting Football: The Need for League Balance' in S. Hamil, J. Michie and C. Oughton (eds), *A Game of Two Halves? The Business of Football* (Edinburgh: Mainstream, 1999), p.125.

19. P. Sharkey, 'Football in a Different League', ESPN Soccernet.com, 15 Oct. 2001, www.soccerne…001/1015/ 20011015featsharkey.html, accessed 20 Aug. 2002.

20. The G14 are AC Milan, Ajax (Amsterdam), Barcelona, Bayern Munich, Borussia Dortmund, Inter Milan, Juventus, Liverpool, Manchester United, Marseilles, Paris St-Germain, FC Porto, PSV Eindhoven and Real Madrid.

21. P. Sharkey, 'The European Question', ESPN Soccernet.com, 3 Sept. 2001, www.soccerne…001/ 0903/20010903featsharkey.html, accessed 20 Aug. 2002.

22. V. Chaudhary and J. Hooper, 'German Government to Bail Out Bundesliga', *Guardian,* 5 April 2002.

23. P. Willan, 'Berlusconi in Middle of Football Fiasco', *Guardian,* 22 Aug. 2002.

24. 'Africa Seeking More World Cup Places', Reuters, 21 Jan. 2002, www.fifaworldcup.yahoo.com/ en/020119/1/4zn.html, accessed 20 Aug. 2002.

25. 'Blatter promises World Cup to Africa', BBC Sport Online, 10 Jan. 2002, www.news.bbc.co.uk/sport/hi/en…africa/newsid_1752000/1752878.html, accessed 20 Aug. 2002.

26. FIFA, *Limits to Growth* (Geneva: FIFA, 2002).

27. FIFA, *Code of Conduct* (Zurich: FIFA, 2001).

28. 'FIFA's Blatter Defends Himself', ESPN Soccernet.com, 15 June 2001, www.socceret.epsn.go. com/, accessed 20 Aug. 2002.

29. N. Adderley, 'Blatter Reveals New Prudence', BBC Sport Online, 6 July 2001, www.bbc.co.uk/ sport1/hi/football/1425895.stm, accessed 20 Aug. 2002.

30. UEFA's 25 questions can be found at www.news.bbc.co.uk/sport/hi/en…otball/ newsid_1386000/1386470.stm, accessed 20 Aug. 2002.

31. 'FIFA Approves Blatter's Explanations over ISL', ESPN Soccernet.com, 7 July 2001, accessed 20 Aug. 2002.

32. M. Collett, 'FIFA Executive to sue Blatter', EPSN Soccernet, 8 May 2002, www.soccernet.com/global/news/2002/0508/20020508blatt..., accessed 20 Aug. 2002.

33. 'FIFA Nearly Bankrupt, Claims Vice-president', *Guardian*, 27 May 2002.

34. A. Jennings, 'The Day Soccer Voted for Sleaze', ESPN Soccernet, 30 May 2002, www.soccernet.com/global/news/2002/0530/20020530blatte..., accessed 20 Aug. 2002.

35. V. Chaudhary, 'Bullish Blatter pledges reform', *Guardian*, 30 May 2002.

36. FIFA, *Activities Report April 1994–March 1996: 50th FIFA Congress* (Zurich: FIFA, 1996), and FIFA, *Activities Report April 1996–March 1998: 51st FIFA Congress* (Zurich: FIFA, 1998).

37. 'Licensing Project Fine-tuned', UEFA press release, 21 Dec. 2001, www.uefa.com...e/news/Kind=128/newsid=14071.html, accessed 20 Aug. 2002.

38. 'UEFA Welcomes EC Decision on Club Ownership', UEFA media release, 2 July 2002; 'UEFA welcomes TV Agreement with European Commission', UEFA media release, 3 June 2002.

39. Deloitte & Touche, *Annual Review of Football Finance August 2002* (Manchester: Deloitte & Touche Sport, 2002).

40. D. Russell, *Football and the English: A Social History of Association Football in England, 1863–1995* (Preston: Carnegie Publishing, 1997).

41. The first live televised Football League fixture was screened on 2 October 1983 following a two-year £4.6 million deal.

42. Russell, *Football and the English*, pp.139, 151.

43. The Football League, *Pattern for Football* (The Football League: Lytham St Anne's, 1961); DES, *Report of the Committee on Football* (London: Her Majesty's Stationery Office, 1968).

44. Ironically, as Russell noted, in 1983 Sir Norman Chester headed a further inquiry into English football whose recommendations were also rejected (Russell, *Football and the English*, p.157); Football League, *Report of the Committee of Inquiry into the Structure and Finance of Football* (Lytham: Football League, 1983).

45. D. Conn, *The Football Business: Fair Game in the '90s?* (Edinburgh: Mainstream, 1997), pp. 40–1.

46. Ibid., p.43.

47. Home Office, *The Hillsborough Stadium Disaster. Inquiry by the Rt Hon Lord Justice Taylor: Final Report* (London: Her Majesty's Stationery Office, 1990), para 26.

48. The key pieces of legislation are the Football Spectators Act 1989, the Football Offences Act 1991, the Criminal Justice and Public Order Act 1994, the Crime and Disorder Act 1998, the Football (Offences and Disorder) Act 1999, and the Football (Disorder) Act 2000.

49. Home Office, *The Hillsborough Stadium Disaster*, para 58.

50. Deloitte & Touche/Four Four Two, 'Rich List', *Four Four Two*, Jan. 2001, pp.43–5.

51. Szymanski and Kuypers, *Winners & Losers*, p.19, note that, from an average annual pre-tax loss of £130,000 between 1974 and 1990, Manchester United plc's cumulative profits from 1991 to 1997 soared to £81.8 million – an annual average of £13.6 million – while shareholders received a total dividend of about £20 million.

52. Deloitte & Touche, *Annual Review of Football Finance 2000* (Manchester: Deloitte & Touche Sport, 2000); Deloitte & Touche, *England's Premier Clubs* (Manchester: Deloitte & Touche Sport, 2000).

53. Deloitte & Touche/Four Four Two, 'Rich List', pp.7–8.

54. Ibid., 'Rich List', p.5.

55. S. Lee, 'Grey Shirts to Grey Suits: The Political Economy of English Football in the 1990s' in A. Brown (ed.), *Fanatics: Power, Identity and Fandom in Football* (London: Routledge, 1997), and S. Lee, 'The BSkyB Bid for Manchester United plc' in Hamil et al., *A Game of Two Halves?*.

56. In October 2000, QPR were reported to have debts of over £10 million ('QPR Send Out an SOS for £££', ESPN Soccernet.com, 25 Oct. 2000, www.socceret.espn.go.com/, accessed 20 Aug. 2002). In July 2001, with debts of over £6 million and weekly losses of £100,000, Nottingham Forest placed their entire first team on the transfer list ('Forest Put Entire Squad Up for Sale', ESPN Soccernet.com, 31 July 2001, [URL + accessed??]). In November 2001, Sheffield Wednesday sought to reduce their £16 million debt through the sale of their training ground ('Wednesday to Sell Training Ground', ESPN Soccernet.com, 16 Nov. 2001, www.socceret.espn.go.com/, accessed 20 Aug. 2002).

57. www.footballfoundation.org.uk/index.asp, accessed 20 Aug. 2002.

58. Until the negotiation of the three-year £1.65 billion deal for Premier League broadcasting rights, the PFA received five per cent of television revenue, worth £8.8 million in 1999/2000.

59. The PFA administers a benevolent and hardship fund, an education fund and a general fund.

Before the formation of the Premier League, PFA funds had been largely financed through a ten per cent share of television revenue, the terms of which had been printed in the Football League handbook. Only with the creation of the Premier League was this agreement abandoned, initially in favour of ten per cent of a fixed amount of revenue and not less than five per cent of the remainder, and latterly from 1997 a share of revenue 'proportional' to television revenue ('The Striking Questions', ESPN Soccernet.com, 22 Nov. 2001, [URL + accessed??]).

60. The deal between the PFA, the Premier League and Football League guarantees that for every additional one per cent of television revenue the PFA will receive a 0.75 per cent increase in its current share. For every one per cent that television revenue decreases over the next ten years, the PFA's share will fall by 0.5 per cent (V. Chaudhary, 'Cherie Booth Helped Union Secure £175m of TV Money', *Guardian*, 27 Nov. 2001).

61. For example, Manchester United plc's share price had fallen to 143 pence on 21 January 2002, and a market capitalization of only £373 million, compared to BSkyB's earlier offer of 240 pence per share, valuing the club at £623.4 million: Lee, 'The BSky Bid', p.92.

62. ITV had invested £240 million per year for Premier League, Nationwide League, Champions League and Worthington Cup broadcasting rights. But audiences for its flagship terrestrial programme, *The Premiership*, declined so far that it rescheduled the programme to a later hour, while audiences for its subscription channel, ITV Digital, fell to as few as 1,000 viewers for a game. D. King, 'The Strike May Be a Blessing for ITV', ESPN Soccernet.com, 30 Sept. 2001, www.soccerne...2001/0930/20010930featkingtv.html, accessed 20 Aug. 2002.

63. For example, Granada Media paid £25 million for a 5 per cent share in Arsenal, £20 million for 50 per cent of the global portal Arsenal Broadband, £22 million for 9.9 per cent in Liverpool and £20 million for a 50 per cent share in a joint venture company with Liverpool. This was additional to Granada's 33 per cent stake in MUTV, a broadcasting company jointly owned with Manchester United and BskyB. M. Garrahan, 'Granada Pools Football Assets', *Financial Times*, 15 Jan. 2002.

64. NTL, the cable company, which had purchased a 9.8 per cent share in Newcastle United and Leicester City, and a 5.5 per cent share in Middlesbrough, had accumulated debts of £11.7 billion, reported to be so large that that it could have been in breach of some of its banking covenants by April 2002 (C. Grande and J. Ratner, 'NTL May Breach Some Bank Covenants', *Financial Times*, 21 Jan. 2002).

65. D. Rockwood, 'PFA Tell Premiership Chairmen: "See You in Court"', *Guardian*, 25 Sept. 2001.

66. 'Leeds Falls into Annual EBIT Loss', *FT MarketWatch*, 1 Oct. 2001.

67. D. Bond, 'Players: Row Is Not Just About Money', ESPN Soccernet.com, 25 Sept. 2001, www.soccerne...s/2001/0925/ 20010925pfamoney.html, accessed 20 Aug. 2002.

68. Strike threats are not confined to England. Australia's national team threatened to boycott a friendly international against France in November 2001 before an agreement between Soccer Australia and the Australian PFA over World Cup 2002 payments. In Argentina in May 2001 players threatened an indefinite strike because professional clubs owed players over $100 million.

69. Lee, 'The BskyB Bid'; J. Michie and C. Oughton, 'Football and Broadcasting and the MMC Case' in Hamil et al., *A Game of Two Halves?*.

70. Nike subsequently issued a statement on 16 October which claimed that only three workers out of 3,800 had misled the Cambodian subcontracting factory about their age. Furthermore, Nike had announced on 29 September 2000 that it had terminated its contract with June Textile Co. Ltd because of repeated violations of Nike's code of conduct standards, including its zero-tolerance policy on child labour. Nike conceded that with over 500,000 workers in 700 factories around the world, monitoring such standards was problematic. Cited in http://www.shareholdersunited.org/nikes_official_position.htm, accessed 20 Aug. 2002.

71. The striker Edmundo and team doctor Lidio Toledo both testified that they had informed Brazil's team coach Mario Zagallo that it was Ronaldo's fit which had occurred 15 minutes earlier. However, Zagallo had previously indicated that he only learned of Ronaldo's fit three hours later (Press Association, 24 Nov. 2000). However, one congressman, Nelo Rodolfo, claimed that Edmundo had toned down his testimony because he had been selected to play in the national team's most recent fixture, against Colombia: *Daily Express*, 23 Nov. 2000.

72. Football's importance to Brazilian society and national identity had been acknowledged by Aldo Rebelo, the Brazilian Community Party politician presiding over the lower house's inquiries. Rebelo stated that football 'integrates all the races that make up our country. . . . It is like a religion, and our players are like its apostles. It is our patrimony. But it has been treated just as a commodity. It cannot be reduced to this. This is the death of football. For the public interest it needs investigation.' Indeed, Rebelo had asserted that 'the main purpose is to fight against the mentality

of the market. We want to preserve football as a culture of entertainment and preserve the nation's self respect': *Guardian*, 11 Nov. 2000.

73. *AFX*, 6 Nov. 2000, cited at http://www.shareholdersunited.org, , accessed 20 Aug. 2002.
74. *Manchester Evening News*, 17 Nov. 2000.
75. Shareholders United press release, 16 Nov. 2000.
76. J. Michie and A. Walsh, 'What Future for Football?' in S. Hamil et al., *A Game of Two Halves?*, p.210.
77. B. Lomax, 'Supporter Representation on the Board: The Case of Northampton Town FC', in S. Hamil et al., *A Game of Two Halves?*.
78. *Independent*, 19 Nov. 2000.
79. Downing Street press release, 27 Jan. 2000.
80. FTF, *Football: Commercial Issues. A submission by the Football Task Force to the Minister for Sport* (London: Football Task Force, 1999).
81. European Commission, *Report from the Commission to the European Council to the European Council: with a view to safeguarding current sports structures and maintaining the social function of sport within the community framework. (The Helsinki Report on Sport)* (Brussels: Commission of the European Communities, 1999), COM (1999) 644 final.
82. European Union, *Framework Document for the Working Party Discussions on the Specific Nature of Sport* (Brussels: European Commission, 2000).
83. S. Lee and R. Woodward, 'Reinventing the Wheel? GPE Scholarship at the Turn of the Millennium', paper presented at the ECPR 4th Pan-European International Relations Conference, University of Kent, 8 Sept. 2001.

NOTE TO EPILOGUE

1. See I. Clark, *Globalization and Fragmentation. International Relations in the Twentieth Century* (Oxford: Oxford University Press, 1997).

Index